AF397986

A GHOST IN THE WIND

DAISY JOHNSON

BookLeaf
Publishing

India | USA | UK

Presentation by *BookLeaf Publishing*

Web: www.bookleafpub.com
E-mail: info@bookleafpub.com

ISBN: 9789369535873

First edition 2025

For Tyler

PREFACE

A Ghost in the Wind was written entirely on my phone notes, in the early hours over three years. If it's not perfect, there's your answer. Then again, if it was perfect, it wouldn't be any good.

ACKNOWLEDGEMENT

The line between fiction and facts is only as good as your memory allows.

"Just because that's the narrative you've told yourself, it doesn't mean it's true."

— something Cody would say if I ever had the courage to give him this book.

JANUARY 2022

It's hard to tell a story when you don't know where to begin, when there have been so many beginnings and endings. My life had been a ritual of flirting between the two—ripping things open and stuffing them shut again.

I was in Brockport, a quiet town tucked away in Upstate New York. I'd landed just a week before, freshly twenty-one, bleary-eyed and bundled into a taxi that reeked of smoke and stale coffee. I was wrapped in layers of winterwear that only seemed to grow heavier with each mile we tore down the highway. The driver kept yapping incessantly, asking about England, my family, about anything she could pry loose. She was smoking and handed me a cigarette. I clung to it as if it were the only familiar thing I knew.

I was a fish out of water—an English girl from across the pond, an exchange student thrust into a world of snowy sidewalks and college chaos. I had left behind my fiancé, Owen, and in my first week, I attended endless orientation meetings and waded in the first thick snowfall of my life. That was my introduction to America, a harsh bitterness, an unfamiliarity, a sinking need to feel accepted, staring down blank walls and empty faces.

Over the first few days, the campus was deserted. Students hadn't arrived back for the Spring Semester; I guess they knew better since there were only three of us knocking around: Meave, Bella, and Valentina — my Cuban roommate, as fierce as she was warm.

But by the end of the week a flurry of students had filled the dorms, and the snow paths had been trodden down. Bella introduced us to her suitemates over dinner in the canteen, they'd come back from the Holidays early— something to do with kissing frat boys and independence. There was a frat party that weekend, and so when Saturday rolled around, off we went.

I guess that's where the story starts—in January, at a frat party, a keg deep. I was drunk and I didn't want to be there. I was surrounded by frat boys and sorority girls, by noise and damage. I felt the walls press in, the smell of beer and grime clinging to everything, the music thudding against my skin. Their shadows stretched taller and their laughter rang louder, booze sloshing out of red plastic cups. I was drowning, sinking deeper into the noise, pulling away into myself as everyone threw themselves out, hungry for attention, for something to grab onto.

I wanted to go home. Home was calmness, solitude; and conversations on the patio under the moon. When I thought of England, I imagined myself there, catching buses and planes and trains, running back with bare feet hitting the concrete, running home to who I am and who I was, yearning for the simplicity of love. The mirror was broken, since landing in the land of the free, I could see how it wasn't mine. It was distant and cold, and I didn't belong. I looked over and saw Meave dancing, and Valentina and Bella hugging. The isolation couldn't have been more apparent.

***

Owen found out that I'd gone to the frat party. He created a fake account, followed me online, saw the photos and responded in a way perhaps most wouldn't. He punched himself in the face repeatedly until he cracked his eye socket, captured it all in a video and sent it to my phone, with a hundred other messages, telling me how much of a "whore" I was.

I looked at my phone, and the screen flashed with his name. My finger hovered, paralysed by a wave of dread. It was as if I could feel his anger radiating through the digital space, pulsing like a bad omen. I swallowed hard and answered.

"Don't send me videos like that," I knew it was futile, but the words felt like the only defence I had. He bellowed down the phone, sharp and fast, like a slap. "Fuck you. You made me do this. You fucking bitch."

I recoiled, his yell like broken glass, cutting through the thin veil of the quiet dorm. I had known it was coming, yet it still landed like a blow. I took a deep breath, trying to steady myself, but the words seemed to fall out of me before I could stop them, "I can't do this anymore."

There was a long pause on the other end, a slicing silence. I imagined him on the other side of the world, hunched over his phone, eyes red with frustration, the angry air between us thickening like smoke.

"You think I'm fucking crazy? You left me. Do you think this is easy for me? You think I don't see what you're doing?"

His words were a storm breaking over the line. I could almost hear the desperation in his voice, the tightness that always gripped him when he was this deep into it. His anger was so familiar, it engulfed me. I was suffocated.

"You think you're better than me? That you can just leave and walk away like it's nothing?" His voice rising again, "You think I don't know what you're doing?"

"I can't keep doing this."

A low, broken laugh came through the line, bitter and humourless.

"Oh, so now it's just about you, huh? Funny how that works. You get to leave, and I'm the one stuck with nothing."

I could almost see him, pacing in the cramped room, running a hand through his hair in that old, frustrated gesture. I could feel his confusion, his need for control, and his iron fist—he could never let anyone leave him without clawing at their soul, trying to pull them back.

"Listen to me," I said, trying to steady my voice, "I'm not trying to hurt you. I can't be who you need me to be anymore, Owen. I'm sorry. I'm just… I'm trying to breathe."

"Breathe?" His voice cracked, and then there was the unmistakable sound of a punch—his fist against something.

I hung up but he blew up my phone like he always did. One heart-dropping, anxiety-inducing *ping* after another. *Ping, Ping, Ping, Ping, Ping.* His anger was desperation, and his desperation was attachment anxiety. I was his mother who had given him life and cast him away. I resented her; she lived in peace while I had been left to save her son from the depths in which she had drowned him.

***

I fell into a restless sleep and drifted into a dark, haunting dream. I was with my Grandpa, standing together in a dim corridor that seemed to stretch endlessly. Shadows reached out, snatching at us. My heart lurched when I saw him—ten years younger than I remembered, fuller, alive. His chest rose and fell, his breath whispering in the stillness.

At first, he didn't notice me, his gaze distant, lost in thought. I called out, my voice echoing down the empty hallway, "Grandpa! Grandpa!"

He turned, his eyes softening as he recognized me, gliding toward me like a memory surfacing from the depths. I reached for him, desperate to hold him close. I embraced him, "Please, Grandpa, stay with me."

But he shook his head, his voice faint yet firm. "I don't like it here."

In my arms, he began to tremble, his body convulsing as though caught in a violent sea. His form started to shift—his frame stretching thin, his face hollowing out, ageing before my eyes. I was terrified, but I held on, refusing to let him slip away. His body twisted and morphed, spiralling backwards through time. I watched as he shrank, each transformation blurring into the next. His gaunt face tightened, his posture straightened, and he became the version of himself that married Granny—a man in his prime. Time kept unspooling, faster and faster, until he was just a boy, standing before me in worn 1940s clothes. He looked up at me, his face lit by a spark of joy, as if happiness was the only thing he knew, "I'm going home."

And then, in the blink of an eye, he faded, leaving me alone in the darkness, clutching only the lingering memory of his kindness.

FEBRUARY 2022

The following days were sad, they blended into one relentless nightmare, and I didn't know how to move forward in the direction I had chosen. Everything I knew crumbled to ash in my hands and I lacked the energy for a grand rebirth; I wasn't a phoenix. I thought of Owen far more than I cared to admit; he had been my every day. Now I had no one to answer to, I didn't know how to answer myself. Yet with sadness, came freedom. A college student's freedom manifested in boys and parties. It was all a distraction: the ritual of getting ready, the alcohol, the dancing, the sex.

I felt myself slipping away, and I wasn't sure if I loved or loathed the person I had become. I got far too drunk, I'd cry while dancing, and I wrestled with the weight of being too big, too mixed, too broken, to despised to be loved. I muddled through the weeks in the nomadic wasteland of my mind. I was in the pit of despair, and I reached for hands, but they all slipped away. I was alone. I wanted to rip the skin from my body and the hair from my head. I needed to be reinvented and I didn't know how. It continued like that until I met Cody.

It was cold and dark and I decided to fill the void with another man, another half-hearted adventure with another stranger who'd give me the world in a night, only to take it away the next morning. I waited by the bookshop on Main Street, it lay quiet under a fresh blanket of snow. Storefronts stood dark and fogged, their displays barely visible through frosted windows, while snow softened every edge, covering rooftops, stoops, and signs in an untouched layer.

Occasionally, a lone car passed, leaving tracks that quickly vanished in the steady snowfall under the soft streetlights, and I didn't know what the hell I was doing there. But he turned up before I could change my mind. He pulled in a couple of spaces over, and saunted out, a silhouette against the truck lights. I squinted and found myself shunted into the past. Life had been a vehicle and suddenly it screeched to a halt, *whiplash*. I was eighteen years old again, in my Primark jacket, with my cropped blonde wig. I was wearing hooped earrings and sat in the November cold, on a bench outside Temple Meads Train Station, and Owen, floppy-haired and bundled in a green coat came walking through the crowd, towards me.

"Are you Cody?" I asked, peering at him shyly.

"Yes, Ma'am," he replied, a slight smile tugging at the corner of his mouth. He was handsome in a quiet way, hands tucked into his pockets, a worn hat shading his face. I gave him a quick hug and he led me to his truck, opening the door for me.

"There's a drive-in movie theatre near if you're up for it?"

"Oooh," I exclaimed, lighting up, "Like Grease?"

He chuckled. "Yes, just like Grease."

We drove through winding roads, leaving Brockport behind, and headed over to the next town. Eventually, he pulled up to two closed gates, the empty field beyond barely visible under the dark sky.

"Darn it," he muttered. "It's closed."

The quiet tension of being alone with a stranger in the middle of rural America started to seep through me. *Darn it*, I too thought, for if he'd taken me here to die, I wasn't prepared for it. We paused for a moment, neither saying anything. If he was calculating his murder move, I wasn't calculating my escape.

"Okay", he finally announced, "I'll take you to Rochester."

Rochester was the closest city to Brockport, a bolthole I'd booked only weeks prior. I met a man and he'd taken me to a bar in the hood, the kind of place where you ate peanuts straight from the shell, dropping the husks on to the floor with a cool carelessness. The whole joint was carpeted in crushed shells, gritty underfoot, a tradition no one questioned. I remembered Rochester to be grey and bleak, the kind of place that seemed to exist between destinations, built for cars and not for people. The absence of high streets had left me disoriented, longing for a center that wasn't there.

"Okay."

"You'll like it," Cody replied, handing me his phone to pull up maps. "Let's get the hell outta here."

He had this way of saying things, a playful confidence like he'd figured something out that no one else had. It made you want to follow him, even when you weren't sure where he was leading. On the road to Rochester, we cracked the windows and lit up cigarettes, the cold air rushing in.

"You smoke a lot?" he asked, glancing at me.

"Only when I'm nervous," I lied, exhaling slowly.

"Nervous around me?" He smirked, letting the silence hang.

At a stoplight on the edge of town, he drummed his fingers on the wheel. "You know, I got pulled over here once," he said, his tone dropping like it was some big confession.

"For speeding?" I asked.

He laughed under his breath. "Not exactly."

I turned to him, suddenly curious. "Then why?"

"Never mind," he said quickly, waving it off like he shouldn't have said anything. "Doesn't matter."

He caught my eyes as the light turned green, grinning like he'd let me in on something he wasn't supposed to. Cody drove me to a lookout point, where we surveyed Rochester's dull skyline.

It stretched flat and uninspired—bars, burger joints, and endless roads.

"Is it what you pictured, huh?" he asked, leaning back on the hood of the truck.

"It's…different," I admitted, watching his face instead of the view.

"Yeah, it's a dump. But hey, you've got me."

He grinned, but I caught the flicker of something behind his eyes, "Come on, there's a bar I want to show you — Hooligans."

As we neared Hooligans, I caught him looking at me, his eyes sweeping over my body, and I wished he wasn't looking so closely.

"What?"

"Nothing."

"It's just…" I hesitated, biting my lip. "I know I'm not, like, skinny or whatever—"

"Stop," he interrupted, his voice firm. "You're perfect."

I blinked, startled, and he turned his attention back to the road like it was nothing.

When he pulled into the Hooligans parking lot, snow was piled high along the edges, untouched by plows, "Hold on, I hope you've got a tight grip."

Before I could ask what he meant, he hit the gas. The truck spun in tight, deliberate circles, tires kicking up snow and gravel as the engine roared. I clung to the door handle, laughing as the world blurred outside the windows.

"You're insane!" I shouted over the noise, but I couldn't stop smiling.

He brought the truck to a sudden stop, and we jolted forward. Cody sat back, smug and satisfied, as if this was his way of showing off.

"Don't worry," he said, winking at me. "I know what I'm doing."

And just like that, the moment felt lighter, I allowed myself to breathe. On our way in, there had been a claw machine with rubber duck prizes, and I had challenged him to win me one. Miraculously, he had. How refreshing, to be with someone who pretended to care, someone bold enough to put a quarter in a machine and hand over a duck. Inside Hooligans, televisions blared sports highlights from every corner, and the waitress, charmed by my accent, asked if I was from London.

Cody leaned forward, telling me how beautiful I was, and I dared to believe him. He played footsies with me under the table as he ordered me drinks, slipping lower in his seat to make me laugh with exaggerated expressions.

"You're trouble," I smirked, the alcohol returning my humour, my sass, my assurance that I was desirable.

"And you're sexy," he shot back.

The words hit me harder than they should've. I didn't know if he meant them, but our eyes met and they lingered there longer than they should've, before I bashfully looked away again. Hopeful, hungry, helpless.

When the waitress brought over our next round, Cody's eyes followed her. He caught me noticing, flashing me a lopsided grid before turning and pretending to watch the game.

I excused myself and went to the bathroom. I stared down my reflection in the mirror, at my blonde clip-on hair extensions tugging at my scalp. I had gone to check if they had slipped, but they hadn't. They were still tangled in my straightened curls, so I returned to the booth, sliding into my seat and sucking in my stomach. My jeans dug into my waist as I adjusted myself, the sharp press of the buttons biting through denim.

"I thought you'd done a runner," Cody said. He wasn't joking.

"Maybe I should've."

I'd promised him sex, and with the drinks draining fast and the night closing in, I knew it was time. His good looks caused me to almost falter. Our eyes met, and I broke the silence with a coy smile. "I'm ready to leave."

In the truck, he ran his hand along my thigh while the radio played country songs, his voice singing along in bursts, grinning at me between verses. I asked if we were going to his place. He muttered something about a roommate being weird about Covid.

"I don't have Covid," I said.

He clicked his tongue, "How about yours?"

"There's no chance in hell," I replied. "I've got a roommate too."

We drove aimlessly, the snow thickening outside.

"Where are we even going?"

He glanced over at me, his mouth curling into a grin. "Wherever you want."

"You're the one driving," I teased.

"And you're the one calling the shots."

His fingers were warm, moving in slow, deliberate circles through the denim of my jeans.

"I guess…we could pull over," I said softly, the words catching in my throat.

Cody's grin widened. "Now we're talking."

He took a sharp turn, and the truck bumped and skidded slightly as he steered into the empty parking lot of a Taco Bell. The snow had piled high against the curbs, and the whole place was deserted. Cody cut the engine, the sudden silence almost deafening, except for the faint ticking of the cooling engine and the soft hum of the wind outside.

He pulled out a small silver contraption.

"What's that?" I asked, watching as he pressed a button and brought it to his lips.

He grinned mid-hit, exhaling a plume of vapor. "This? It's a dab pen."

"A dab pen?" I echoed, confused.

"Yeah, it's weed, just, like…concentrated. Pure THC. Way stronger than a joint." He offered it to me, holding it out casually like it was the most normal thing in the world. "You wanna try?"

I hesitated, staring at it. "How concentrated?"

He laughed, tapping the pen against his thigh. "Relax. You'll be fine. One hit won't kill you—might make you feel like it, though."

I couldn't tell if he was joking or not.

"Comforting," I said dryly.

Cody leaned back in his seat, taking another drag before blowing the vapor toward the cracked window. "It's cleaner, too. No smell on your clothes. Plus, it hits faster. This little thing," he said, holding up the pen between two fingers, "will knock you on your ass."

And it did, and I was high. And we sat in silence for quite some time, not strained nor awkward. A knowing silence, a stoned silence. Until he broke it, and bought me back to him and the parking lot, back from wherever it was that my mind had ventured.

"You shy?" he asked, his voice low, teasing but not unkind.

"No," I lied, my voice too quick, too high.

"Good," he said, leaning in closer. His hand moved up my thigh, his touch firm now, and I felt my breath hitch. The windows fogged up quickly as he kissed me, his lips warm and eager, the faint taste of cigarettes and beer lingering on his breath. I kissed him back, trying to match his rhythm, but my hands trembled as they found their way to his shoulders.

Cody pulled back slightly, his eyes searching mine, and for a moment, I thought he'd say something mean. Instead, he smirked, brushing a strand of hair away from my face. "You're so goddamn beautiful," he murmured.

I wanted to believe him, and perhaps in that moment, I did.

He unbuckled his seatbelt and shifted toward me, his hands moving with an ease that felt both practiced and spontaneous, tugging at my jacket, then my sweater. I laughed, the sound awkward to my stoned ears.

"What's so funny?" he asked, as he pulled his own jacket off and tossed it into the back seat.

"Nothing," I said quickly, shaking my head. "I just… I've never done this in a car park before."

"Car park" he murmured, "Miss England", his voice dripping with charm. And all of a sudden the nerves were replaced with something electric, something raw. Stoned, giddy, and reckless, we made love in the truck as snow slammed against the windows, the rhythmic beat of the wipers keeping time. And, when all was said and done, this curious stranger leant back in his seat, zipping up his jeans with a satisfied grin. He hit his dab pen again, exhaling slowly before glancing over at me.

"Don't go falling in love with me now," he said in his American drawl.

We drove back to Brockport and a couple of young deer ran across the road, magnetic in the headlights, brown against the snow. Cody almost didn't see them for the weather was worsening. We screeched to a halt, and I asked him if he liked to hunt since he liked to fish.

"No", he retorted, surprised I'd asked, "I don't kill animals, bro."

He dropped me off at the parking bay, and I kissed him goodnight. I told him to let me know when he got home, secretly hoping I would see him again.

Don't go falling in love with me now.

Oh but Cody, I already had.

MARCH 2022

After telling all the girls at the frat party about my Taco Bell escapade, and receiving gleeful laughs, questions and admiration, I felt like I somewhat fit in.

"Your life is a movie", one of the girls laughed, pouring me a vile concoction of vodka and coke.

"Yeah, you could write a book."

I tried to remember his surname. With Owen out of the picture, the temptation of social media stalking lured me in, and if I hadn't wanted to play it cool, I would've asked Cody straight up. But, the thrill of the search was a fun insomniac pastime and I lay in the dark after the party, drunk as I replayed our date.

And then, just when I had rolled over and given up, deciding to ask him in the morning, my heart leapt, and I opened Facebook and jabbed in his name. A profile appeared and lo and behold, there he was. Cody. *Oh, Cody.* I smiled. There was a woman in his profile picture, and I was smug that I'd get to stalk his sister too. Perhaps they were close. I appreciated a family man.

"Fuck!"

"What?" Valentina's head hovered above her desk.

"What the fuck!"

"What?", she pressed.

"Nah, fuck this", I exclaimed, "I'm going for a cigarette."

I left the dorm, shoving on snow boots and headed to the loading dock, where he had dropped me off the night before, lit my cigarette, and poured over my phone. The cigarette burned too quickly. Another followed, but it didn't settle me. My fingers were numb. I needed to look again, to confirm it. Heart pounding, I tapped back into his profile, holding my breath as the profile picture came into focus.

Cody, smiling, his arm around a woman—no sister, no cousin. She wore a ring. I stubbed out my cigarette, nearly stumbling as I rushed back to my dorm, heart racing with adrenaline and a sickly sort of clarity.

"What is it?" Valentina asked impatiently, her Cuban accent thicker with a mixture of concern and excitement.

"He's fucking married."

***

I met Cody again on Main Street. He was idling in his truck, one arm draped out the window, as if he hadn't a care in the world, and I felt the nerves wash back. Seeing him was probably a mistake. Valentina and Meave had insisted I block him. But he was still here, as real as ever, a loose end I couldn't quite cut. "I'm starving," he called out, springing from the truck, and tossing his arm over my shoulder.

I couldn't help but wonder where he'd hidden his ring. Was it tucked in his glove compartment, shoved into a corner of his wallet, or did he simply leave it at home, out of sight?

"The Sub Shop is good," I said, remembering the place one of my classmates had shown me earlier that week. It was the only place I knew to recommend.

"Bet!" He gave me a quick grin, and we went inside. The woman behind the counter recognized me, her eyes crinkling into a grandmotherly smile.

"What do you want?" Cody asked.

I chose the cheapest sub because I wasn't accustomed to the man paying, and half expected I would be covering the bill. But he put his dollars on the counter as if it was second nature, and the woman gave us free cookies. We sat by the window, and I wished the sub wasn't so messy. I didn't want Cody to see that side of me, the ugly-eating, human side. Cody's voice dropped low. "There's something I need to tell you." He shifted, the smile gone, his fingers tracing the edges of his cup. "I'm married."

I lifted my eyebrows, performing the surprise he seemed to need. He looked away, gazing out the window, eyes far off. "But we're divorcing," he added. "I'm moving out."

I debated telling him I knew, but that's probably not what he needed to hear. Instead, I offered the only thing I thought I'd want to hear in his place. "Do you need a hug?"

He looked taken aback but said he did, sadness clouding his childish aurora.

"I broke up with someone I was engaged to two weeks ago."

I had spent three years dead, three years locked up, tormented by tongue lashes and steely fists, the shock treatment of being woken up in the middle of the night and thrown out, waiting out in the cold, back leaned up against my car, for I wasn't even allowed my keys, denied even my small Renault car seats, to hunch my back and fall asleep. I was something to fuck and thrash about. I was new to this American existence, I was new to the promise of freedom. I didn't know how to navigate it.

"We're going to Letchworth", Cody suddenly announced.

"What's that?"

Cody chuckled bemused, as if it was common knowledge, "The State Park."

We hit his dab on the way. My job was to pack the bowls and his job was to take smoky inhales, behind the wheel, passing it back just before all the weed had turned black. Letchworth wasn't far, and by the time we had gotten there, my mind was clouded, my words clumsy. I stepped out of the truck, hit by the air, trying to busy myself doing nothing, a pitiful attempt to fight the pull of being stoned. But it was no use, the haze crept in like a slow, inevitable tide. Cody headed to the truck bed and started rummaging around, as the world around me sharpened into something foreign.

I was too real. Too *alive*. Golden light sliced through the tall American trees, like some kind of hymn, a silent cry of a nation's fading hope. The birds' tired cooing twisted through the air, and I felt the urge to run, but I was spinning, falling inward, collapsing in on myself, unable to stop it. Cody's truck was the only one in sight and the only vehicle I had seen since leaving Brockport, and Cody blissfully unaware, was the only person I had seen since Brockport too.

I could taste the fear on my tongue, sharp and bitter, a premonition that I could not shake. The world had shifted in a way I couldn't hold on to, and I was terrified. Terrified of the unknown, of what might be waiting behind it. The dread gnawed at me, the feeling of something terrible about to happen.

I was sure of it then. I was sure I was going to get raped.

"There's a trail down this way!"

Shit. He spoke, his voice cut through me, a sharp break in the silence.

"I don't know," I mumbled, my voice a thread.

"What do you mean?" Cody was curious now, but there was something else too—concern? I couldn't look at him, I didn't know him. I didn't trust him. The fear crawled up my throat, thick and suffocating. Who was this man? This American who had taken me to a remote part of an already remote State Park?

"Is everything okay?" Cody asked, confusion laced his tone.

Run. Make him take you home. He was a stranger in the woods, and *you're a girl in his hands.*

He took a step towards me, and I took one back.

"We don't have to go if you don't want to."

I looked away, my eyes lost in the blur of the woods. The sunlight seemed too low now, too cold. I smoked a cigarette, though I could barely taste it. My mouth was dry, the smoke thick. "We're going to get lost," I said, the words escaping in a rasp.

No, we won't," he replied, his tone steady, too steady. "We have cell phones. We just follow the river. We'll find our way back."

He's thought this through. He's equipped. The knot in my stomach only tightened.

Silence: long, awful, awkward silence.

"I don't want to do anything you don't want to do," he continued cautiously. He was close now, too close. I felt the heat of his presence. I dropped the cigarette; it made it impossible for me to swallow. I wondered what expression was on his face, whether he would hurt me, whether it had come to that, and I couldn't shake the feeling that it might, "Do you want to do something else?"

"Yes."

We got back in the truck, the heavy silence settling around us like fog. I stared out the window, turning my body away from him.

"You're stoned."

"I know."

"There's a viewing point not far from here," he said, and I could hear the gentleness in his voice, or maybe it was just a way to fill the hollow space between us, "We can just go and sit there if you like?"

"Okay."

***

Cody told me he wanted to take me out to dinner and that he was going to pick me up, all I had to do was choose between Mexican food or cheeseburgers. It was a no-brainer. Since I had entered the States, I had replaced greasy doner kebabs with the saturated goodness of burritos; Mexican it was. I got ready, clipping my extensions in, painting my face with pink and pulling on a black top and denim skirt; I wanted to look pretty. He told me I did.

In Cody's style, he picked me up, spinning his truck into the snow of the loading bay, and getting out of his truck to open my door. He took me to Rancho Viejo, the little Mexican spot in Brockport that I'd been raving to Meave and Valentina about as if he'd plucked the idea from my mind. The restaurant was packed, but I didn't mind. A busy place felt like a good sign, and having more time with Cody was no small bonus.

We slid into a booth in the corner, and he immediately shifted in his seat, adjusting his posture like he couldn't quite find a comfortable spot. He tugged at his shirt, stretching his legs under the table, looking like a man who couldn't quite sit still.

"You good?" I asked, raising an eyebrow.

He gave me a crooked smile, tapping the side of his foot against the table leg. "Yeah. Just—" He paused, glancing around the restaurant, "You ever notice how bad the tiles are in these places?"

"Hey, they're functional," I said with a grin, "they're not here to make an impression. They're here to support the quesadillas."

He chuckled, a little more at ease, but he was still fidgeting, tapping his fingers against the edge of the menu.

"Fair enough. But if I were running the show, I'd have gone with something more… you know, clean."

I laughed. "It's just tiles, Cody. It's not like they're the foundation of the universe."

He shot me a playful look, "Oh, they definitely are. You just don't see it."

He told me he was a laborer, specialising in tiles, his gaze flicking around the room, pointing out all the flaws with the place. I couldn't help but notice the little things—his restlessness, how his words came fast when he was thinking, the look in his eyes as if he was always scanning for something just beyond reach.

It was a night of tostadas, chips and queso, and the kind of easy conversation that unspooled endlessly. Cody talked about fishing, and his love for the water, how the world seemed to stand still on a lake, and I told him writing was my version of fishing,

"How so?"

"I dunno, it helps me order all the chaos in my head."

Cody smiled and for the first time that night, I saw something softer in his eyes. A real warmth, a kind of understanding. "You've got a lot going on in that head of yours, huh?"

I shrugged. "Yeah, I guess you could say that."

He told me he was a quarterback for a semi-professional team, and I laughed, telling him I could finally cross, "sleeping with a quarterback", off my bucket list. He laughed too.

I was drawn to his laughter, how he would scrunch his face and his eyes would glisten, and no sound would come out. Later, he admitted he'd felt self-conscious that night, worried people might wonder why "a guy like him" was sitting with "a girl like me." I thought it would flatter me but instead, it made me feel sad. He didn't see himself the way I did, though no one ever does. I ate slowly and he ate fast, and we smiled at each other. Cody was a messy eater and it made me feel at ease, for the best company are those who enjoy their food, who talk and eat and care.

The meal was over and yet the night had only just begun. We headed back to the truck and I slid close to him, resting my head on his shoulder as he started the engine, headlights brightening the night. Out on the road, I felt like Kerouac, as if I were in some story I'd only dreamed about. Cody wrapped an arm around my shoulders, pulling me closer, and I let myself fall into him, savouring the warmth and his soft hoodie, hoping the night might never end. He kissed my forehead, and I sighed, feeling a quiet peace settle over me, "Where are we going?" I asked.

"I have no idea."

"Good", I peered up at him and he down at me. Cody reached into his pocket and pulled out his Hyde and placed it in my mouth. I drew on it and a cloud of misty strawberry haze engulfed us, it tasted of happiness. We drove around aimlessly like we always did back then, it was the drive we enjoyed, the company, the music, and the dark roads. I felt alive when I was with Cody, he unlocked a part of me that had been oppressed for so long. He made me want to see everything; it was limitless the things that I felt we could do. I caught him looking over at me, one hand on the wheel, one around my back, and I hoped he could read my mind.

"If you're here in the summer, I want to take you out on my boat."

"To fish?" I asked.

"To do whatever you want honey, it's so beautiful here in the summer, I hope you get to stay."

"I hope so too."

I really did hope so, I wanted more than anything to stay. I couldn't imagine a life back in England now, I had burnt too many bridges and amidst the blaze, I had tasted freedom. I enjoyed the comfortable silence, there was a feeling of something new on the horizon, something within our grasp, "I want to cuddle you", I said.

"Then let's cuddle", he beamed.

We were young ramblers on the search; a quest to find the perfect cuddle spot. The roads in Upstate New York were wide and despite being in the countryside, there were no little tracks or back lanes, no privacy for lovers looking to cuddle. I didn't mind the wait, it gave me more time to feel at peace, to drag on a night with an inevitable end. We drove past a small church with a quiet car park, "Bingo", Cody grinned and swung his great truck in.

He sank into my arms, and I held him tight, I held him as I would have liked to have been held. The radio hummed the local station's country tunes, and I rested my head on his, the low engine rumble calling for sleep. I dozed in between counting his breaths, I wondered what he was thinking and how many other arms he had found himself in. We were silent and we were one. I thought about what it would be like to love him, and whether I already did. I felt content and as he melted into me, my life melted away; responsibilities, heartache, racing thoughts and pain, all erased at the side of the road in someplace unknown.

"I really like you", he sighed.

I paused to savour the moment, "I like you too."

It was there, in the car park, by the small church and vast road, that I suddenly realised it wasn't the destination that interested me. I had been focused so long on the end goal, the dazzling possibilities of the future, but I had gotten it all wrong. I wanted the passion, the fleeting moments, the hellos, and the goodbyes. I wanted to be consumed with love and adventure and hold onto the ideas of possibilities, for possibilities are all we'll ever have. Life isn't about where you end up, it's about how you get there, and I wanted to be everywhere and nowhere. I wanted to be held and to whisper promises, to explore and to cry, to feel and to think, to propel forward in one direction only to change my mind.

I wanted to be fluid and transparent; the chain of others had weighed me down for so long that the burning desire to be free had finally dawned on me. I wanted Cody and no longer wanted to be chained to myself. I wanted to take a chance and to see where, with what roll of the dice, life would take me. I'm not sure how long we lay there entwined nor how many songs had trailed on, but eventually, all good things must come to an end and Cody prised himself away.

It was late and we were tired, and the inevitable drive home awaited us. We kissed at the stoplights, barely noticing when they turned green. I wanted the minutes to drag, but they didn't. We parted ways, "Send lots of pictures of you in Los Angeles and have a great time!"

"I'm going to miss you", I replied holding onto his hand in the loading bay.

"I'll miss you too honey", he kissed me, and I watched him disappear into the night, his taillights fading into the darkness.

***

Spring break was here. I spent the morning packing; dresses, skirts, crop tops and my passport, I was excited to leave the dreary winter behind and step into the promised land; Los Angeles. Meave, Bella, and I caught a taxi from the Dinner Hall to Rochester Airport, rearing and ready to go. The taxi had a sticker on the window, 'God, Guns and Country', and if that didn't sum up small-town America, I didn't know what did.

The flight from Atlanta to Los Angeles was long and so my thoughts began to wander. They wandered to New York and the dirt track roads and trees. I thought about country music and Rochester, Brockport and everywhere in between I thought of Letchworth State Park and Main Street; Upstate New York pulled on my heartstrings up in the early morning sky, up amongst the clouds. I watched the little plane on the flight tracker venture further and further West, towards California and the city of the stars. I couldn't help but look backwards at how far New York slowly became.

I thought about Cody, and how I wanted to tell him I loved him when I journeyed home. I missed him, and I would have switched in an instant to be sat in his truck instead of on that flight. Los Angeles was getting closer with every second, my childhood dreams in reach, and yet all I could think about was Cody and how far he was already slipping away. It dawned on me as dawn broke over England, that I had found a new home, and since meeting Cody, Upstate New York had become quite possibly my favourite place on Earth.

***

The Californian sun danced along my back, and I closed my eyes, basking on the beach. The waves crashed along the shore, and I rolled back out with the tide. I rolled out to my childhood, to my brother and sister, to my Mother, to my Granny and Grandpa; I was back again in Cornwall. I was young and the youthful bliss of sunshine and sandwiches, the rock pool and crab fishing, rolled back to me. Trevone, Millook, Crackington Haven, Widemouth Bay… all the beaches I had loved so much seemed so far away, but Redondo Beach pathed my way back to them.

Sometimes life fades to black, the switch to the world flicked off, leaving us groping through the shadows. I hadn't realized how long I'd been living under a shroud until I found myself lying alone in California, and suddenly I could see again. The world was bright and beautiful, and as my heart beat the waves washed me clean. I'd forgotten what it was to be alone, to sit still, to feel the deep and ordinary rhythm of the sea.

The ocean invited me in, and I walked out into the water, the vast stretch of enchanting blue. I was baptized anew. I was a child of the universe and for all my battles with the world, I knew that something out there was looking after me. Something out there, just beyond the horizon told me it was okay, that I was loved. It's surprising how adaptable we human beings are, now that I had been removed from Brockport, I questioned how I had managed to stay there so long; and how College life seemed to be all I had ever known. Yet, there in the ocean, I was reminded of my adventurous spirit; California reminded me of how I felt in Pokhara, the mist-wrapped mountains of Nepal, of how one can fall in love with a country all over again, just by changing locations.

I was already hurriedly thinking of where I wanted to venture next; I thought of Australia, the great barrier reef, or perhaps Thailand; or maybe I'd build a little boat and paddle across the blue until I arrived in Honolulu. I had lost so much in my life that loss no longer seemed like an obstacle. I wanted to be on the move, I was a nomad and I no longer had to fight for my freedom, I was mobile, the world was my oyster, and the sea gave me my clarity. At that moment, I was glad that Owen was no longer in my life, for I wouldn't have had peace, I wouldn't have had quiet. California would've been tarnished with arguments and accusations, a battle fought on hallowed ground. But now, California could stay pure, unmarred.

The next day we all cycled from Redondo Beach to Hermosa Pier. We had gotten up early and walked to the nearest bike hiring store, and a big wad of cash and four bicycles with baskets later, we were zipping along the Southern Californian Bay. We pedalled past suntanned pedestrians, roller skaters holding hands, volleyball teams and stoners. My senses were alive, a breeze blew in my hair, and sea salt and marijuana filled my nose, music from other cyclers and the beach trailing in and out; hip-hop, classical, and R&B. I smiled as we raced on past miles of blue and yellow, ducking under kite lines and swerving to avoid skateboarders.

We partied on the tables that night, dancing to the beat of our lives; an Italian, an Irish, and an English woman in California, drunk under the palm trees of Los Angeles, claiming America for our own. I hugged strangers and embraced the oneness of us all. Meave chatted excitedly to the girls in the toilet, Bella and Dan swayed side by side and I waltzed up and down the bar, hypnotised.

I needed a cigarette and so I disappeared, wandering out onto the strip. The night was winding down and it was almost deserted, no longer buzzing with drunks and anticipation. It was peaceful; the simplicity in quietness is often ignored and I felt that was a shame. I wandered down the pier, surrounded by an ocean I could only hear for the black water was invisible against the night. I decided to loop back to the club, but I was in L. A and I were fat, and they didn't let me back in. I protested and that only made it worse. I watched a trail of girls leave and walk back in, tall and thin and beautiful. And I fat and ugly and alone, furiously phoned Meave and Bella back and forth, the phones ringing out.

I sat there still and angry, smoking through my packets of cigarettes, until the club closed some hours later and everyone came piling out. A woman saw me crying, she was with Meave and someone else whose face I struggled to picture. She handed me a tulip, I thumbed its silky stem and looked at the petals, before crumpling it in the palm of my hand.

"Why'd you do that?"

I pulled a face and shrugged, walking away from her. Meave chased after me and so did her newfound friend.

"Can I have a cigarette?", the girl I didn't know asked.

I looked to Meave and barked, "If one more person asks me for a cigarette, I swear to God I'll kick off."

***

I was in Santa Monica when Cody asked me to be his girlfriend, he said I was the only thing keeping him sane. I told the girls back at the motel, and they were unimpressed,

"That's too soon."

"He's moving too fast."

"But you're going to have to go home."

"He has a wife."

I told Cody to ask me again when he next saw me, and that I would decide then. He was adamant. I was secretly overjoyed. The L.A. hot nights and ocean-swept days had come to an end and we were heading home again.

***

Life felt stagnant when I got back from California. The things I was excited to return to were dull. I was back in the snow again. I liked the snow when I first arrived, the pretty white blankets which reminded me I was someplace else. Yet now, it felt like spring was blossoming across the world and I was stuck in the place where it was always winter and never Christmas. The day I got back, I had a couple of hours of sleep and then was off again.

It was time to see Cody. I had projected so much of my hopes and dreams onto him, that I was disappointed when I didn't get the rush of excitement of seeing him. He was nervous and I clung to his anxiety like a spider clings to a web. We drove to Hamburg – a town outside Buffalo, where we had a night in an Inn ahead of us. I fought off tiredness as we ploughed onwards through the night. Upstate New York flew past my window; it was a wasteland, a barren void of red barns and large country houses, of fields and small-town America. I told Cody I liked it better than California, and on that night, for some strange reason, I did.

We pulled up to the Inn and I was glad we were someplace other than campus, that I was standing someplace other than the Dinner Hall. Cody went and checked us in, the clerk was large and friendly, he had a red face and a cap too small for his large head.

"Anywhere we can get Hydes around here?", Cody asked, then gesturing to me, "She wants one."

"Let me call my wife, I'm not good with directions."

The clerk lazily fumbled for his phone, showing us how it flips in two – overly impressed with himself and between talking to his wife and looking over at us, he started giving hazy directions. But it didn't take long before he gave up and leaned back in his chair, it creaked and the whole place creaked with it, "you know what, give me 20 bucks and you can have this one", the clerk pulled out a packaged Hyde from his pocket, "it tastes like an ice cream cone."

The deal was done, Cody's pockets were twenty dollars lighter and mine a Hyde heavier. We dropped the bags off in our suite, a dingy room with character. I think Cody was embarrassed by its cheapness, but I liked it. The night was slow, and I was glad for I felt slow myself. Cody made me bottomless Sex on The Beaches as per request, and I downed them one by one. We watched Harry Potter and The Goblet of Fire, and I told him of my autograph collection, of the Harry Potter wallpaper I once had plastered across my bedroom wall. We connected; I enjoyed hanging out with him.

Cody told me that he really liked me, and I believed him. We spoke about his love problems, and I kept trying to understand him, gazing into his hazel eyes, hoping he couldn't see into mine and unravel all the horrible things I had ever done. He told me about his wife, "I never loved her, I settled", he said, his face plastered with an expression I couldn't figure out, "she was the first woman I met in Rochester, and she wanted to marry me."

We talked slowly and then excitedly and slowly again, I wanted him to think I was excited about life, and in many ways, I was, though I mostly listened. I find people talk more when you listen. I wanted him to see me as I wanted to see myself; a young hopeful, full of promises and adventure, and without me voicing it, he told me he did, "You're different."

I looked at him and cocked my head and decided that he had earnt my vulnerability, "Promise you won't turn mean?", I asked.

Cody gestured at a pinky promise, "If you promise you won't leave me for someone else."

I promised, and we gazed at each other. Had we finally found the one?

"Play me a song that makes you think of me", I said and got up off his lap.

He obediently went over to the television stand where his phone was charging, and I waited in anticipation. He played *Love Story* by Taylor Swift, and I told him that was my favourite song before I grew up and got hurt before I gave myself to anyone, so I told him I loved him.

"I love you too, honey."

The bed was comfy, and his skin melted into mine, I was glad for the ropey Inn and for whatever the fuck Hamburg was, I was glad for Cody. In between hesitant conversations, fast-talking declarations and comfortable silences, Cody would hit his dab. The room had a hazy aroma of marijuana smoke, liquid nicotine, vodka and sex. I hit his dab too, and then crawled into the sheets, his arms blanketing me from the world, and we fell asleep.

The next morning rolled around, and I awoke to the taste of the last night; I felt nauseous and excused myself to be sick. A hungover clung to me as promises had clung to the room hours previous. Cody seemed unfazed, and I joked that he had been making his drinks weaker than mine, "You caught me there, honey."

We had to check out by eleven, which suited Cody for he was ready and raring to go, onwards to the next adventure, Niagara Falls. We weren't far from the Falls, but my stomach was in knots and the truck was too hot. I cracked the window and wished that Cody would stop talking, for every American drool was making my stomach churn.

The only part of the journey I enjoyed was driving along the U.S.-Canada border, seeing Canada mere feet away, the houses, the fields – another country, another place awakening the travel bug within. The Falls weren't as I expected, everyone always would say that the Canadian side was better, and they were right. I had envisioned cliffs and beautiful foliage, and yet it seemed to be randomly plonked amongst concrete and tall office buildings. I didn't think much of Buffalo, it reminded me of Rochester; they were both big cities and yet filled with vast emptiness. I found it peculiar how a great waterfall, mother nature's creation could be nestled between car parks and miserable grey. Though, I was excited to be there and thankful that I could tick another small wonder of the world off my travel list. The fresh air cured my hangover. Cody and I were the fresh new couple; poking at each other's ribs and holding hands, enjoying nature together.

We walked down the length of Niagara Falls and onto Goat Island, where a great tree in the woodland had toppled over.

"Let's climb it!"Cody turned around, eyes wide.

And so, we did. Cody hoisted himself up onto it and walked with large strides along the hundred-year-old trunk, before turning around and yelling over to me, "Come on!"

I followed tentatively on all fours, edging my way up and along the trunk towards him, "Don't look" I laughed, "this is the lamest thing ever."

We sat side by side, listening to the birds tweeting in the trees, squirrels rustling in the leaves and the waterfall rushing into the river. A wash of browns and oranges spread as far as I could see, and it was as if we had gone back in time to Autumn. The snow hadn't dared to fall on Goat Island, for it didn't wish to spoil its beauty.

"I love nature,"Cody sighed, his eyes following a little blue tit across the sky.

"Me too," I replied, running my hands along the twisted knots of the trunk, the rough bark, "Let's sit here forever please."

Cody looked over at me, and smiled, pulling me in for a kiss, "Yes, let's."

But, before I knew it, we were following the yellow line of the American road back to Brockport, Cody stopped for gas at the 7-11, and I knew he was stalling. We shared the sunken disappointment of the realisation that the day had come to an end. He had bought us both a soda and we clamoured into the truck bed and sat on his toolbox which was forever planted there. We drank our Coke and sat in silence, soaking in the day.

The night was cold, and we were shadowed by the world. Parked at the side of the road, no cars dared to intrude on our solitude.

"Can we be soulmates?", Cody suddenly asked, his gaze tilted up at the stars, as if he were asking the sky itself.

"Oh, but I thought we already were", I teased.

"I've not felt like this for a very long time", he confessed, finding my hand in the dark and squeezing it softly, the pressure somehow both firm and fragile.

I pulled my eyes away from the heavens and scanned his face, detecting the truth, "If there's anything I'm sure about it's you", he continued.

My words caught somewhere between my heart and throat, "What if I can't stay?"

He didn't flinch. "Honey", and there was something fierce in his voice, "I bend the universe to my will. I'll make sure you stay."

***

The weeks went on like they always did, sleeping through my morning classes, dragging myself to my afternoon ones and canteen dinners with Meave. I went out to the Frats once or twice, but the thrill it had given me, wore off weeks ago. It had become yet another routine; a ritual amongst the booze runs for my underage friends, walking to U-Hots for a 3 am burger and getting drunk to forget there'll be yet another tomorrow. Meave and I excitedly talked about New York City, the yellow cabs and tall buildings beckoning us, which shows we'd watch on Broadway and exploring Times Square. It kept us going, or at least it did for me.

Some days were a burden to shuffle my way through, studying in the library, lunches in takeaway containers and long nights of homework and overthinking. Some days were alive, electric with friendships and creative projects, frantic bursts of applying to internships and falling in love – my mini breaks coming in the form of Cody, spontaneous drives and meal outs, outdoor trekking, and kisses. Brockport again meant having a boyfriend.

I enjoyed how fast-paced it all was, I didn't have to stop, to think, to feel. It was a whirlwind, a race to see who could fix the broken pieces of their heart first. Cody was my happy distraction, and I was his. One date was as exciting as the other, and I would countdown the days from the last to the next.

Cody took me to High Falls in Rochester, where he stood by the roaring water and told me about geology, and how rivers shape the world over millions of years. There was a little island in the river below, barely more than a slip of land in the current, and he told me he'd like to live there, in a small, weather-beaten shack, away from the world —just him and his fishing rods and the pull of the water. I joked that I would stand on the bridge with a little zip wire and send him down food.

"As long as it's Pizza", he agreed, turning around with a bounce and a goofy smile sprawled across his face.

"Oh of course", I assured him, "only the finest pizza. Pizza worthy of an island King"

Later that day, he took me to Lake Ontario, laughing as he called it "Poopy Beach" because the water's edge bore signs of city runoff, the waves dull and dark like some great inland sea, with sand that wasn't sand, just silty layers of soil washed ashore. We walked down to the water's edge, and I stared out, almost unable to believe that I was looking at a lake and not an ocean. Everything in America expanded into extremes—the buildings, the rivers, even the sky. America was a land on steroids. I picked up a piece of driftwood and pretended to chase him with it, but he dodged, laughing.

"You're different today," he said, his smile softer, "I like it."

"Maybe I'm just in a good mood," I replied, spinning along the lakefront. "Maybe I'm excited."

"Oh, are you?" Cody caught up to me slinging his arm around my waist. "Excited about me?"

Without warning, he lifted me off the ground, all of me suspended in his arms as he spun us around. I squealed and we fell with a great *thwack*.

"Why'd you wiggle around like that!!"

"I don't like being picked up", I exclaimed, and stood up, taking his hand, hauling him up, "I'm heavy."

"Oh honey," he said, grinning as he brushed off his jeans. "Don't emasculate me."

***

I met his grandparents as the weeks evolved, they lived in quiet suburbia, in a ranch house, his Sicilian grandmother feeding me watermelon slices and pork. She piled asparagus and bread with sage stuffing onto my plate, and apologised that it wasn't "her best."

"This is her first home-cooked meal in nine weeks, that's what she told me", she barked in her New Yorker-Sicilian accent at her husband, who rarely spoke.

I smiled, "It's really good!"

"Honey, I'm Sicilian", she said, passing me more bread, "I like to feed."

"I'll never complain about that", I laughed.

They had a little dog, Mindy, she was the most hyperactive dog I had ever seen, a King Charles Spaniel. I watched the way Cody would pick her up, and I imagined he'd be a good father, cradling his children like he cradled her ball of fur. Their kitchen was small and tidy, his grandmother was a good wife and I felt sad that her life, which I knew nothing about, amounted to a silent husband, a clean house, and endless mealtimes. Perhaps she found her solace through cooking, I hoped she did.

"My grandparents really like you", Cody told me as he drove me back, "and I really love you."

I wondered if this was my life now, impressing grandparents and being polite at mealtimes. The bed of Cody's truck was full of masonry waste from his last side job, and he told me how he needed to get rid of it before he dropped me off. So, we threw bricks out of the back of the truck, stopping at intervals on deserted sides of the road. "Oh my god, this is so illegal", Cody groaned, concern over his face as he grabbed massive hunks of concrete and tossed them into the New York wilderness.

"You're going to get me deported", I joked.

"You probably would if we got caught."

I laughed at him, curious as to why he was so concerned about the law and the government, but I was glad to help. I enjoyed feeling as though I was doing something I shouldn't have been. I would have to convert him into being a rebel. And so, it continued like that: studying, friends, studying, friends, Cody, friends, studying. Not a whole lot ever happened in Brockport, you had to create your fun, and the weeks of mania that had consumed me were slipping away. My new normal grew exhausting.

***

I dreamt of Owen again. I was nineteen and we were in Bristol. I was staring across the room at him, to where he was sitting with tears rolling out of his blue eyes, his brown hair falling sad across his face. I felt defeated for I couldn't stand up and walk away. He deserved better than what the world had given him, but I was too young and naive to understand that his battle was not my own. The man before me was a reflection of my Father, and I was a little girl – and just as little girls aren't accustomed to leaving their fathers, I couldn't leave Owen. I couldn't bring myself to rip open the wound I had spent a lifetime sewing up.

I felt trapped again and I began to wonder if it was I that was the problem. I fantasised about running away, back into the arms of Owen. I missed him. I lay in bed at night and imagined my arms wrapped around him, I thought of our embraces; our magical, long loving embraces. I daydreamed about England and about returning – leaving Cody at the alter that didn't yet exist and down the aisle towards Owen; I wanted to be home at last. I felt heavy and slow, my face was too tight, and my bra dug in too deep; my whole existence – was uncomfortable.

I didn't feel good at anything. I couldn't commit to ideas, to people, to time, to places. I didn't like people, I wanted to drown them out. I had been sharing a room too long, living on campus, surrounded by Americans too long, and the American Dream was a rug that I was pulling out from under my own feet. I wanted to escape the world to escape myself. I couldn't string two sentences together or distinguish the good from the bad, life was murky – a horrible splash of desperate grey. I didn't want to be here or there, I wanted to be with Owen, I wanted rollies by the side of the bed, smoke-stained sheets, and alcohol. I wanted to let loose, I wanted to *fuck*.

I needed to get away from everything. I was an enigma, the girl with the clip-in extensions and thick thighs and big stomach and self-hate, the girl who couldn't be held down, the girl on the road, the girl running, always running. I hit Hydes until they were burnt, and smoked cigarettes until my hair smelt and my fingers stained. I lay night after night with racing thoughts and an annoying mind. I detested everything and couldn't settle on what I wanted. I decided to drink myself to death, but I didn't have any booze, none of that Angry Orchard I liked so much. I, myself, was an angry orchard; maybe the only thing left were the trees, nature, and the great outdoors. I wasn't good at anything. Good for nothing.

I tried to make sense of everything, piecing together the broken shards of my life, but the more I tried the more the shards sliced me, cutting at my fingers and digging into my palm. I gave up. My life was a mystery, a puzzle that could not be solved, and I only bled anytime I tried. I wanted something to hold onto but when things held onto me, I shook them off with venomous ferocity.

Valentina interrupted me, rapping on my desk, "Have you ever heard yourself typing?"

"No"
"Well, you type like a mad person."
"Good."
God, I wished she would go away.

***

It had been a week since I last saw Cody. Strangely, I didn't find myself missing him; maybe the intensity had faded quicker than expected. Our texts had trickled down to small talk, and whatever excitement I'd once felt for him had turned into a kind of lingering curiosity. But when he pulled up that Friday afternoon, in the thick of a snowfall, I thought maybe this time, something would shift back into place.

"So," he said as he leaned over to kiss my cheek, "we're going on an adventure today—I'm taking you to the Indian reserve."

"Oh?" I raised my eyebrows, catching his sly grin as he put the truck into drive, leading us out of Brockport.

"They sell weed there, and cigarettes, dirt cheap," he explained, eyes on the road. "Gonna buy you some bud and rolling papers."

The reserve was nearly an hour away, and soon Cody's usual ease faded into fidgety silence. He looked uncomfortable, shifting in his seat and glancing at me every few minutes like he was trying to gather his thoughts. Finally, he exhaled and confessed, "Listen… a woman I met a few weeks back messaged me. She wanted… you know. I talked to her for a minute, but then I blocked her."

My stomach twisted, and I turned toward the window, watching as the snowy landscape sped by. I was annoyed and told him not to tell me crap like that when I was out of cigarettes. I looked out of the window as he apologised. I shook my head and ignored any attempts of trying to reconcile, my silence a shield. He offered to take me home, and I told him I was disappointed in him.

"Let's not talk about it anymore", I said, "but if you do that again, I'm gone."

He bought me a carton of ten cigarettes, two pots of bud and edibles. I decided that was a good trade-off for a small betrayal. He asked to kiss me several times and I didn't let him. I was toxic, I let him pander.

"So, do you wanna go to a bar, or do you wanna go back to mine and have those edibles and drink there?"

"Yours."

"Yes, Ma'am," he replied, a relieved smile breaking through his worry. "You hungry?"

"I could eat."

"Well, where to then?"

I hesitated, feeling a strange mix of gratitude and resentment toward his ease. "Taco Bell?" I asked shyly.

"Taco Bell it is." He grinned, taking my hand briefly as if to reassure me.

"Thank you", I said studying the profile of his face, he always looked so good in the truck. I wondered whether I was biased for that was the version of him that I loved, "I appreciate you."

"No problem honey."

We ate tacos and drank Pepsi, debating communism and capitalism, educational systems, and England versus America. Cody got a kick out of it, talking wildly about politics and law and taxes. It went over my head, but he didn't seem to notice: Ambulances, VAT prices, children from the hood going to Yale. All this excited talk flew from his mouth and went through one ear and out the other, through the open window alongside my cigarette smoke and patience.

Once back at his grandparents and in the comfort of his basement we took the edibles. He gave me three glistening candies, and I chewed on them. They tasted just like strawberry gummies. I watched amused as he did crunches and wandered around the room, potting about, and then before I knew it, the weed seeped into our systems, and we were in a country music trap. George Straight, Keith Urban and Kenny Chesney all rolled into one. We lay on Cody's bed, consuming one patriotic music video after another. I laughed my head on Cody's stomach.

"What', he asked, pausing the music video for the hundredth time, "What's funny?"

"It's so American", I chuckled.

"You don't like it?", he sounded disappointed.

"No, I like it, baby, you can play it."

And so, Cody played it, and continued to play it, queuing songs which were always "the best country song" and yet were continuously more diabolical as the minutes rolled on. I laughed again, louder this time.

"Oh my god", Cody groaned, "what's funny?"

"Is this a spoof?", I asked, watching a man in a redneck hat and cowboy boots strum his guitar singing about God, Country, and red, white and blue.

"No, it's serious."

"I don't think I realised until this moment how different we are", I giggled.

"You want to play something else?"

"Listen, I'm gonna play you a song that summarises British culture. It doesn't get any more different."

"Okay, let's hear it."

I took his phone and jabbed Parklife by Blur into the search bar.

"They're not even singing!" Cody exclaimed, "Bro, they're talking, they're not singing."

I laughed.

"I don't get it", he continued, "What's Park Life?"

I couldn't explain it to him, but I realized I didn't need to. He was sprawled out beside me, revealing himself, in all his American heartland glory. I felt his vulnerability, his pride in his world and his values. The ease with which he shared these pieces of himself—without embarrassment or hesitation—was endearing.

"You're really sweet," I teased, resting my head on his shoulder, and letting my hand rest over his heart. "You're lying here, playing an English girl all your favourite country music. You're showing me who you are."

He shrugged, a little shy, but his voice was firm. "I love my country."

And there was a simplicity in that, an unbreakable loyalty that I both admired and felt distant from. As we lay in his dimly lit basement, high and half-asleep, with his beloved country music humming in the background, I felt a strange warmth for him. I was beginning to see him clearly: flawed, earnest, fully open. We beamed at each other, and he kissed me. I was in an American basement, listening to American music with an American boy, high off my face on Native American edibles, and yet we could've been anyone, doing anything. We moulded together perfectly. I thought it peculiar that I ever doubted our connection, for the first time in days, he felt real and obtainable. He wasn't perfect, but maybe that was the point. His world was raw, messy, and stubbornly hopeful. And, for that night, I was part of it too.

***

The edibles hit me. I was peeing too loud, I was taking too long, I was breathing too much —the lights too bright. I analysed the reflection taunting me in the mirror. My eyes were red and my hair messy; I was greeted by a different girl than the one I had last seen. I stumbled out to the bed and sat perched on the side, my mouth dry. I looked over to Cody, and if he hadn't looked so wasted, I would've felt embarrassed.

"I think I'm having a panic attack."

My skin felt taut as if the fabric of the T-shirt had wrapped itself around me, a constricting coil tightening with every breath. I yanked it off, gasping for air. I couldn't breathe.

"It's okay honey, come here."

I lay down and rolled over to my side, my heart beating out of my chest. Cody rolled over to me and his arms enveloped me, pulling me close, his body warm and solid against mine, a steady anchor. His breath was gentle, his face pressed into the curve of my neck. "You're okay honey, I promise."

"I'm having a heart attack."

"It's just the weed honey, I've got you." His voice low, familiar as he held me against him, his warmth seeping into me, "Focus on your breathing."

I tried, but the more I focused, the louder and out of sync it seemed. I was acutely aware of every breath I took, the way it seemed to hang in the air, thick and heavy. I was clumsy, I was fat again.

But then Cody's voice reached me, his arms solid, his presence real.

"In and out, in and out." He murmured, breathing deeply through his nose and out through his mouth, his warm breath reassuring me.

I imitated him, in and out, in and out, into hell and out again.

"I love you honey", he kissed the nape of my neck, "Just ride it out, you'll be okay, I promise."

Cody was good, I could feel the goodness of his soul seeping from his body into mine. As he cradled me the panic left as quickly as it had come. Cody rubbed my back, and I was glad I was soon to be entering the world of dreams, a rest bite from the Earth.

"Goodnight honey."

APRIL 2022

Cody's alarm sounded and I was back again, a physical being rooted to this plane. Whilst we had slept, we had left March and entered April; April 1st 2022, the start of Spring. The day ahead was going to be busy, but I was already craving my ethereal self. I wasn't ready to be propelled into a new day, "What time is it?"

"Five-thirty honey, you can sleep a little longer, I need to sort the rods out."

Cody had decided he wanted to take me fishing, to teach me how to cast and reel. He wanted to share his passion, perhaps in hopes that it would become mine. I dozed on the bed with Mindy, she had been curled on my feet all night. I lapped up all the comforts of sleep until the day could no longer be postponed, and up and out the door we went, rods and lures in hand. I rolled for us on the way to the creek, and Cody teased me, calling them prison joints.

"Why?" I asked, "because I've rolled them shit?"

"No", he laughed, "because there's hardly anything in there!"

"Oh, sorry", I joked, "roll them yourself then if you're so bloody bothered!"

He pulled that face he always pulled when there wasn't a comeback good enough and reached out for my hand. I held it, I liked how his hands felt big against mine. Cody made me feel like a woman. I was drawn to his masculinity, his practicality and his outdoor nature.

"You look gorgeous honey."

I didn't, I had eyebags and my face was bare. I was wearing a grey fleece and my hair was pulled into the bun I had slept in. I was sure that my fleece was tucked into my back fat and that my belly bulged from under my seatbelt, but I thanked him anyway.

We pulled up to the creek and Cody taught me how to cast the line. My first few throws were shoddy, and I was glad it was early, for I would have been embarrassed if there had been anyone around to see. It was cold. I wasn't sure if I liked fishing, but I found peace in being with Cody. I enjoyed watching him in his element, strolling up and down the bank. He possessed an air of knowingness.

I got a bite on my line and then a fish wrestled my lure. I reeled it in, excited by the promise of a smug catch on the other end of the line. But, the fish had bit the lure right off the hook. That's about as close as either of us got to catching a fish that day. Cody blamed the creek and so we climbed back into the truck, to the next creek and the one after that.

I learned that Cody was impatient. He was always flipping from one direction to another without any time to settle. It wouldn't even reach half an hour in one location before he decided the wind was too strong, the creek too shallow or the water too clear. It amused me. I found it funny how his brain worked. His fishing reflected his life, bouncing from one place to another, forever casting a line and forever reeling in the weeds.

We spent the whole day by the water, the plop of lures hitting the surface and sinking to the depths. It was peaceful and tranquil, and time stood still. The sun came out and the sky was blue, and I was happy. I hoped the whole Spring would continue like that, with good company and good weather, with the outdoors and fresh air. April beckoned a turn for the better, for blossoming, blooming and rebirth.

***

The days after seeing Cody were filled with interviews for a videography position at a summer camp near New York City. I had willingly thrown myself at them in hopes that they would be my lucky break, and they were. I was going to stay for the summer. I told Cody and he was elated for me, but the elation was short-lived when I told him I would have to go back to the U.K. in August, as my visa would expire after my internship. The summer job only postponed the inevitable ending of America and our chapter.

"Then marry me, and we'll make it official—green card and all."

I stared at the words typed so carefully, so precisely. I didn't know what to say. I waited until another message appeared, *"We could just go to the courthouse and get married. You'd get your citizenship, and I'd follow you anywhere. Honestly, I see you as more of a partner than I ever did with Rochelle."*

I was in disbelief; *"You love me that much?"*

"You're my soulmate."

I turned off my phone, pushed it aside and cried. How could he be my soulmate when I had another? How could I love him and yet love another? And so, I cried. I cried and cried and cried. My heart shattered into two. It broke like I could never have imagined it to break, it broke for my twin flame; for the lost. I was devastated. I was devastated for I couldn't stop loving Owen. I couldn't stop wanting and needing him and I howled, a long terrible howl, and a hand came and grabbed my heart. It squeezed it and yanked it straight out of my chest, wringing blood and clots all over the floor. I wanted to die.

My knees buckled. I desperately tried to scrape the squelching pulp of my heart from the floor, but all it did was bloody my shaking hands. "Fuck", I exclaimed, "Fuck! I change my mind!"

I screamed, I couldn't stop screaming, "I changed my mind!"

Screaming turned to sobbing and I couldn't undo what had already been done. I had chosen to let Owen go and I couldn't pull him back from the ether, all was lost.

What if I had been living in my head? What if he didn't care about me anymore? What if he didn't want me? I scrambled up from the floor, slipping on my blood. Blood started falling from the ceiling, it was all around me, it coated me, I couldn't see through it, it poured into and out of my eyes, what if he didn't love me? What if he had moved on?

I opened my mouth to scream my long-drawn-out scream but this time nothing came out. God had cut out my tongue. "Give him back," I thought, "Give him back. I want him back."

I couldn't have him; it wasn't meant to be. We hurt each other, he hurt me, I hurt him. There were years of hurt, of bruises, and yet his loss was the most excruciating blow. It knocked everything out of me, and my innards dispersed. I was naked and hunched for I could no longer stand. I was feral and I regressed. The room was my womb, and I succumbed to dying. Blood turned to acid rain, and it plummeted down, paintballs on my ripped-up skin. It sizzled and burned, and I couldn't feel a thing, a great numbness washed over me. *Please be mine. Please be mine. Please be mine.* But he wasn't.

I had gotten rid of him and yet he had wanted to marry me, he had wanted forever, he had told me repeatedly for years. I was the only one he ever wanted, he wanted my children, he wanted my life, he wanted my brain, he wanted my heart, he wanted me. I had fought him off and snatched myself away. I had decided to protect myself from his hands that soothed me. All this time I thought I had ripped out his heart, but his was alive and beating and healing, and mine was nowhere to be seen. I no longer knew what was real, I had fictionalised my whole life.

When you put love on a pedestal, it comes crashing down. I fell through the floor; I plummeted down into the black. I was in the dark, journeying down and down and down,

I was Alice in Wonderland, and I was hurtling through the rabbit hole. Finally, when I could no longer possibly fall any further, I landed on my neck. It cracked. I was sprawled, pasty white, distorted in the bottom of the world's well. I looked up with my glass eyes, and there was no light. I had died.

My soul didn't leave my body for it was already gone; it had left with the last goodbye. There were no more fumbled words to be said. White butterflies crawled out of the walls of the well, their wings were broken, and they could not fly. Their spindly legs carried their dust-laden bodies, their torn wings towards mine. They fed on my body, camouflaged against my skin, drinking my blood until they too died, for I was poison.

***

The rain started to fall. The April showers were here, and with the water came the cleansing of my small world; it brought rebirth. I had decided that if Cody was serious about marrying me, I would, for he was kind and whole. He loved me and although a non-tumultuous love was unfamiliar, I knew it was right. I needed to stop branding Owen as my penultimate lover for that love was tainted, and time was running on. I needed to be cared for, to live in the light, to have fun and to pour my energy into something that would blossom, rather than a bottomless pit of pain.

The first part of overcoming a problem is to recognise it, and I knew my loyalty was misplaced; I wasn't ill as I often deemed myself to be. I was traumatised. I was a survivor.

I took a deep breath as the rain sounded on my window; I knew I needed to calm down. I needed stability. I had made bad choices after what had happened in Germany, I knew I had. I had chosen the wrong people and done the wrong things; my thoughts were rushed and so my life was rushed and frantic, never slowing down. On the third anniversary of what had happened, of my womanhood being destroyed, I knew it was time to grow and to slow. I had to think in my head. My heart was oozing with past hurt far too much to be a reliable advisor.

Everything with Owen had been so difficult, the universe kept forcibly pulling us apart. Yet, things with Cody came easy; so much so, it was if someone on the other side placed him down right in front of me. A guardian angel got fed up with waiting for me to figure it out, so they gave me this charming, young American, whose heart was kind and honest, and said, "If you don't choose him I give up."

And so, I chose him. My whole splintered past had led me to him, and with that realisation, I was excited to give myself over to him, and I was sorry I hadn't surrendered sooner. Weekends were reserved for each other, and that weekend we had a trip to Newark, a small Finger Lakes town.

***

Cody had picked me up late, and we drove through the night. The sky was mottled grey; the moon must've been shining through the clouds. We checked in around midnight, and I was underwhelmed. We drank as that's all there was to do. I didn't feel entirely invested in it, but I enjoyed Cody's company.

"Should we jump on the beds?", he asked a smile on his face.

"Sure."

We bounced up and down. The bed, our springboard, up and up and up and away. I hoped I'd jump so high I'd go right through the ceiling and land on the moon. The thrill lasted only a moment and then it was back to sitting and drinking, listening to a mix of Bruce Springsteen, Dizzy Rascal and Snoop Dogg, and then that thrill wore off too.

I wanted to feel, to burn, to be struck by lightning. And yet, the only thing I felt were sheets and pillows and the rise and fall of lumbered breaths. I was frustrated by something I couldn't put my finger on.

"Simply wonderful sleep for a happier you", a commercial on the TV chimed. I scoffed. What is a wonderful sleep? I was yet to discover it. And a happier me? *Fuck off.*

***

"Do you want to go to a bar later?" Cody asked, clinging onto the side of the pool.

"No," I rolled my eyes and looked away.

"Really?" He puzzled, "you don't want to go to a bar with me?"

"Go with your wife."

"My wife was a stepping stone to you. I love you with my whole heart."

I swam away from him, clinging to the pool wall, looking down at myself, at how my stomach hardly fit in my bikini bottoms, how my thighs touched.

He swam after me, and turned me around, hauling my great weight up, and held me there in the water,

"I never thought I'd enjoy being around someone this much. I really believe you were made for me, and I you."

***

The bar was small and dimly lit, its cosy corners buzzing with quiet laughter and low music. Behind the counter, the bartender—a wiry, blonde Italian with an easy smile—seemed to be everywhere at once, slinging cocktails and sliding beer across the polished wood with practiced finesse. Cody and I were tucked into two stools, the world narrowing down to the clink of our glasses. Between rounds of mixers and bites of juicy burgers, I felt the edges of everything blur: the bar, the crowd, time itself. We leaned into each other, laughing as though nothing could touch us, feeding off the glow of shared secrets and a never-ending tab.

Cody looked at me with a playful seriousness, his eyes glinting. He reached over, gently lifting my hand in his rougher one. "Will you marry me?" he asked, sliding his thumb over my knuckles as if smoothing out the invisible ring he pretended to slip on.

"I'd marry you", I smiled, letting the warmth of his words settle over me, but there was a spark of something real, like the thrill of standing too close to the edge. My fingers brushed his leg, feeling the worn denim beneath my hand. "I'd make a very lucky wife indeed."

We shared a look—part tease, part dare. It felt more real than it should have, charged with the possibility of things we both knew would likely fade by morning. But in that dim bar, with Cody's thumb tracing circles on my hand, it was easy to believe in anything.

At some point, Cody caught the bartender's eye, raising two fingers in a way that seemed casual enough, until the wiry blonde slipped through a door behind the counter, leaving a pause in the rhythm of drinks and orders. Cody glanced at me, his face unreadable.

When the bartender returned, she leaned over the bar, sliding Cody a small, folded paper in a way that was almost too subtle to notice, like a magician's sleight of hand. Cody took it, slipping it into his pocket as if it were nothing, flashing me a grin.

I felt the air shift. A hungry desire spread through me, sharper than before. Cody leaned close, his eyes dark, alive with something almost manic. "Wanna go?" he whispered, his hand brushing the small of my back as he slid off the barstool, and left a pile of dollars on the bar.

We slipped out the side door, into the cold. Cody's breath hung in the air as he fumbled in his pocket, pulling out his truck keys. His expression was somewhere between excitement and desperation, chasing something that was always just out of reach We got back to the hotel and continued drinking. Cody made the best mixers, rustling up pineapple and vodka concoctions which we guzzled down. Cody moved quickly, almost frantically, over to the TV stand, where he started racking up lines with the same precision he had with the drinks. His driver's license, the edges worn from use, slid across the glass, the crisp white powder forming neat lines one after the other. I lay back on the bed, letting the music fill the room, the soft pulse working its way into my veins. There was something about the way the night was unfolding, how easy it was to get lost in it. Cody rolled up a 100-dollar bill. We took turns inhaling lines, choosing songs and professing love. We shared our secrets and our innermost thoughts, we loosened up.

"I'm writing a best-selling book," I told him, mocking myself, but somehow, it felt true at that moment. "You're in it."

"Oh yeah?" he smiled, his eyes flicking to mine with a knowing gleam. "I'm sure you are."

"Don't doubt me," I said, the words a little too forceful, "I'm a good writer."

"Oh, I'm not doubting you, honey, I promise."

Cody kept the alcohol flowing and I stretched out in the sheets feeling the linen across my body and thought of my friends in Cornwall. In particular, I thought of Sadie, of our acid trips and coming up on ecstasy, how we would lie side by side and admire small comforts. I would get up in intervals and pace around and Cody would do the same. He opened up to me about his past, about his first love who had cheated on him and his wife who hadn't understood him, both having left him for women.

"You don't have to worry about that", I declared, "I'm straight as shit."

And then I told him about Owen, how he had cried at the airport and begged for me to come back. I spoke of the guilt which haunted me for I had promised him I would. I felt I had let my character down for I don't promise lightly. I was worried I had betrayed him. My feelings poured out of my mouth, and I tried to vocalise my confusion about navigating a healthy love. I struggled with the fact that Cody didn't possess nor control. It was hard for me to take his love at face- value,

"That wasn't love honey, that's Stockholm syndrome."

Perhaps he was right. I felt a twinge of sadness though for Owen was often painted as all bad. I wouldn't have stuck with him for so long if he was. I thought back to Normandy and of my conversation with Owen's mother. I had told her I was in love with her son for he was the most beautiful person I knew, and that had been true. Even reflecting on that moment, I refused to believe he was terrible.

"Do you still love him?" Cody asked.

"I have a love for him," I replied softly, my mind spinning with memories. "But if I was in love with him, I wouldn't be in this hotel room with you."

Cody pulled an expression I couldn't read, and for a moment, I saw a crack in the armour he wore so well. He looked away, then back at me, his eyes dark with something unreadable.

"I feel vulnerable," he said, his voice tight with something raw.

"I know," I replied, my voice steady despite the adrenaline buzzing in my veins. "I've known since we went to Rancho Viejo and cuddled by the church."

Cody's eyes widened slightly. "Oh? You knew I was vulnerable because we cuddled?"

"No," I answered, my gaze steady. "I knew because I held you. I could feel it. You've got deep sadness in you, don't you?"

He paused, his breath caught for a moment. The vulnerability that he always tried to keep hidden slipped out then. "Yeah," he nodded, his expression wistful, distant. "I do."

I didn't press him, but my next question was simple. "Is it because of your parents? It's often because of parents."

Cody sat up, silent for a moment, as if the question had hit too close. He finally mumbled, almost too quietly to hear, "I was never good enough for my Dad."

He got up and walked back to the little pile of cocaine, snorted another path of crystals into his brain, another break from the world through the 100-dollar bill and into his sorrowful soul.

"Do you want to see my vulnerability?" I asked, my hands behind my back, proud I had figured it out.

"Sure, show me, honey."

I snatched up my hairbrush from the side table and strolled into the bathroom where tins of pineapple juice, half-drunk bottles of vodka and spilt cranberry juice littered the basin. I analysed my body and my face. I decided I was beautiful. My hair fell in blonde curls around my face, edging towards my necklace that I never took off, for it was my spiritual link to my Mother. I took the brush and took a breath, running it through my curls until they became fluffy, expanding around my hair into a mass of delicate frizz. I brushed harder, spirals separating into a cloud of hair, an Afro halo.

In childhood, my Dad had called it a lion's mane. I apologised to the mirror, for bleaching my hair and breaking it, for straightening it, for ironing out my race. I had felt undeserving of my natural hair for it didn't match my skin; the world perceived me as white, and it was easier to pretend I was.

I walked back into the bedroom where Cody was waiting,

"Well, here it is."

"You're gorgeous honey."

I hugged him and then we were back to talking again, *yapping, yapping, yapping,* a flurry of wanting to be understood. I can't remember what I had said, but it must've been something about Grandpa, for the next thing I knew Cody was lying on the bed sobbing. His paternal grandmother had passed, and he regretted not having spent more time with her. I was surprised by the emotional display, and sat quite hopeless wiping his face with my hands, "I okay."

"No, it's not", he sobbed, "I was a piece of shit. I sat on my ass smoking weed all day instead of seeing her, and now she's gone."

"That's what kids do", I said soothingly, "don't blame yourself."

"But I do", he cried, and I let him cry. He looked like a little boy. I often forgot he was twenty-four for he seemed to have his whole life together; his independence and job, his truck and money. Perhaps that was merely a disguise, steered by his wounded inner child, lost and afraid. Finally, his sobbing quietened, and his body soothed.

He lay in silence for a moment, his eyes planted to the ceiling and then they wandered to me. "Can we go fishing now?"

I looked into his eyes, tears coating his lashes and replied, "Of course we can."

"You better catch a fish." He said as he got up and sat by the television stand, racking up two lines of perfect white powder, "Well this is the last of it now, honeybun."

I was disappointed. Cody snorted his line and I mine, and then off we went.

"I don't feel high yet."

"Trust me baby you're high."

We crossed over the bridge, down the steps to the water where we'd fished that morning, the same cold stone now softened by the night. I smiled to myself, thinking how, earlier, I'd had no idea I'd end up back here—a creep in the dark. Cody was already at the water's edge, busy with his line, bait box open as if fishing was all that mattered. But I lingered, feeling the night air stir through me, a restless energy rising within. The act of fishing required patience and effort, but I wanted only ease. I enjoyed the fresh air and outdoors and a great energy bubbled within. Yet, fishing required effort, and I desired ease. Cody had left the tub of live bait open. I ogled the worms sinking in and out of the soil, impressed they were still alive. I watched their fat bodies twist and turn and bury and emerge.

"Can I let them go?" I asked Cody, whose back was turned, casting a line into the canal.

"I don't care honeybun, you can do what you want", he replied.

I marvelled at them for quite some time, repulsed and enamoured, I could almost see their hearts beating through their long slimy bodies. I reckoned they'd pulled the short straw by being born a grub, "do you think they're related to slow worms?"

"What's a slow worm?" he asked, reeling in his line and flicking the rod. The line whirred, followed by a distinct plop.

"Don't worry", I muttered and put the tub down, I needed to walk. I hopped onto the small stone wall, balanced my way along it and turned around, pacing back and forth until it no longer sufficed. I needed to walk. I hummed to myself, once conscientious of appearing like a crackhead, I was now too lost to care.

I looked across the canal and saw a bandstand, a relic under the moon's glow, shining white at 3 a.m. It called to me like Gatsby's green light across the bay, a beacon in Newark's forgotten corner, my small Taj Mahal. Daffodils lined the path that led there, bright against the dark. Where had they been this morning? When we had come earlier all I had seen was concrete and dead fish, rotting carcasses at the wayside. However, now I was drug-fuelled and alive, I could see the world for how it always existed but was rarely noticed, the nature, the breeze, the beauty in the everyday. The street lamps cast long yellow stripes over the water, and I imagined the daffodils leading a golden path straight to the bandstand, and my feet jittered.

A warmness washed over my aching body, and I was innocent. Cocaine went to my brain, and it rattled, *"Where is the love?"*. I had blazed through life, leaving behind a trail of smoke and fire.

I had been on a self-professed journey for love. It was clear now that I was merely looking for my Dad.

I wandered down the canal until I came face to face with the branches of a winter tree, the bare bark reaching out to me, its gnarled limbs stretching out like an invitation. I stopped and stared; it stared back. I swayed where I stood and wished the breeze would turn to wind and whip the branches to action so that we could dance. I touched one of the veined branches, running my hand down the bumps of the buds and I was glad it would flower in the coming months. I didn't want it to live in the cold. The air was crisp, and it blew through the branches onto me, and I smiled. I loved nature and in my haze of ecstasy, I understood why tree huggers existed.

Cody wandered over, his hood up, shuffling past the water, and stopped, watching me with that familiar, easy grin. "What are you doing?" he asked, amused.

I laughed. "Listen, I know it looks weird—"

"Twenty minutes ago you said you weren't high," he teased.

"Nah but listen," I said, I reached out, pulling him up onto the bank so he could stand under the branches with me, "If you actually listen you can hear nature, it speaks."

He stood there, silent, waiting for something profound to happen. But there was only the night, still, deep, holding us in its silence. "Come on, honeybun," he said finally, "I'm cold."

"But we only just got here."

"I know, but it's freezing, and I've hit a wall."

I took his hand, leading him under the arch of branches, ducking into the embrace of the tree's shadow. I sighed, taking in the expanse of dark sky above us, the empty stillness around. "I wanna live here, under this tree," I announced.

Cody lay back, his head amongst the daffodils and I lay back with him, raising my arms to the sky, feeling the breeze on my skin, and marvelling at my limbs. My body was a trunk, my arms and legs branches, my fingers and toes twigs,

"Cody!", I exclaimed, "I'm a tree."

He laughed, "I don't know about that, honey." He tugged on my arm, gently. "Come on, let's go."

We ambled up the steps. Cody stopped to sort out his fishing gear as I consumed everything around me, gulping down the electricity of the world, and its glorious buzz. The neon signs of petrol stations gleamed, the reds and blues seeping into the atmosphere, floating away with the air and the ether breathed. *Tick. Tick. Tick.* The traffic lights sounded louder, and I was drawn to their vivid green, the dictator of the roads.

"Don't cross without me honey", Cody called up and paced up the steps, but I crossed anyway.

"Why'd you do that?" he asked, catching up.

"No cars were coming."

"I know but I told you not to."

"I'm sorry."

The hotel corridor seemed longer than when we'd left, the carpet welcomed us. It put on a display, swirling its patterns in the excitement of our return., "You were right."I said to Cody, taking his hand, "It's better inside."

"I'm so high", he replied as we got back into our warm room.

"I like it here", I observed, and then suddenly, electric, "Let's have a bath."

We bathed in the dark, a faint bluish light crawling across the floor from under the door. The only sound was the slow drip of the faucet and the gentle slosh of water against porcelain. Lavender and liquor hung in the air, bubbles foaming up and spilling lazily over the edges of the tub, slow, lethargic.

Cody sat behind me, his legs stretched out on either side of mine, knees bent just enough to cradle me against his chest. His arms draped loosely around my waist, slick and warm. I tilted my head back, resting it against his collarbone, feeling the slow rise and fall of his breath against my neck. Although I couldn't see, I could feel, I felt something deep inside me bubbling alive, in the bathtub with my American boyfriend, my rites of passage, my life. His fingers traced lazy circles on my stomach, dipping into the water.

He reached for a handful of bubbles, spreading them across my shoulders, slow, deliberate. Tender. He smoothed the foam down my arms, his hands light. I twisted slightly, turning to face him. My hands found his chest, tracing the planes of muscle I pressed a palm flat against his heart, feeling its steady, comforting thud.

He cupped my cheek, his thumb brushing against the wet curls. I leaned into the touch,

"Bedtime." He cooed.

"Bedtime." I echoed.

And when we crawled beneath the sheets, he held me close, "I'm happy", he breathed and that breath melted into a deep sleep.

***

I dreamt again. I dreamt that I was in a field, the grass covered in ash, the clouds above were sad. God had painted them orange. I raised my palms and awaited the rain, but it never came. My heart weighed heavy as it often did, but I told myself that was okay, it proved I still had life left. I squinted into the orange, and I saw figures dancing, ghostly silhouettes, shadows amongst the clouds. They were laughing, and rejoicing, and I yearned to join them.

"Hello", I whispered, my voice echoing, it made the ground quake, "Hello?"

They were too far up, and I was dismayed they couldn't hear me. Yet, a boy who I hadn't previously noticed was sitting on a cloud of fire, his legs dangling over the edge, and he let down a great rope. I leapt for joy; I too was going to dance in the sky.

The rope was taught and hovered above my head, and I started to climb, hoisting myself up to the heavens. Though, I couldn't have made it up more than a mere foot before it started to burn. It seared my hands, blistering my soft skin and I couldn't hold on any longer. I let go and fell on my back. The boy laughed, and I combusted into an array of reds.

I woke up and found I had missed another class; I'd slept through it and at that point, I didn't care. Everything else weighed too heavy, studying didn't seem to matter anymore. I wasn't sure what I was going to do. Home seemed to be getting closer by the day, and although I had made up my mind to stay, the logistics of it all seemed far too complicated. All the rules and regulations tore me, and I felt tangled in a mess of scratches and dead ends.

***

I no longer wanted the job at Camp Sunshine because it meant I'd be away from Cody for six weeks and long distance had never been kind to me. I hadn't had my period since before Los Angeles, and the thought of quite seriously being pregnant plagued me. My silky daydreams and cushioning denial weren't present as they usually were, and I felt depressed again. Perhaps I was doomed to go home and finish my degree. Maybe one day I would see Cody as nothing more but a holiday fling, a passing romance in this always passing world, a kiss in the breeze. I wondered if he'd flutter away as all beautiful things far too often do.

I wished I was a man and he was a woman. I would propose to him, and he would accept, and I was frustrated that although he had asked me to marry him, it didn't seem foolproof, it wasn't yet cemented. I didn't want to be at Brockport anymore, I didn't want to go to Camp Sunshine. I didn't want to go home, and yet I did. I wanted to go for a weekend back to Cornwall, to hug my Mother and then to be back in the States with it all figured out. I no longer wanted to fall in and out of love, and I wondered why I was bright and yet hollow, and how I was always too full and yet always empty, perhaps I had a puncture.

I told Cody about how I was feeling. I felt bad because he felt the same, a mess. Perhaps I should've kept my mouth shut. I was scared he was going to leave me; it would be easier for him to love an American woman. The day ached and the night ached, and I wasn't sure if it always would ache.

I felt angry with myself. Why couldn't I have forged a normal experience? Why couldn't I be like Meave or Bella, or the hundreds of students every year who go abroad and make friends, sight see and study? I was too chaotic. How is it possible that in eighty days I had ended a three-year relationship, fallen in the hands of another, acquired a half-hearted proposal, lined up an internship and felt far more than I could've bargained for?

Why was everyone else's life centred and yet mine seemed to lack gravity? America had handed me a shovel. I had spent the weeks burying myself in a hole and frantically digging myself out again. From day to day, I had no idea whether I would awake to soil in my mouth, or my head above the ground.

***

"I care about you so much, but I'm not emotionally ready for marriage. I think we need to part ways for now, until our lives are in a better place. Our paths have always been linked, and I believe they'll cross again someday, but this isn't goodbye—it just feels like it."

"I don't think we should break up. We can just live in the moment? I'll turn down Camp Sunshine."

"I can't ask you to do that."

"Are you seriously breaking up with me?"

"We need to."

"But that breaks my heart. I'm in love with you."

"I love you too."

"Then please don't do this."

"I have to honey. This isn't goodbye forever, it's just goodbye for now."

"Then it shouldn't be goodbye at all."
"This is the hardest thing I've ever done."

***

I walked up the cracked stairs, the slabs of perfect grey; charcoal blocks pathing the way. I didn't know if I was a traveller, a woman on a journey upwards to heaven or hell, or somewhere in between. I inhaled, and the air was musky, but it tasted sweet. I touched my hair, expecting to feel thick locks and a brazen mane, but my fingers ran through the white wisps of a balding crown, and I realised I was slumped in my frame. I was heavy and I oozed out of a wheelchair. The steps folded in on themselves and before I knew it, I was whizzing backwards on a ramp. I stretched out my wrinkled arms, fat flapping in the wind. I raised back my bulging chin and cackled.

One of the wheels got caught in a crack and I went flying off the seat, the ramp shifting ominously back into stairs, and I thudded onto the hard steps. I was 21 years old again, my skin was taught, yet supple enough to bruise. I smiled and pulled myself up, perching on the steps, attending to my wounds. Dressing my scraped-up knees with Band-Aids and dabbing my blood with cotton wool. A great many stars were out, and I realised I had made it. I was above the clouds, and it wasn't hell that awaited me. It was heaven. The blackness was strewn with glitter of milky ways and galaxies. I saw a star shoot past, it was beautiful and radiant, and I waved as it hurtled by.

I laughed, and tears of joy cascaded down my young face, I closed my eyes so I could feel them in my lashes.

I stood up, and stretched, taking a moment to soak in the galaxy, to consume its wonderment, its twinkles, its void of beautiful black dotted with astrological fireworks, *bang bang, bang*.

"Cody", I marvelled, "You're good and true, you rolled up your sleeves and decided what needed to be. Just because the timing wasn't right, I still think it's an honour to be your friend, friendships are so much stronger than lovers."

I sighed. As I exhaled, stardust left my mouth, and hovered around me, suspended by the lack of gravity. I was a star and my dust shone and I was so proud of the spectacle I had become.

"Grandpa", I beamed, "Look at me! I feel I am a granddaughter you can be proud of, and my oh my, am I so gloriously happy to be just that. I love you. I love you more than I think you ever knew, thank you for guiding me, for supporting me, for being here with me. I can't wait to see you at the golden gates, you can measure how tall I've gotten with your ruler, against God's wall of white."

I burnt bright as a star; I was so bright that those down on Earth would be able to see me there, a million miles away. I was the most golden star in the sky, and I wondered if an astronomer in a tower, somewhere forgotten, was writing me down somewhere, on a sacred parchment. The stairs had now vanished, and I was floating. I wondered if all the other stars were also girls like me, I hoped they were.

"Dad", I said, "Life is full of lessons and yours were full of hard ones, but you have three children, and each child is a blessing. You have three blessings, count them, every day, day and night, on your ageing fingers, one two three. Three beings who will continue to bathe in the light."

"Mum", I twinkled, "Oh Mama, I chose you, the last time I was here. The last time I danced amongst the heavens, I looked down on Earth and granted myself a wish. I wished for a mother, and I scoured the Earth, and through a windowpane, I saw you, with plump cheeks and blonde hair, sitting on a chair. I think it was brown, but life then was hazy as it hadn't started, not really. I decided you were gentle. You were selfless, you were beautiful, you were caring, but you had pain, and I blinked my ethereal baby blinks; your pain saddened me, and I shot right back up, through the ceiling, back to heaven and the ethereal plane. I told God I wanted to be given life again, that I had found my Mummy. That was the single best decision I have ever made, in all my life on Earth."

It was time to go back down, I had had my cleansing. I looked back around at the heavens, and I was excited, just as anyone who has ventured too far from home is excited to return.

"I'll see you when I see you", I said ogling my beautiful astronomical realm for the last time. I floated back down, to my sleeping body, and enjoyed the warmth of not being. I had a few hours left until morning would come around, and I would awake as a human again. They were the best few hours of slumber I had ever needed, and ever longed for. My physical body snoozed under the American sky, and I trusted when it awoke, it would be to the most magnificent journey, the journey of life.

***

I had fallen back in love with life, and I was perplexed as to why I ever felt otherwise. Where there had been a match, burning, whittling to black in the depths of my heart, there was now a spark — a spark that sometimes at night, would become a full-scale sparkler, fizzing white, convivial flickers of sentience. I was alive, lit up on something sacred.

New York City was a rush, a giant thrill, an escape from the *blah blah blah* of the mundane. I went with Meave and Bella.

We cycled around Central Park, explored the Empire State Building and caught a ride on a party boat amongst many other dazzling things. I felt alive to be with my friends and to be in the city. New York City was the apple of my eye. The depression which had nestled itself into my heart like a benign growth seemed to shrink in the April heat. We went to Brooklyn and splurged at the thrift shops, ate pizza and bagels and marvelled at the dinosaur bones in the Natural History Museum. I felt the world open like a giant rose, and the city was the bud. It was a blooming mess, heaven on Earth. We went and saw Pamela Anderson on Broadway, starring as Roxy in Chicago, and cried in the seats at the front of Moulin Rouge. New York City was a slot machine stealing my quarters and leaving me for dead, but I loved it.

I loved everything about the city, it was more exciting and magical than I had ever imagined. The hustle and bustle, the enormous buildings and tiny coffee shops, the night lights and Central Park. I wanted to stay forever.

Ping.

I scrambled amongst crumpled Broadway tickets, restaurant receipts and lip gloss, pulling my phone out of my bag. A message from Cody appeared on the screen; *"I just want us. I'd follow you anywhere"*.

I'd follow you anywhere, I read and laughed. I wondered if all men had a script, and how many had used that line as easily and carelessly as they did on me. I was surprised at myself for having lapped up his bullshit like a cat on milk.

The red hand shone down on me, ordering even the most daring not to cross. *Tik tik tik, wait, tik tik tik,* the little pedestrian speakerphone reminded me of earlier mornings at Redondo Beach, and I smiled. I looked up at the New York City street, at the traffic honking, cars packed like sardines on a road wide, but not quite wide enough. I watched the yellow taxis as they zoomed off with the turn of a green light, and pedestrians bustling their way through a crowd. My eyes averted upwards, and I cranked my neck back to see whatever small patch of blue sky I could, the skyscrapers so tall that New York was indeed a concrete jungle. I felt alive here and I didn't want to be followed. I only wanted to follow my dream, my destiny, my vision of a Manhattan townhouse, of lunches and friends, of lazy afternoons in Central Park, and evenings applauding glittering stars of Broadway.

The red hand switched to the little walking white man, and with a surge, I was swept across the road, 42nd Street behind and onto 43rd, from one adventure to the next. I was unobtainable, standing on top of the world, waving to all those who looked my way, only to disappear into the crowd again. I wanted to move to the city and live in a high-rise flat with a balcony, or a townhouse with flowers potted at the sides of the steps. I wanted to be a dancer, an actor, a poet, or a fiddler. I wanted to be a deep dark brooding creative, drinking a bottle of harsh liquor from the closest deli, and sleeping until noon. I was always drawn to being unhappy, perhaps under the facade New York was unhappy too.

MAY 2022

Cody had been messaging me as the weeks had dragged on, little "hello's" here and there. Then it progressed to short conversations and half-hearted plans. I had come back from class one afternoon, to find he had sent me a video of a policeman gunning down a perpetrator, proper weird American shit. He'd sent it with the message, "I'd protect you like that", and I guess in *Hillbilly* that meant he was still into me. The initial shock and sadness which had consumed me had subsided: walking to Walmart in the rain, asking Meave to analyse his texts, law of attraction meditation, and overthinking his cryptic Facebook posts. It was liberating to not care as deeply, to not hang on so hard.

In New York City he had become more distant, leaving my messages on reading. I thought he must've seen that I had moved on. I thought he too must have been adjusting to the fact that our time had rolled on. I should've seen his unpredictability coming; the night after I'd gotten back to Brockport he told me he loved me.

"*Fuck it*", he had messaged, "*I love you, and I'm not sure what to do with that feeling.*"

'I was shocked and slightly annoyed. His unknowingness of how to deal with his emotions, and his lack of accountability were irritating.

"*Well, what do you want to do about it?*"

"*I want to take you fishing.*"

I almost laughed, but it wasn't funny.

I had missed him, and although I felt myself slipping away from him with my newfound confidence, I agreed to meet. I suggested we meet on Main Street outside the bookstore, for no reason other than nostalgia. I was nervous as I walked through campus and up onto the street, I hung back in the alleyway, preserving the moment. I enjoyed the taste of uncertainty. Cody was late as usual. When he eventually pulled up, he was on the phone to his insurance company, and I felt disappointed. There were no grand gestures or declarations, but looking back, perhaps that was good, we had instantaneously slotted back into normalcy. I sat and looked out of the window, at the sunshine and rolling fields – his phone call gave me time to settle my anxiety.

"Your hair looks great", he mouthed and I smiled. It felt like I had been sitting in his truck for days, and that no amount of time had stretched by, it was commonplace again. Isn't it weird, the fluidity of life?

I gestured as to whether he had any water in the truck and he shook his head. And then, at the next gas station, he turned in and disappeared, phone to his ear, and emerged again with a carrier bag: soda, water, candy… he knew how to impress. I thanked him.

"No problem."

It's curious as to how people's voices are the first thing we forget, for his nasally American accent filled the truck and I realised just how much I had missed it. Cody drove us to Rochester, and we stopped at a sports store so he could buy more fishing gear. There were taxidermy deer, elks and otters, and antlers placed on the walls,

"Bit grim innit", I observed.

"Why?", Cody asked, distracted by spools and spinners.

"Well, because they're dead?", I replied, but he wasn't listening. I doubted if he ever really bothered to hear me. I looked at the glass eyes of an otter, I wondered how long ago it had died, and of what cause. I didn't always understand Americans, people would have a fit back home if JD Sports filled their walls and shelves with stuffed carcasses. I wondered if veganism would ever sweep through Upstate New York, but it was only a flitting thought, for I didn't too much care.

I snaked through the aisles, feeling self-conscious of my weave, I kept trying to catch glimpses of it in glass cabinet reflections. I had called Cody insecure in the parking lot, but it was a projection. I was always confident until I liked someone, and then it would fall apart.

"Are you mad at me?", he asked, "I'm sorry I'm taking so long."

"No", I said, "you're fine. I'm just gonna go find a bathroom."

The restrooms were nestled between yet more taxidermy, and I looked into the eyes of a dead stag, and he looked back at me. I was glad I wasn't stuffed and put on display. In the bathroom, I busied myself fixing my hair and smeared on lip-gloss which was far too red for my face. I told myself to stop acting off with him, but I couldn't help it, I didn't know how to act or how to feel. Cody was at the checkout when I returned, "look away", he joked as the numbers on the till racked up. When we got back to the truck, he demanded I drive it.

"Okay then", I said and slowly walked over to the driver's side, expecting it to be another joke – a trivial comment to disperse the tension.

"Go on then", he exclaimed, and so I got in. He clamoured into the passenger's side and looked at me expectantly.

"I'm good at driving", I smiled smugly as I fastened my seatbelt.

"Then prove it!"

And so, I did, I whizzed around the parking lot and cranked the music up. I was alive again. He laughed and I glanced over at him and laughed too. Pedestrians hurried out of the way, and I felt the eyes of drivers in parked cars, if nothing at all, Cody knew how to cheer me up.

"Now you gotta go onto the road!"

"Fuck off", I scoffed, "I'm not gonna kill us!"

"But I thought you were good at driving", Cody replied, raising an eyebrow.

"And I would've thought you'd like to make it to old age", I swung into an empty parking space, our brief adventure over, and we switched sides.

"Are you hungry honey?", he asked.

"Are you hinting that you are?"

"You got me there, what are you feeling?"

"I don't know, just not cheeseburgers."

"Damn, you didn't like Tom Wahl's, did you?"

"Tom Wahl's?", I asked, although I knew what he was referring to.

"You rated it a six", he said.

I felt bad. It must've stung him. I should never have publicly rated it. I was spoilt and careless. I hated being either of those things, though often am. I should've apologised but instead, I bit back,

"Is that why you dumped me then? I was dumped over a Tom Wahl's someplace near Newark?"

"I meannn", he said, and then must've caught a glimpse of whatever expression was on my face, "I'm joking, let's get pizza."

We pulled up to a fancy-looking pizza place, and I couldn't decide what to choose from on the board.

"You know, they have an option where you can make your own", Cody said, if he was impatient, he masked it well.

"Yeah, but then I won't know what to say when I get up there. Can you go first?"

"You can chill out", he said, "You can take your time."

"I am chill", I snapped.

"I'm just saying."

I rolled my eyes and folded my arms.

"Can I get a hug?", he asked.

I wrapped my arms around him, and our hug was brief, but long enough for him to start calling me babe, "Let's order babe."

I followed his lead, and we ate messily, on the stools in front of the window. We could've been hired as restaurant deterrents.

"I've got three weeks after Brockport where I don't know what to do with myself", I hinted as we shovelled pizza into our mouths, "I think I might go to Vegas."

"I want to go to Vegas", Cody replied, "I'll go with you."

"Really?"

He nodded, and I doubted he would, but I made a mental note to ask him again nearer the time.

"Gah", Cody exclaimed, "Your anchovies stink!"

I laughed and picked one off my pizza, wriggling it in the air, "Try one!"

"Nope", he recoiled, "I'll be sick!"

"But you're a fisherman", I giggled.

"But they're so gross!"

"Don't knock it until you try it", I said and leaned back on my stool, "I'm so full."

"You ready to leave?" Cody asked, scooping up my plate and taking it to the bin.

We drove to the movie theatre and parked up, we had an hour to kill before Fantastic Beasts: The Secrets of Dumbledore was to start. So naturally, we got stoned. Cody grabbed his "Captain's Logbook" from the dashboard and gave it to me to roll on. It grew dark as we sat there, it reminded me of when we pulled up in the snow, in Avon. I felt sad about how quickly everything was disappearing, but I assured Cody I was still going to find a way to stay. He said he was happy for me, that he wanted me to have figured it out. I wanted him to fancy me, to tell me he was sorry, to ask me back, but we just passed the dab back and forth instead. The headlights of the truck bounced onto the wall, and a shadow cast over Cody's face, hiding half of him in shadows. I wondered if he was a moon, waning away.

I was always just so thankful to be around him, he had a pull, and he was a magnet. I didn't know if I was a moth attracted to the light or a fly attracted to shit. I hoped it wasn't the latter. I didn't want to end up hurt, I didn't want to forgive easily, I didn't know how to proceed. Cody had a quiet beauty, I don't think he found himself attractive, despite being athletic and young, and the owner of a good nose— good noses go far. I wondered whether I was a magnet for him too, something must've beckoned him back, and I hoped it was more than my accent.

"You get to watch Harry Potter with a British girl", I said, as he came round to open my door.

He grabbed my hand and we strode into the movie theatre together, "Dreams really do come true, huh?" He twinkled. I hoped they did.

***

The next day Cody offered to take me out on the boat. I had seen so many photographs and heard so many stories, that I almost felt like I'd already been on it. We woke up early and headed to the lake. I was excited. I'm a naturally lazy person, and to know I could sit all day, drifting around on a blue oasis, was far more appealing than fishing with frozen fingers and aching legs, like earlier that Spring. We were surrounded by lake houses and woodlands, squirrels rustled in the trees, hiding amongst the leaves which were slowly budding back to life.

I sat in the truck and waited for Cody to sort his fish finder. I had offered to help but he told me to sit and look pretty, and that was fine by me. My eyes were full of sleep, and the 7 am sun filtered through the windscreen, and Toby Keith filtered out of the radio.

I could hear Cody mumbling along to the song through the open truck door, followed by an occasional exclamation of "Fuck" and disgruntled sighing.

"You okay?" I shouted out.

He didn't hear me. I clambered out of the truck and went to investigate. He was hunched over a bunch of wires, analysing the blues and the reds, "now listen here honey, I've never claimed to be an electrician."

I laughed, "Oh I could've figured that out."

I realised I'd be more of a pain than a help, so hauled myself up into the truck bed, sitting on his toolbox. I amused myself with the perfect view of a sexy man, doing some sexy electricity stuff, and hummed to the music. When we finally got out onto the lake, the sun stretched across the blue. Dazzling white rays danced along the water, and we trundled on in silence. Cody was irritated from the lack of sleep and fish, and I wasn't sure if I was too hard on him the day before. I wanted to tell him I loved him as he sat stony-faced, threading a line onto a rod, but the words got stuck on the tip of my tongue, and I gazed out instead. I wondered if this was the last time I'd ever see him, on a warm spring afternoon, on the boat he fulfilled his promise of taking me on. But if it was, why did the constant drone of pet names linger in the air?

"Tighten your line baby!"

"I want you to practise your flick for me, honey!"

"Babe, can you pass me my Hyde?"

He'd made us sandwiches, I told him mine was the best I'd ever eaten, and it wasn't a lie.

"You're easily pleased", he had replied.

Perhaps, I was indeed easily pleased. What was his game? Why was I here? If the sex hadn't felt so transactional, I would've thought it was because he wanted to get back together. I almost wished we had ended in tragedy, for I wasn't sure what was worse - the heartbreak of parting, or the small talk about the weather and scenery. We bickered in the intervals between silence. I felt the absence of friendship; I was his fishing companion, and in return, I'm not quite sure what he was to me.

I was puzzled whether he viewed life at the surface level, or if he was a deep thinker. On the surface, he would've thought I came along because I missed him, or because I was easy; and that I was cold and sometimes distant because I was disinterested or reserved. If he thought deeply, he'd have known I never get up at 5 am, and that I had bounced out of bed for the eagerness of purely existing with him. He would've known I didn't cuddle him for I was scared, I was scared he had gotten sex and a cuddle would've been too needy, too clingy, too desperate. He would've known that I wanted to kiss him when he had asked in the dim lights of the cinema and merely said no so that he could ask again. He would've known that three hours fishing would do me nicely, but I sat patiently for twelve for I was afraid of parting again. He would've known I cared.

I reached for his hand when he wasn't looking, and changed my mind, reaching past him for a lure. I decided that not all goodbyes are simple, and yet they are inevitable.

***

Life had been a giant sand timer, weighing on my shoulders, particles of time and love running empty around my blurry head. I went out to the Frats, and I enjoyed it for the first time in months. I liked letting loose; dancing to music with my friends, letting my shoulders sway and feet weave in and out of drunkenness and music.

I was in love, and I had tried to repress it; I was in love with Cody as much as I had been with Owen, only we beat to a different drum. I thought of Cody driving down an Upstate road, a small smile, crows feet by his eyes, shining on through the night. I thought of him silent and contemplating, content in my company as he mulled over everything. I thought of him flicking a line and reeling it back in, feeling like he belonged in his comfort of nature and promises. I thought of him sad and lonely, happy, and loved, I thought of him in bed, and in the morning. I thought of him wanting to say words that escaped him, and to wrap his hands firmly around mine, I thought of him in the summer and the winter, of his misery and his feelings. It was a magical thing to love, and an unhinged part of me found joy in loving someone I didn't understand.

Boys and girls filled the room like swarms of bees, the desired and the undesired, all dancing as one under the shut-off lights, to hip-hop and R&B. They were alive, buzzing to the night, and I buzzed too, in my yellow dress against the black, *buzz buzz*. We were sitting ducks, all the girls on the dance floor waiting to be harpooned, waiting for that sharp jab of being claimed, and for me, it never came. I didn't mind though, I enjoyed being with my friends, we went and partied at the Lacrosse house, and they had a gazebo with lights and a DJ. I shouted out to Meave that it was like a "Shitty U.K festival", "Yesss", she beamed back, followed by our usual chant, "U.S.A!"

The mood was high, there were hugs and dancing, beer spilling and handshakes. It was the last Saturday night, the last Frat party. The cops were out, three cruises slowing down, past gaggles of girls and groups of boys. They'd shut down three parties and so at 2 am we all surged to Omega, it was a tight pack; we were either students or sardines, I'm not sure, but we were alive. *Love Story* by Taylor Swift blasted out of a speaker, and I laughed, the song Cody had played for me all that time ago. I found it hilarious. Meave, Valentina, and I linked arms and screamed the lyrics from the top of our lungs, into the night, "Romeo save me."

As the night wound down, we started our trek up the hill towards U-Hots. Hannah, our favourite burger flipper, drove past, screeched on the breaks and turned around, "You girls need a ride?"

We piled into the back of her car and gushed about how much we loved her like all drunk girls do.

"Aw, you girls are gonna make me cry", she drooled as she dropped us off, three wasted friends in need of bacon egg and cheese.

The next day I scraped through my hangover and went to class and then on to see Cody. This time he was left waiting for me. I was unprepared as ever, rollers still in my hair when he turned up. The weekend went as per usual; he drove me to his grandparents, and I had dinner with them, and then fulfilled my womanly duties in the basement, followed by a 5.30 am start and twelve hours of sitting on the boat, in the wind, without catching a fish.

Cody seemed distant and I couldn't figure him out, his mood from the previous weekend seeped into this one, and I started to feel as though he didn't love me as he said he did. As he dropped me off to my halls, he made a special effort to get out of the truck, open my door and kiss me, but it seemed lacking. Our fire had died out and I didn't know what to do about it. I had attempted to relight it, but I decided perhaps he wanted it to blow cold. I no longer trusted his words nor his actions, as the spark which had existed previously seemed strained.

Relationships are complicated, and it was naive of me to enter one, naive of us both I suppose. I wanted him to desire me but it was always half-assed. He had given me a half-assed promise to have me over until Sunday until it was an "I'm gonna drop you home now" and a swift packing of my bag and drop off. I didn't know whether he was worth chasing anymore. I had loved and let go before and this time it felt like loving and accepting; romance was shallow, but friendship was firm. I didn't know how to make a conversation with him anymore, and instead of growing sad with it, I grew tired of it.

He had held my hand before we fell asleep, cuddled into me, "I love you."

But if he did, why did his love feel empty? I wasn't sure if I was overthinking, or if my hunch was right, and although the story wasn't quite over yet, I could already anticipate how it would end. I enjoyed partying again, for the first time since before I let Owen go, and that told me everything I needed to know. I only enjoyed the alcohol when I didn't enjoy my life.

***

I was suddenly in the last week of classes, it was seven days before Bella would fly home, and then soon to be Meave. I had a month before I would be propelled into Camp Sunshine and then with a visa expiration, I would be thrust home. Things had been slipping away, Cody's feelings, time, and college life. In my own little way I accepted it. I accepted Cody's loss by no longer listening to the law of attraction meditation, trying to get the divine to will him my way. I accepted the end of college life by preparing for finals; writing a fifteen-page essay I'd left to the last minute in six hours the night before it was due.

I hadn't given up, but acceptance and throwing the towel in are a thin line to tow. Life will always keep moving, it's like a treadmill you can't get off. Nothing stays the same. That's a realisation we'll always have at some point. It's far harder to realise you're living in the good old times whilst they're happening— we always tend to look back and pinpoint those times when it's too late.

My days were numbered, and numbered still was the final chapter of Brockport. A semester abroad, filled with frat parties, late nights at bars, forged friendships, and spontaneous trips to Los Angeles and New York City. Yet, none of it compared to those golden days with Cody. That haze, warm and fleeting, felt like home. I wished I could have preserved it, bottled it somehow, but deep down, I knew it had run its course. Life always does. And as I stood on the brink of something new, I wondered: when would I end too?

Would I have decades left, half a century of adventures stretched out before me—or mere weeks, months, or years? Would I marry next year, the year after that, or maybe not at all? I wondered when the next blow would come, the aching loss of a loved one. I wondered about the journeys ahead, the places still unseen, and the strangers who would become friends, lovers, family. Would I have children? How many? What would their names be—or would I never know the chaos and joy of parenthood at all?

We drift forward, blind to what lies ahead. That's the thing with a life in flux. You never know what's going to happen next, what awaits, or how long we'll go on. I felt very temporary, just as Brockport and Cody and Meave and Bella and Valentina, and my classes, and America, and being twenty-one was all temporary. My golden age was Cody, being picked up for dates, taken out, hugged and held, being excited, sweet nothings, telling each other how much we loved each other, discussing marriage and life, wanting to be the penultimate and knowing we weren't. I was sad, but that was temporary too. I wanted to shout at him, to tell him to wake up, that he still had me, but I couldn't figure out the shallowness of our communication now. I think he lost his feelings, but he couldn't explain why or how.

I asked him how he felt about me and he said "I like you" and I liked him too, our whirlwind, our stretch of romance, our yellow-lined American road. I could've cried right there and then thinking about it all. I'm never ready for the next wave of life, it scares me. I almost wanted a hole to hibernate in, and to wait for it all to blow over and emerge again as old, with everything figured out, with stability. But even then, things change, and we kid ourselves that anything can ever be stable. I hadn't had a cigarette in eight days, and I guess that was something. I'd quit cigarettes after six years of smoking just as easily as Cody had quit me, yet puffed every day on a Hyde, for despite not needing cigarettes, I still needed nicotine, until one day I wouldn't, and one day he wouldn't need me.

I thought about when I poured over Jack Kerouac's *On The Road*, desperately googled American road trips, and daydreamed about roaming across America like Sal Paradise and Dean Moriarty, and I did. I drove in the passenger seat of Cody's truck for miles and miles around Upstate New York, doing doughnuts, and taking my turn at the wheel: going to seedy bars, doing drugs, fishing, hiking, and making love. I hung out in basements and partied, and met people, people, people, so many people, passing faces, fleeting friendships: warm people, kind people, lost people, afraid people, loving people, old and young. It blew my mind.

I thought of all the times I had doubted, or other people had doubted my abilities, my capabilities, my limits, my success, and yet I had had far more successes in my early career and personal life than failures. Although I had faced many closed doors, it was always the ones I truly wanted which came true. So, a part of me knew or so deeply wished, that I would be returning to America. I thanked the universe for that, but I also cursed it for each wish came at the penalty for love. I could never have it all, to win something, I had to lose something. I felt like I was always doing a trade with the divine or the devil, or whoever it was that was up there receiving parts of my soul, and strips of my heart for another rung in the ladder to prosperity. The irony of it all was that I would probably get to the top of the ladder, only to look down and find each rung was fashioned from an artery. The whole thing would sway and topple with any blow of a strong wind, for arteries if not rooted to the heart are very weak things indeed.

I willed myself to stop being so distracted by men because I knew deep down, that they would always lose to my ambition, and I always knew they would hinder it with their smooth talks, good looks, and declarations. But, if there was one thing, I ever wanted more than a successful career, it was love, in whatever form that came in. In some twisted turn of fate, I thought that perhaps men were simply there to be my muse, a fuel for another sad prose or poem, or a film about heartbreak and tragedy. It was such a pathetic notion that I hoped I'd grow out of it.

I watched a lot of movies and documentaries in my last week in Brockport, lying in my bed, in my room, watching hours upon hours of lives which weren't my own. I devoured escapism, until I stumbled across a film about two sailors, who fell in love on their travels, only to be brutally ripped apart, by circumstances out of their control, and I cried. In the dark shroud of the early morning, I sobbed, muffling my face in my pillow, tears and snot stinging my cheeks. It dawned on me that I was leaving, and it hurt. It hurt like hell. And that's the thing about travelling, you kid yourself until you can't, your daily life is a lie for it's one you can't secure. You're always going to have to leave one way or another. Camp Sunshine felt purposeless, it was a void, a last-ditch attempt to bid Cody into staying with me and to prolong the denial. I understood why my Dad binge-watched television from morning to night every day of every month of every year, why Owen was glued to the gaming screen for every waking moment of the day, and why Cody would fish. When life is unbearable, you escape; into hobbies or entertainment, into love or hate …into anything to keep you afloat. People numb the pain, and I had chosen to travel to escape mine, and that's why with each ending, it hurt just that bit more.

I wasn't a college student. I wasn't an American. I wasn't going to be a part of Cody's future. I wasn't from New York, and neither was it my right. I was a silly girl from Cornwall, a student at

Bath Spa University, and a British National. I belonged to a small island 3000 miles away, across the Atlantic, and yet going home seemed less hurtful than venturing four hours south of the State I loved, for I would've rather lost Cody to the vast stretch of the sea than to a road. I would've rather been in a different country than unobtainable in the same State.

That night I fell asleep as the birds awoke outside my window, and I dreamt. I saw flashes of my life go by, a silkscreen projector of all my moments, of all the good, of all the happiness, of the pain, the tragedy…of the truck, the drives, yelling, fights, friends, parties, crying, hiking, swimming, dinners and dreams and kisses, art and exploring, school and smoking. I slashed the silk with a knife, tearing through the images, slitting the memories in two, and it hung ragged, but the movie kept rolling.

I pointed the knife towards myself, the tip of the blade at the top of my forearm, and I pulled it down, it slid through my skin. I took it to my other arm and slowly forced the knife down right towards my wrist. My bones were exposed, they were black. I drained my arms over a constructionist's bucket until it filled with my perfect pool of scarlet blood. It was heavy to carry, with my flesh flopping in loose folds, but I lifted it into the air and chucked it onto the screen. Large splashes of red, I painted my world with pain. It sizzled and burned through the projector, staining my life and scolding the screen until there was nothing left.

When I woke up, I was angry. I was red hot, burning, furious. Cody was ghosting me. I wasn't sure what was next in store, or if I would enjoy Camp Sunshine. I hoped Miami and New York City wouldn't be tainted with the sadness of change and parting ways. But who knew?

***

My days of insomnia caught up on me and I collapsed on my bed for a 3 pm nap. My nap turned into astral projection, something I hadn't done for years, something I'd tried to train myself to do, but which often happened spontaneously.

As I was sleeping, I felt a great weight on my back, as if someone was sitting on me—"Ah", I had thought to myself as I dozed, "the hag at the end of the bed!"

I felt at peace though, I wasn't startled or scared. The weight became heavier and the heavier it got, I could feel my soul getting pushed out my front. Something was squeezing me out. I heard a whisper by my ear, "Get up."

I telepathically replied to this intruding stranger, "So help me."

I was in sleep paralysis, and I tried to move my astral arm, but it was stiff. I was rusty. I managed to free it from my physical arm and flailed it in the air, "pull me out", I telepathically asked my ethereal friend.

They did. And I was suddenly up out of my body and in my dorm room. I was hovering above my sleeping body and felt clean. That's the thing with astral projecting, every time I've ever done it, I've felt fresh, reborn, alive again. Everything was cleaner, the mind, the atmosphere. In the corner of the room was a floating tiger's head, glowing purple, the entity which had removed me.

"You're a tiger's head!" I said dumbfounded. They didn't reply but I knew they had heard me, "What am I?" I pressed.

"You're a teacup."

I didn't question it. I could sense I was glowing green.

"Follow me."

The tiger's head disappeared through the wall and out into the campus air. I followed suit but I was moving a lot slower than my companion, I forgot how hard it is to move in the astral realm. I had to will myself with my mind to push through the ether and along behind the tiger's head. I looked up into the blue sky and suddenly had the desire to travel to England and see my Mother, I pushed myself up as high as I could, but I couldn't leave the confines of campus.

I remembered when the last time I had projected in Cornwall, I had travelled out into my village at home, along the road and over the bridge. I had tried to will myself to Germany, to visit my first love, but for some strange reason, I couldn't then either.

I was supposed to be following the tiger's head, it was some way ahead of me waiting. So, I carried on gliding through campus, among the trees and the pavements, between buildings. It took me to a building I hadn't been to before, and we floated through the window of the top floor, into a deserted classroom. There at a table was another entity, for the life of me I can't remember its form, only that it was also an animal's head. The tiger's head took me to it, and we gathered around the table. This entity was shining blue, it had an authoritative nature. I knew it was wiser than the tiger's head, and it was the one that had summoned me.

I received the telepathic message, "Cody is sleeping with his wife."

The news didn't startle my astral being. Instead, it came as news I somehow already knew. I felt no different hearing it. I glided away, through the window and back out the way I had come. I was getting better at moving, faster and nimbler. I rushed along the pavements, enjoying the feeling of the air rushing by. And then, *smack*, *bang*, I collided with an unassuming college kid, walking along by himself. I'm not sure what he saw, but he jumped out of his skin and snapped his head around in shock. This confrontation propped me back to my physical body and I startled awake.

Later that day Cody resurfaced again. I didn't feel any ill toward him, if anything I felt liberated. If he was sleeping with his wife, I would've much rather been the other woman than the wife he didn't want.

***

The next morning Cody called me at 7.30 am, "Are you free today?"

"I have my final film screening for my Video Production class", I said, "but I can skive if you tempt me."

"I've skived off work" he told me, "want to spend the day on the lake?"

"Sure, only if you take me to Walmart and the Smoke Shop though."

"You got it. I'll pick you up in an hour."

I rushed my make-up whilst Valentina slept, creaking around the room, and rustling in draws, looking for bobby pins and eyeliner. I always made an effort for Cody. I went to the dining hall and was one of the first students there. I ate a bagel in the corner of the hall and hoped I wouldn't be detected by any early risers. I licked cream cheese off my lips and thought about how many meals I had eaten in the canteen, and how now they were limited, perhaps four more at best.

Cody was parked up in the loading bay by the time I had finished my breakfast, and as promised he took me to Walmart and the Smoke Shop. I thanked him and he said he was happy to do it. We had held hands down the aisles, and I thought about how one day soon, we'd be holding hands for the last time. We drove to Cody's favourite lake. I liked it too, it was funny though, how accustomed to lakes I was becoming. Who would've thought?

We got into the water in the late morning, and Cody was impatient. We did the routine motor-sputtering ride to the middle of the lake and then allowed the threader to direct us to the bank.

"Cast in that direction", Cody said pointing out towards an island of trees. There's a drop-off."

I flicked my line obediently and fumbled in my pocket for my Hyde. But just as my line had hit the surface, I didn't have time for a nicotine hit nor to reel before I was wrestling with a great big bite, and suddenly I was struggling against a flurry of fins and splashing water,

"Babe!" I shouted, consumed with a sudden thrill.

"Yoo-hoo, reel him in", Cody yelled, tripping over rods in his rush from the bow to the stern, "reel him in baby!"

The chug on the line sounded, and my rod top arched.

"It's a big one", Cody grinned, "Relax your line, tire him out."

I did as he said and then on his command, reeled as fast as I could. Cody stooped down and snatched the net up from the floor. I flipped a great big pike into it.

"Oh my god", I exclaimed, "Oh my god."

Cody unhooked him, "Look at that beauty!" he laughed, placing the fish into my arms.

I grinned triumphantly, posing for a photo, the weight of the huge pike in my arms. I held it steady, I had caught my first fish with a lure after months of nothing. The bluegill I had caught from live bait in Newark hardly counted, as Cody said, that wasn't real fishing.

"I did it!" I jumped up and down in excitement after we'd thrown the pike back into the water and watched it swim off.

"That was a good one!" Cody replied.

I outstretched my arms and he squeezed me tight.

"That's made my day", I gleamed.

"And mine!" he said, kissing the top of my head. "You're a pro now, fisherwoman!"

The pike was my good omen, my sign from the universe that everything was going to be okay. It was a fluke by design. I had caught my fish, I wasn't going to always be reeling in the reeds, my life wasn't one empty cast after another. Patience pays off, and a big catch awaits the resilient, and better days awaited me.

As we drove back, singing to whatever song came on the radio, he kept glancing over at me, his face beaming with pride, posting the pictures on Facebook behind the wheel, praising me with "I knew you could do it" and "That was one big fucker."

Back at his grandparents' house, the unspoken shift between us fell into place. We unloaded the boat and headed down to the basement. Daytime affections were always light and easy, but once hidden from the world, the intimacy became real.

I held onto Cody, pressing my face to his chest as he cradled me. His smell was a mix of stale cologne and weed. The smell made me realise I was going to lose him, and I compensated by wrapping my arms fiercely around his waist.

"I know I shouldn't say it", I mumbled, "But, I love you."

"I love you too. I wanted to say it, but I felt bad", he kissed my forehead and tucked my hair behind my ears.

I peered up at him, my chin resting on his chest, "are you going to miss me?"

His answer was a grin, pulling me closer, "I'm going to harbour you", he tickled my ribs, "You're gonna be my illegal immigrant!"

I laughed and then buried my face again, inhaling deeply, feeling a pang of bittersweet, "It makes me sad."

Trust me—I know the feeling," he whispered, his voice low and reassuring.

I hugged him as tightly as I could, and his strong arms engulfed me, and we lay there in a perfect cuddle.

"I'm excited you're going to be in South Wedge for two weeks, I won't have to drive to Brockport, so I'll be able to see you nearly every night."

"I'm scared you're going to hurt me."

"Look at me", he cocked my chin and I scanned his face, trying to hold back a sob, "I'm not going to hurt you, I promise. You think I'd do that?"

"You can do that without meaning to. You ghosted me this week."

"I was in a bad headspace, I didn't want to talk to anyone", for a moment, we lay there together, his hand on mine, and it felt as if time had slowed, carrying us to some distant, peaceful place where everything was easy. I hoped I would never forget how his hands were rough and calloused against mine.

Cody puckered his lips, "Can I kiss please?"

I planted a dainty kiss on his lips and then we pecked each other repeatedly, mushing kisses in a comedic style all across each other's face, *mwah, mwah, mwah, mwah.*

"God, "Cody exclaimed, "you're beautiful."

"You're warm", I replied and ran my hands up his hoodie onto his soft warm skin and nestled into him again.

"I love you", he said.

"I love you."

"You're pretty."

"You're pretty too."

"Come here."

"Why?"

"I want to make love to you."

He scooped me up, and I sat on him, drumming his stomach, and poking his armpits.

"You're mischievous."

I nodded, "I am."

"Come here", he said again, and kissed me, long and hard. It felt whole again, it felt like it did all those months ago, those moons ago, when we fell in love.

On the drive back to Brockport I dozed in the dark, *Comfortably Numb* playing through the radio and drifting around the car, I felt safe and happy and warm, the aura was good, and for the first time in a long time I felt like everything would fall into place, my pike a good omen. I felt grateful I was going to have a girl's holiday with Meave, to explore Florida and return to Rochester with Cody on my doorstep. Perhaps Camp Sunshine wouldn't be as bad as it seemed. We stopped at McDonald's.

"Are your fries the same in England?"

"They're not as fatty and salty" I replied.

"Sucks to be you" Cody said mouth full, shoving his hand in my carton, "You commies."

"Fuck you", I laughed.

"You already did."

***

The waves crashed along the shore, kite surfers whizzing by. White sand dusted my legs and I watched in quiet distaste as pelicans dived into the water, their sharp beaks like swords, guzzling down Floridian fish.

Florida was different to California, Miami a tropical Los Angeles, and yet it distinctively felt the same and foreign all at once. The air was thicker, the people laid back, a more body-positive, down-to-earth world, and those who did have money and glamour had a different kind of new money in a different kind of style to those in L.A. Miami was Miami.

Miami Beach was long and thin, and the sea was crystal blue, it was warm. "Watch out for the sharks" everyone had said, and from my brief swim, I could see how it was habitable to sharks. I had to keep reminding myself I was in America, for it was nothing like the America I knew. The few places we had been were predominantly Spanish speaking, and the climate and the palm trees and the warm sea, the sand, the tarmac pavements hot to bare soles and the lizards scurrying about tricked me into thinking I was somewhere in the Caribbean— though I suppose, I near enough was.

***

I hoped I'd be able to sleep in Miami. I wanted to sleep forever, to switch off and shut down. I hadn't heard from Cody, he'd gone ghost again, I'd only received a message in the morning saying *My mental health has deteriorated again, and I can't stop it.*

I wondered what plagued him, whether it was his divorce or his job, whether it was that I was leaving soon, or something entirely foreign I didn't know about. I told him that he didn't deserve to feel like that. I prayed that Cody's depression which would always seem to come about after seeing me, wasn't something I was responsible for. Cars flew by on the highway, as Meave and I headed to the Everglades, and I thought of him and how he had driven over 24 hours from Florida to Rochester when he'd moved there. I don't know why but I found it attractive.

***

Pink clouds streaked the sunrise sky as we flew over the white skyscrapers of Miami towards New York City. It was Neverland, little islands and palm trees, a vast sea and rose clouds. I was in a cotton candy sky. The plane glided through a sandwich of blue, pink and yellow. A lone boat chugged along the sea towards the beetroot horizon. I had left Florida and entered a world waking up.

***

We clattered down the subway steps, the stale air hitting like a wall. The 1 train rumbled somewhere in the distance, and Meave glanced at me with a furrowed brow.

"Downtown, right?" she asked, her boots echoing on the concrete.

"I think so." I wasn't sure. I never was when it came to directions. "Isn't it the 1?"

Before Meave could answer, a voice cut through the underground hum. "Y'all going downtown?"

We turned to see a guy a few steps ahead, leaning casually against the railing. I hadn't noticed him before, but now he was all I saw—short, skinny, with a head full of locs and eyes that felt too kind for New York City.

"Yeah, we're trying to get to Nebula," Meave explained.

"You're on the wrong side," he said, shaking his head. "Need to be across the street."

"It's closed," we said in unison, like some tragic chorus.

The guy shrugged. "42nd's not far. You could walk."

We froze, mentally tracing the grid, trying to summon up a mental map that wasn't there.

"Come on, I'll show you." He was already heading back up the stairs, barely waiting for us to follow.

Meave and I exchanged a look. *Fuck it.* Shrugging, we trailed after him.

"What are your names?" he asked, glancing over his shoulder.

"I'm Meave," she said, quickening her pace to match his.

"Daisy," I added, lagging behind.

"Max," he smiled. His teeth were white against his dark skin, his voice smooth. "Can I hit that?" He nodded toward the vape in my hand. "Don't worry. I'm Covid-free."

I passed it over, watching as he inhaled deeply. "You got any weed?" I asked, "I'm not paying twenty bucks for some sketchy pre-roll."

"Not on me. Got some at home, though."

"Where do you work?" Meave asked, always quick to keep the conversation going.

"Havana Central," he said.

"No way!" Meave and I exclaimed together. "They wouldn't let us in," she added, still a little salty about it.

"Yeah," Max chuckled. "It fills up fast." He studied us for a moment. "What's your accent?"

"We're from the U.K.," Meave offered. "Northern Ireland, actually."

He nodded slowly but didn't seem entirely convinced. "You gals just visiting?"

"For now," I said, letting my eyes drift over the chaos of Times Square.

Max grinned, bemused. "This is random," he said, laughing softly.

"Are you a creep?" I blurted.

His expression shifted to something between amused and apologetic. "Nah. Am I freaking you out?"

"No," Meave interjected. "But if you are, our mums will send you straight to creep jail."

"Yeah," I added. "Lifetime sentence."

Max laughed, shaking his head. "Why don't we go to mine instead of creep jail? We can smoke and listen to music. No clubs. No weirdness."

Meave and I looked at each other, talking with our eyes. We unanimously agreed we would but kept promising jail for him if he tried anything. We turned around and walked back down to the subway, taking the next train to Queens. Meave was a gifted socialite and seemed to talk to Max with ease, I hung back, looking at myself in the subway windows as we tunnelled through blackness. I felt uneasy.

"What do you think?" Meave asked.

"Huh?"

"About getting drinks? Max says there's a 7-11 by his house."

"Sure."

The subway to Queens took a fair while, Max ordered us an Uber for the rest of the journey. In the dark car, we learnt that he was twenty-one, he lived with his parents, but they were away, he had a cat and dropped out of a CUNY school. He'd always lived in New York City and wasn't sure if we were faking our accents.

"It's weirder for him than it is for us", Meave kept interjecting, trying to bring me into the conversation which I was continuously dropping out of. As promised, Max took us to the 7-11 by his house and he bought Bud lights. He lived on a quiet street, and I announced that "Peter Parker's from Queens."

"That would be true if he were real", Max said.

His room was small, but it was cosy, I felt better after seeing it. It was any old room for any old guy, a double bed, bongs, ashtrays a smart TV hooked up to the wall.

"Sit where you like", Max gestured to the floor or the bed. I took the floor, Meave the bed, and then he passed us a can each. We drank it, slightly awkward, slightly anticipating, slightly not feeling anything at all. Max took the bed too and started rolling joints, and then looked apologetic again, "Awdamn, did you gals want bongs? I didn't think to ask."

Meave looked at me, she hadn't smoked before. The can was going down nicely, and my bad influence came out. I was excited to see her stoned, "Nah joints are fine", I assured him, "Thank you."

To my surprise, he'd rolled one for us each and then excused himself to go to the bathroom. Meave looked at me, "How do I do it?"

I laughed, "Just smoke it like a cigarette", though she didn't do that either.

We got blazed, just like that. One joint after another, one can after another, taking turns in choosing songs. Meave chose Lizzo's new song, the one about needing a *sentimental man or woman* to *pump her up*. I chose *Call Me the Breeze*, by J.J Cale, which then caused us to fall into a Bob Dylan trap. The room filled with smoke, it smelt of beer, and Max seemed cool. He had cool dreads, cool clothes, cool piercings and a slow, long, cool accent. Meave told him he was perfect. I think he didn't know how to take it, perhaps he took it too much to heart because he asked us if we'd ever had a threesome.

Meave and I, of course, assured him that we had not, and started laughing maniacally when he suggested we have one.

"No offence Meave mate, I just don't see you like that", I joked.

"Cody wouldn't like it if she did that", Meave explained to Max.

"You have a boyfriend?", he asked me.

"Something like that."

I think Broadway rubbed off on Meave and I for we did a pretty convincing job of creating a boyfriend for her, and the subject wasn't brought up again. Max said we could stay over, but that he had work in the morning, he said he would call in sick. We told him we'd come into Havana Central for happy hour to see him instead.

It was 6 am by the time we stumbled out of there, the world was bright, and commuters rolled by in their cars. Early morning runners and dog walkers gave us a wide birth as we stood waiting for our Uber, smelling of boozer and weed, make-up smeared, hair ratty, eyes puffy. It was time for sleep.

The Uber to Amsterdam Avenue was long, and we racked up a hell of a bill. But I liked watching the yellow sunrise even further up in the sky, glinting in the windows of the skyscrapers, the golden hour of the morning. New York City was beautiful, a work of art, I loved it. I looked over at Meave, I loved her too.

We grabbed a McDonald's for breakfast, chewing up disgusting McMuffins and washing them down with orange juice. We were fucked and slept in the next day.

****

It was Sunday, and we walked to Central Park, I dropped a soda on the way, and it annoyed me somewhat. When you've got $30 in your account, a $2 loss is a bit of a blow. We found a quiet spot and I lay back in the grass, looking up at the trees, the canopy of green leaves and the wash of blue. It was a cloudless sky, and I felt the blades of grass on my arms. I felt tired, and my eyebags felt sticky as if the creases under my eyes were permanently edged there. An occasional ant crawled up my neck and I'd crush it between my fingers. I sighed. I could breathe. We had come full circle.

The day was somewhat lazy, until the evening when we ventured back into Times Square. We'd bought overpriced tickets to see Beetlejuice on Broadway, and we were bustling with excitement. Meave had seen it already and told me I'd love it more than Moulin Rouge. I was dubious, but hey, I'll give anything a shot. We clambered onto the subway, reminiscing the night before, and laughing about our adventure. Perplexed at our stupidness for having gone, despite having left unharmed.

"That was a one-off okay," Meave said.

"You don't need to tell me, "I agreed.

A couple got off at the next stop and we managed to sit down. I'd always look at New Yorker's feet on the subway. Every single time. I was fascinated by how they posed their feet, what shoes they were wearing, the brand, and the age. You can tell a lot about someone by their shoes. I'd often look down at the shoes and try and guess the person before adverting my eyes up to them, to see if I was right. I was lost in mindless thought, coming up with a vague idea for a coffee book idea: The Shoes of The Subway. And then, a homeless man got on, and my heart dropped.

I'd feel sad when black, homeless men would wander the subways, wishing the passengers a safe journey, and a life of love. They'd shuffle along, sometimes with a cane, with a bag, a hat or a cup in hand, asking for a nickel or a dime, a dollar. I never had anything to give, my pockets were empty, and my bank balance was in the two digits, money borrowed from my Mum. They often looked like my Dad, I could envision him with his stick and a missing tooth, his broken face and worn hands shuffling along the New York underground, or sleeping on bags, and I was glad he wasn't. I saw his face in theirs, and that's why long after we'd reached our destination, their face would linger on.

***

Meave and I sat on the bench outside the hostel and decided to call Valentina. We had planned to go to Coney Island, to have a beach day, to see her one last time. But, her parents, strong Cuban people, with strong parenting ideals, didn't want her to come into the city. There had been a string of unrelated gun attacks on the subway, and they thought she ought to stay home. Meave and I couldn't afford to get the train to Long Island to see her, and so, that was that. I was disappointed.

***

Times Square suddenly jumped alive like a Jack in the Box, bright lights, luminous reds and blues shining down on us, us specks of human dust milling about along blocks, like beetles scurrying to the scarab. Boom boxes and ice cream van jingles, chants and street dancing, microphone preaching and people chattering. And when we'd had our fill of watching the billboards switch and change and dance against the lights, and of Broadway musicals whipping by, we decided to surge into the crowd and disappear into the bobbing heads of 42nd Street. The crowds swept us along, like a great current, and a tidal wave of hot dogs and balloons, street artists and taxis, NYPD officers and tourists rippled through New York with the great white rawr of electricity.

We saw the same cyclist taxi as the night before, and he waved us over,

"Girls", "did you find it?"

"Find it?" We asked unanimously, swaying, legs of jelly.

"Ohhhh it's him!" We shouted pointing at each other and running over, spinning the tale of Queens with twisted tongues.

He looked confused but a smile stretched across his face as he said, "Well enjoy Times Square", throwing an arm out in gesture, like a Broadway showman, and we looked on with a colourful "ooooo" spread across our faces and trotted off obediently back into the rush.

***

"Look," Meave said as I scrolled through our selfies on my camera roll, she clicked on one of the photos of us stoned out of our minds on the steps in Times Square, "I'm looking at you like I love you."

I paused and looked at the photo, it made me happy, if I was rich I would've bought Meave a place in NYC, she did love me, and I loved her too. The city was hers, it suited her, "the city only sleeps when you're not here", I said.

***

I climbed onto the bus and found a seat; it was more packed than I had thought it was going to be and I faced the window. Resting my hand on my chin and just like that, I started to cry. Tears ran down my face in tingling prickles and I slid an AirPod into my ear to drown out my sniffling.

The bus pulled out and before I had time to process the end of what felt like a small era, the skyscrapers of New York City rolled passed my window and behind us.

The journey was long, and I was tired of looking out of the window, at the trucks and cars, continuous roads, buildings rolling into trees. I was glad Cody was meeting me on the other side. I felt vulnerable, and suddenly very alone. I was always very conscientious of time and with Meave somewhere up in the air ploughing towards England, the hands of time didn't feel like they were on my side.

***

I pushed open the door and was surprised at the flat. It was spacious, with a beautiful wash of white and large rooms. I peered through a door and saw a queen-sized bedroom with an en-suite. The kitchen had teabags in a small pot and the living room looked inviting, a cosy set up of sofas and a telly, it was bright and clean, it was everything I had ever wanted.

"Wow," Cody exclaimed, giving himself a tour of the home, "This is nice!"

"Yeah," I said shovelling the McDonald's spicy chicken deluxe he'd bought me into my mouth, "Thank fuck for the amount it cost."

I wondered if he thought I was rich, the paradox was that I was dirt poor, completely skint, with maxed-out overdrafts and student loans pissed down the drain. I was a fraud.

Cody stripped off, his clothes landing on the floor around him and climbed into bed.

"This isn't to become a boy's pad", I joked, knowing that soon enough I'd make it messy too.

"What?"

I didn't bother repeating myself and paced around taking in my surroundings, from hostels for two weeks to a large swanky apartment. It was a new chapter, and I couldn't keep up. I wondered how far across the sky Meave had now travelled. I did the maths in my head as to how much longer she had left before touching down in London, and it made me sad.

"I'm gonna have a shower, I'll be quick."

"Take your time, honey."

There was a bath and a shower in the bathroom off from the kitchen, and it smelt nice, with store-bought shampoo, conditioner, shower gel, and moisturiser all lined up and waiting to be used. I let the hot water pour over me, cleaning my bus oil skin, the dirt from cheesy trainers and unwashed clothes running down into the drain. It was unlike anything I'd experienced since January, from a college dorm to shared motel rooms to hostels, I finally had my place. I hoped I'd wake up in the morning and be able to soak it all in.

I wrapped my towel around me, it smelt fresh and headed to the bedroom. The light was already off and Cody was already under the sheets. I crawled in to join him.

"Hello," I whispered.

"Hi."

I edged closer to him, feeling the warmth of his body and pressed my cheek up to his chest. He ran his arm down my arm and to my hip and pulled me closer.

"I missed you," I mumbled.

"I missed you too." He kissed my forehead.

"Too bad I've had my fill of Americans now." I joked and looked up at him, a grin on my face.

"Oh is that right?" He said, his breath on my neck.

"Yeah, I'm over it now." I prodded and playfully shuffled away.

"Oh, are you sure about that?" Cody replied, pulling me back.

"Mhmmm."

"I think I can change your mind."

He reached over me and switched off the lampshade before engulfing me in his arms and we made love in the dark.

I struggled to sleep. I listened to the blare of the AC and whir of the fan, I counted Cody's breaths and hit my Hyde. I tried to meditate on the noises, but it wasn't them that was keeping me up. I finally had peace, I had solitude and yet after months of rush, of voices, of friends, of adventure, the first night away from it all echoed around the walls. I had been in the waves, bobbing up and down in the current and then bashed through a rip tide, I'd made rafts to keep afloat, and they had sunk, I had wrestled sharks and swam with dolphins, and now I had washed up on a shore of aloneness and the land was foreign, it was time to unwind.

JUNE 2022

Cody's alarm sounded at 6 am and he woke me up with a morning cuddle. I dozed as he got ready to leave for work, half-heartedly pondering my day ahead.

"I'll leave my stuff here?" Cody asked threading his belt through his jean loops.

"Okay", I smiled.

"I'll be back around three", he said and stooped down to kiss me. I stretched out my arms and wrapped them around his waist. The sunlight filtered through the blinds, and little spotlights of white waltzed the floorboards, reflecting off the cream walls and I sighed, "Have a good day."

"I will", Cody smiled, "see you later honey."

He let himself out and I stretched in the sheets, June 1st, 2022, alone in my apartment in Rochester, two weeks to live out my lonely writer fantasy. Cody had left me a handful of weed on my dresser but I didn't have any rolling papers or tips, so I paced about the apartment. I placed the caricature of Meave on the shelves in the dining room and then examined the books, running my finger along the dried flowers and ornaments.

There was a radio, with a CD section and clunky buttons, I picked it up, I hadn't seen one of those in years. I wondered if it worked and took it to the kitchen and plugged it in. Rochester Radio, Country 100.5 clicked on, and the room seemed brighter. I liked the noise. It comforted me, just as words on paper do. I wasn't sure what else to do with myself, so I made my bed and walked to the grocery store in the rain, past coffee shops and spiritual stores. I watched daytime television and stared at the clock.

Cody was late back from work, and by the time he showed up at the door, I felt like my day could finally start. I was bursting with stifled co-dependency.

"Hey", I smiled.

"Hey", he said dangling his truck keys in front of me, "you ready?"

"Where are we going?"

"To go get food", he said, "aren't you hungry?"

"I could eat."

Cody took me to Schaller's, a joint not too far away which reminded me of U-Hots. I got loaded fries, and Cody's tray was full of onion rings, a burger, a strawberry milkshake, and a coke. He'd just been paid, so it was time for a feast.

We sat in a little booth by the window and stole glances at each other over our mountain of food.

"You make me happy", Cody said, reaching for my hand across the table.

"You make me happy too", I replied, "do you want a plane ticket to Florida?"

"Huh?"

"I have a credited flight, you should have it, so you can go back."

Cody let go of my hand, dumbfounded and fumbled in his pocket for his phone. He pulled it out and jabbed on the keypad, holding it to his ear.

"When have you got time off work?" He asked into the phone, a glint of excitement in his eyes, "I've got a flight."

I leant back and smiled, touched at his immediate phone call to whoever was on the other end. We finished eating and then drove back to my apartment. It was an evening of telly watching and slow cuddles, I'd made the bed earlier that day and Cody was surprised.

"Wow", he had said as he entered the bedroom, "you're a fully-fledged American housewife."

I was glad he was impressed, "English housewives are better."

"Oh yeah?" He said, "Why's that?"

"We come with humour."

"British humour?"

"Unfortunately, so."

***

I started to grow impatient. It was one long day after another in the apartment, and I was restless. I was in a faux married life, Cody staying over each night and disappearing to work early each morning. He had told me he would be back at four and it was fast approaching six. I had been stuck watching mindless daytime telly all day, and I was bored out of my mind.

Cody never was punctual. Yet, all was forgiven when he opened the door and stepped inside. He was stoned and stumbled into the kitchen, bumping into the coffee table, and dropping both his lighters.

"Hi!"

"Hello", I laughed and threw my arms around him. We cuddle-side-stepped into the living room and collapsed onto the sofa. I bear hugged him and he wrestled me back, "I'm glad to see you", I said.

"Oh yeah?"

"Yeah, I've been like a puppy all day."

He laughed, "A puppy waiting for me to come home?"

I nodded and he kissed me, "you free all weekend?"

"Yeah."

"I was thinking we could take the boat out Friday and Saturday."

"That would be nice, I leave on Monday."

"This coming Monday?"

"Yep", I sighed, trying not to think about it, "and I've got an interview at six on Sunday."

"What's it for?"

"A photography internship in Miami."

Cody pouted, his arms around my shoulders, "I don't want you to go to Miami."

"I don't wanna be anywhere but with you", I said, "but if I want to be in America I have to take what I can, beggars can't be choosers."

"Yeah", he sighed, "I know."

"Let's not think about it", I said, and led him outside by the hand, "the patio is cute, we could sit here if you like, it's a nice evening."

"Sure", he smiled and then disappeared inside, emerging again with towels which he chucked onto the outdoor chairs. He had his pipe with him and packed a bowl which we shared.

I was paranoid about the smell despite Cody's reassurances that it was legal and that it was no one else's business. We lit up one bowl after another and drowned the angst of the coming week in inhales and spluttering exhales. I watched the smoke evaporate above us as we spoke about the future, our goals, our wants, our needs, and our demons and paused in thoughtful ponder in between.

We headed back inside, our minds comfortably sedated. Cody lay down on the sofa, and I slotted in next to him. He was soft. I clamped myself onto him, our legs entwined, my arms around his middle obscuring my view of The Walking Dead. I didn't mind though; I closed my eyes and regulated my breathing. I always hated how conscious I would be of my breaths when I was stoned. I always thought I was breathing too loud. I tuned my breaths out, and meditated, inhaling, and exhaling to Cody's rhythmic heart. I felt at peace. The sofa was moulded to our weight. We were hibernating in a cave of zombies and melodramatic music, of body warmth and yawns.

Cody stayed up longer than usual and I was glad for I knew it meant he was having a good time. It'd been a fun evening, and I realised that the barriers which I had felt for several weeks had melted away, and it was distance and time which had caused them. I appreciated how Cody made every effort to come over, and to make the most of the two weeks like he had promised. There was only one day when we hadn't seen each other, and I felt closer to him than I ever had. I thought about the simplicity of human beings, how bonding is animalistic, and how the psyche is pure and easy. Spending time with someone in great quantity creates a connection. We were in the best place we had ever been, love had turned to lust, and finally, lust had rolled back over to love again.

When we finally got into bed, we lay in a quiet haze of slumber. Our stoned minds coated us in loved-laden honey. His hand ran the edges of my body, his wide palm stroking me, and I held onto his waist, my face on his chest. We moulded into one, a soothing mass of sleepiness. I thought about how much I loved him, how his body felt perfect against mine. I had travelled far and wide and found myself nestled next to Cody, our heartbeats drumming as one. I savoured it, and he savoured me. I felt the wave of love channelling from his body to mine, we were weaved together. I inhaled, tasting the unsaid, licking the truth from the tip of bruised tongues.

He started to kiss my forehead, and I kissed his chest, his stomach, and his hands, and he placed his lips on mine. Silence turned to desperation, and we were eager, hungry, desirous of everything our broken beings had to give.

I soaked in that night with Cody, it was my favourite, for we devoured what we could, a linked effort to fight time, to battle the current, to love. It's rare to feel love, the kinetic warmth of the energy, I could've almost held it, this great white sphere of unfiltered love, radiating from his heart to mine.

Cody held me through the night, his arms around my chest, my hands cradling them there. Leonard Cohen floated in and out of my head as I floated in and out of sleep.

And, when the morning rolled around in a rude awakening, he gave me an array of kisses and told me he'd be back after work. I sighed happily, stretched out across the bed, and back into a world of blissful dreams, and it was as if the whole sky above me opened, and the rain fell in mid-June droplets.

***

Later that day, we found ourselves locked out of my apartment in our pyjamas, stumbling around, knocking on doors, and cursing under our breath as we tried to find a way in. It felt like an hour of aimless knocking, with neighbours who didn't come to the door but merely twitched their curtains, before we finally managed to shove the AC unit up and wriggle Cody through the gap in the window. I thought we had successfully broken an entry without detection.

I was wrong.

By the time my phone buzzed with a message from the landlady, I was already stoned on the boat in the middle of the lake. I glanced at my screen, Cody standing at the bow, oblivious. My heart dropped.

"For fuck's sake," I muttered, clicking on her message. "Shit."

"What?" Cody asked, turning around, largely unconcerned, "Is it about us being locked out?"

"God", I said, sitting down, "she's pissed off."

"What is it?"

"The neighbours called the police on us; she said you can't stay anymore and she might lose her AirBnB license."

"What?" Cody's face shifted, the calm slipping away. "Wait, are you serious?"

"Ugh", I exclaimed, "I shouldn't have checked my phone", I put it down and continued, "She said that neighbours reported you banging on their door."

"That's ridiculous", Cody retorted.

"I didn't realise it was a crime to ask for assistance", I snapped.

"You should tell her that we got locked out and were tryna get help."

"I can't believe that", I continued, "I'm annoyed now. Is that an American thing? Who calls the police for knocking on a door?"

"Democrats", Cody muttered bitterly "They're so annoying bro."

And just like that, we slipped into silence, the fragile mood shattered, leaving nothing but the cold slap of water against the boat as we drifted across the lake, tossing our lines over our shoulders. I didn't want to go back to South Wedge.

A heaviness lingered between us, as thick as the clouds rolling in. I felt the weight of it, that unspoken truth hanging over us—that this was going to end, that everything was unraveling. I could feel my body curling inward, the weed seeping an uncomfortable fear through my bones. I cast aside the rod and sat hunched at the end of the boat, hoping I'd become invisible. I was so much in my head about the whole thing that it startled me when Cody bellowed, "Fuck!"

His voice echoed across the choppy waves and wash of grey, bouncing around the boat, the wind grumbling back, disgruntled. He had managed to hook a fish but reeled too fast and it had flayed free.

I hadn't seen him angry before, it took me aback, but I wasn't surprised. I wanted to roar too, to stand up on the bow of the boat, beat my chest with tight fists and scream a long, blown-out, "*FUCKKK*". Good on him, I thought.

The water was a midnight blue, the waves beating the boat, shunting us from side to side and the black clouds rolled in. Rain started to pelt down, and I zipped up my coat, the wind blowing curls across my face, and I looked out, across the dark bay. The water rumbled like God's empty stomach. I had managed to hook three fish and like Cody's pike, they'd all come straight off the hook. I was fucked off and I hoped the northeast wind would blow my annoyance right out of the back of me and far away past the bridge and the State, across the continent and to someplace else. But, it didn't.

"You okay?" I finally asked.

"Just great", sarcasm laced his tone.

I didn't push it.

"Are you ready to go back?" He asked, but it wasn't a question, he had already cast his rod aside and was stumbling across to the driver's seat.

"Okay."

"You want to stay?"

"I mean, I'm having fun."

Fun was an exaggeration, but I enjoyed being in the storm. I almost hoped something drastic would happen, like a capsize or for a great wave to come crashing over the side. But, it didn't.

"It's seven now, we should get going, honey."

"Okay."

We drove against the wind on the way back to the dock, water splashed over the windows, and our bodies lurched up and down as we rode the waves. Everything seemed to be going belly up.

"I guess I can't stay tonight then", Cody shrugged as he loaded the boat onto the back of the truck.

"Yeah, I guess."

"I hate that", he groaned, "stupid democrats."

"What are you?"

"Libertarian."

"I don't like Democrats then", I said, looking down, scuffing my feet.

We pulled away from the lake, the rain thudding against the truck as though it had something to say that we couldn't bring ourselves to voice. Cody kept his gaze forward, one hand on the wheel, the other drumming against his thigh, and I sat there beside him, looking out the window as we sped through the slick streets, neither of us speaking, neither of us needing to say it. I could feel it—that sense that this was slipping, that we were running out of things to hold on to, like the rainwater trailing down the windows, disappearing as it pooled at the edge and spilt away.

We stopped at a McDonald's on the way back to South Wedge, and Cody helped himself to my fries,

"Rochelle would hate it when I do that", he said, a faint, bitter smile playing on his lips.

"That's because you were together a long time", I replied, thinking that if I was with him long enough, I'd hate it too.

He didn't respond, just watched me for a moment before looking away, and there was something in that silence, in the weight of it, that felt like the end of something, "She hated it from the beginning", he finally muttered.

I didn't know what to say but settled on, "How are you feeling about that all?"

"I talked to her the other day."

My heart panged.

"She said she doesn't have the mental capacity to go get the divorce papers", he continued, "but if I do she'll sign them."

I took a long, hollow sip of my drink, the straw crackling against the ice, and looked out of the window.

"Like she's just taking so long with it, she won't meet me in the middle", he said.

"Maybe she's stalling."

"Why?"

"Well, I'd stall if I was divorcing you."

"Why?"

"Because I like you."

"It's just so… wild. She's living in my house with her girlfriend, sleeping in my bed, with my dogs. Three months ago she was my wife." His voice cracked just slightly, like a bone bending under the weight, and I felt my heart twist, watching him drift somewhere I couldn't follow.

I wanted to tell him it had been nearly five months, that the timeline had grown longer than he was allowing himself to remember. I wanted to tell him that maybe part of him didn't want to let it go, that maybe he didn't want to be here with me. But I kept my mouth shut. Instead, I just watched his fingers, twitching, restless, like they were holding onto the air around him, searching for something solid, something that was long gone. I wished he wanted me the way deep down he must've wanted her, but that's not the way life works. So, I stayed quiet and wondered if he would miss me when I went to Camp Sunshine, but six weeks is a long time. I didn't trust he wouldn't slip away.

When we got back to South Wedge, the rain was falling harder, slanting down, blurring the streetlights into smudges of yellow and white. Cody opened my door and walked me to the steps. I hugged him and held on longer than I usually would, he embraced it and kissed my hair.

"I'll see you tomorrow and we can go do something", he said.

"Okay."

I watched him walk back to the truck, his shoulders slumping slightly as he climbed in, and I stayed there on the steps, the rain streaming down my cheeks like tears I couldn't bring myself to cry.

***

I had nightmares in the night and ripped my sheets right off my bed, knocked a glass over and awoke to it shattering on the floor. Cody didn't come over. He said he wanted to go on the boat by himself. So, I spent the afternoon at Highland Park. I sat on top of a grassy hill and looked out at the trees and road. I played my music and lit my joint, appreciative of the little love tokens of bud that Cody would leave for me each morning.

I enjoyed the comfort blanket of weed, I enjoyed having a moment to sit still and forget in the silence of everything. To ignore how bad I truly felt. I had no money, I was broke. I had no friends left in America, they'd gone home. I had Cody temporarily but in a few days that would be gone too. I always felt anxious. The dread of the unknown and the undone chores and of time escaping me clung to my back and only with a smokey inhale did it disperse. Light relief. I started to feel like the only way to shake my angst was to return home, and I hoped the camp would be worth hindering that journey across the Atlantic.

I looked at the squirrels climbing the trees and the woodchucks snuffling amongst the flowers and leant back to the sound of kids playing in the park behind the hedges. I envied how easy they had it. I wanted to throw myself into a car, blare *Jackson* by Johnny Cash on the stereo, and propel forward to someplace else. I wanted to feel free again. I was stifled, stagnant. I wanted to break the speed barrier, travel at the speed of light, shoot up to space like a rocket, explode in the Big Bang, and start something else all over again. I wanted peace. I was heavy, maybe I needed cigarettes again.

I lay back and listened to Bob Dylan swirling through the sky, I raised my hand as if to try and touch him, somewhere up in the ether, my fingers outstretched to heaven.

Tears ran down my cheeks, and I drowned in them as the music faded out and my high wore away. That night I lay in my bed, my first night alone in months. Complete darkness crawled in from under the floorboards, in the spaces between the walls, it stepped through my open doorway. I was cloaked in black. I felt a deep depression crawl up into the bed with me, it lay down on my chest, draining my soul with its leech-like mouth, feeding on me, taking all that I had. I didn't resist. I simply pulled its head towards my breast and nursed it. I only knew I was alive for its teeth hurt, and its claws dug deep, sinking into my skin, into me.

I had nothing to do when Cody was at work or fishing with friends, and to his credit he came and saw me near enough every day when he could. I understood he had a life, and I couldn't have been in every facet of it, and nor did I want to be. I cried a lot. I'd cry in the bath, the shower, before falling asleep and when I woke up. I felt lonely and isolated, I felt acute anxiety, as if my world was soon going to be turned upside down—which it was. I had a terrible problem with being by myself, I couldn't hack it, and come to think of it, I'd never been able to hack it, and after such a prolonged period of never having a second to myself, it seemed that much more unbearable.

I didn't want to go to Camp Sunshine, the dread of that chapter coming swarmed me like bees in my ears and eyes, I couldn't get rid of them. The future seemed too heavy, and my heart raced at the thought of Cody drifting away, of this fragile thing slipping from my grasp. I could already feel the loss, like a cold weight in my chest, and the closer I got to leaving, the harder it became to imagine him waiting when I returned.

***

It was suddenly my last day in Rochester. Cody had made me choose a lake to visit and I had chosen Lake Ontario. I was in a reflective mood. I decided we only have ourselves in this blue abyss of land and sea. We don't belong to anyone, and no one belongs to us, unless child to a mother, we are free. I thought about how lucky I was, in all my emotions to be here. To have my hands at the wheel of Cody's boat and steer onward to the horizon. I thought about how I had joked about going off to America with a few belongings over my shoulder in a polka dot handkerchief, off to find my fortune. And, I had. It was no small feat and although the journey ahead daunted me, I knew I'd be back, following my favourite road toward Brockport and Rochester, towards where in my heart I knew I wanted to be.

I'd come far, and I had further to go, yet I knew when I finally touched English soil again, I'd be returning with the experience of a lifetime in tow, and that's all I ever wanted, an experience of a lifetime after another, until the greatest experience of them all, *death*. And, when I part this world, I'll know I part ways with the luckiest, fullest, well-lived life known. That's all we should ever hope for.

I looked down at Cody lying on the stern, his head buried in a towel, napping under the noon sun. I smiled to myself. He looked good—he always did. I replayed the words he'd said the night before: I love you. My chest swelled. I loved him too, truly. Meeting him had been a twist of fate, one I was grateful for. He'd restored something in me—hope, perhaps. Hope for men, for healthy communication, for kindness and decency. A part of me I thought was gone forever had returned.

It was a Saturday afternoon, the June heat pressing softly against my skin. The water stretched endlessly before us, a mirror of the sky. I was content. My thoughts wandered to my Grandpa, to my Mum, to the adventure I was living now. For all my grumbling about existence, I was thankful for my life. Later, we gave up on trolling for fish and drifted closer to the shore. Cody leaned back and lit his pipe, exhaling a cloud of smoke that drifted lazily into the clear sky.

"I'm going swimming," I announced, already pulling off my clothes.

Cody raised an eyebrow. "It's gonna be cold," he said, glancing at the water.

"How do I get in?" I asked, peering over the edge at the turquoise waves below.

"Jump." Cody chuckled, his grin teasing.

And so I did. I bent my knees, reached my arms high, and leaped. The water met me with a tremendous splash, and the coolness enveloped me in an instant.

"I'm a mermaid," I teased, slapping my wet hands against the boat's side and pulling myself halfway up. "Come swim with me."

"I think I'm good from up here," Cody replied, amused.

"Boring!" I laughed, kicking off the boat and treading water. The thought of weeds brushing my legs or fish darting too close made my stomach tighten, but Lake Ontario was too inviting to resist. The water soothed my tired muscles as I floated on my back. The day was painted in shades of gold—sunlight buttercup-soft across the horizon, the vast lake stretching all the way to Canada.

"See you later," I called, splashing as Cody drifted farther from me on the boat.

"Yup, it was nice while it lasted," he joked, waving.

"All good things must come to an end, Cody!" I shouted after him, grinning.

"You never know. I might see you in the next life," his voice echoed back.

"Or the one after that!" I yelled, but the lake swallowed his reply. I let him drift uncomfortably far before dog-paddling back toward the boat, ready for the day to carry us to shore.

Later, Cody decided he wanted to buy drugs.

"We're gonna go pick up Carl," he said as we packed up. "He knows the dealer."

"Okay," I replied, rolling down the window as we drove. The sun kissed my hand, still damp from my swim. I hoped the drug run wouldn't take long—I wanted a shower.

Carl was small, as thin as a rake, and settled in the backseat with a smoker's cough that rattled the air.

"It's Covid," he announced nonchalantly.

I blinked, bewildered, as he and Cody launched into a rapid-fire exchange of pandemic theories.

"At the end of the day, it's population control," Carl drawled, his accent thick and sticky like syrup on a too-hot day.

"Covid? What Covid? It's a hoax, man," Cody replied.

They volleyed conspiracies back and forth, each statement more ridiculous than the last. I stared out the window, half-listening, amused at my situation: riding around Upstate New York with two American men, on a cocaine run, three thousand miles from home.

Carl eventually disappeared into a house, leaving Cody and me in the truck.

"I really like you," Cody said, turning to me. "I love going on the boat with you."

"We always have a good time," I replied, leaning over to give him a peck.

"Careful—I might just follow you back to England," he teased, his voice low and playful.

"I dare you," I whispered, sliding my hand into his.

Carl returned soon after, carrying the cocaine. Cody stopped at Sunoco on the way back to buy him cigarettes. The truck filled with the acrid tang of smoke as Carl lit up immediately.

"I fucking needed that. It's been two days," Carl rasped, hacking like his lungs were about to collapse.

I envied him. It had been six weeks since I'd quit.

When we finally pulled up at South Wedge, Cody wasted no time racking up a line. I joined him, snorting a couple myself to take the edge off packing and cleaning the apartment. I dashed around like a headless chicken while Cody watched The Walking Dead, offering half-hearted help before giving up. I didn't care. I was just happy to be leaving.

The cocaine worked, and before long, we were back on the road. Rochester Country 100.5 blared from the speakers as Cody cranked the volume higher than usual.

"I can't get this song outta my head," he said as we sped down the highway. I could hardly hear him over the radio blaring.

"Yeah, it's catchy" I agreed.

"You know why that is?" He said, angling his body to me, his face lit up with an eureka, "It's because of the Illuminati."

"The Illuminati?"

"Yeah, they make songs addictive", he smacked the radio, convinced in his declaration, "Listen."

I listened as the lyrics swirled around the truck.

I pondered it, "Well yeah, I mean, the song's what the government wants for you guys, like for Americans? To be a good, well-rounded family?"

"Right?" Cody exclaimed, "Right! It's wild."

He swerved into the next lane over, "Rack me another line, honey."

I rustled around for the bag and took too long because he suddenly exclaimed, "Pass it here, pass it here, I'll do it."

The next thing I knew, we were zipping along the highway, in and out of traffic, a phone with a line of coke up to Cody's face, hands-free steering as he thrust a dollar up his nose and made the crystals disappear.

"Take the wheel, honey."

"What?"

"Take the wheel!"

We were on a great wilderness adventure, of drugs and danger, of yellow lines, and number plates, of the Empire State.

"Yoo-hoo!" Cody crowed.

"Yoo-hoo!" I roared.

We were the lion and the eagle on a one-way journey to a collision. Cody screeched into his grandparent's driveway, and we manically climbed out of the truck. I watched him carry my bags into the house, thinking how sweet it was that he would always do that.

He reminded me of my Grandpa. My Grandpa was the best man I ever knew. He was kind, caring, and considerate, he was generous and fair. I saw so much of him in Cody, and I hadn't realised until that moment that the humble, thankless qualities that Cody possessed touched my heart so dearly for I had missed the presence of that safe masculine space. I truly loved Cody, it was the healthiest love I'd ever felt, and whoever ended up with him would be one lucky woman, and his children and grandchildren would be incredibly lucky too.

We went down to the basement to drop off my bags and then into the kitchen. His grandmother greeted us, "Catch anything?"

"Not today Nonna", Cody replied opening the fridge and pulling out watermelon slices with his large hand, shovelling them into his mouth.

His grandmother looked at me and barked, "I like you with no makeup on, you have a pretty face."

"Thank you", I replied, taken aback. I was way too high for this. I hoped we wouldn't be standing in the kitchen for long. Her eyes adverted to Cody, and she shooed him out of the way, be-lining the fridge.

"You like zucchini?" She asked me.

I was pretty sure a zucchini was a courgette but like I said, I was high and instead of a straightforward "Yes", I rambled about not knowing what a zucchini was. Cody's grandmother was visibly distressed at my response and so decided to rectify the situation by giving me a zucchini tour of the fridge. I felt like the Joker hanging over her shoulder, a grin too large for my face, nodding and laughing in all the wrong moments.

"And this is my zucchini salad", she said grabbing a Tupperware box and opening the seal, thrusting it in my face, "looks good, doesn't it? And this", she said getting distracted and shoving the box on an already bursting shelf, "This is my pork steaks. You know what that is? Have you ever tried a pork steak before? Real good with zucchini."

She seized large slabs of pork steaks with her tiny hands and peeled off the clingfilm as though opening a candy she'd been savouring for years. I almost thought she'd start salivating, turning into the wolf in grandma's clothing, "Smell them, smell them, see that, eat that with zucchini."

I was in a nightmare of boiled eggs and zucchini, potato salad and zucchini, chowder with zucchini. I thought zucchini would start growing from her fingers and pour out of her mouth as she poured over me.

"Nonna", Cody said, and I suddenly snapped back to reality. The fridge door slammed shut, "Nonna can we get salad, I wanna start eating salads for lunch."

She shuffled away and towards him spouting about Wegman's lettuce and Aldi *tomados*, I was spared. Once Cody was spared too, we disappeared into the garage. We watched an array of television, images and voices splurged the screen and they all moulded into one. I'm pretty sure Cody said we were watching *Jackass* but if it was *Jackass*, man I went on a trip. I watched in eye-bulging, jaw-dropping horror as some dude thrust a crab in a screaming guy's face.

And, at some point, an astronaut floated across the screen, amongst stars that my eyes got lost in. It took me what felt like an eternity to realise that the heavy breathing was the astronaut's tank and not my fat self. I sat edge over a table in cocaine terror. I started gnawing my fingers with gurn relief, shoving my hands in my mouth and chattering down on them.

Cody sorted out his fishing lures unbothered, and I liked the sounds of the rattling and plopping as he shifted them from box to box. Everything was heightened, like a strike of lightning, bolting straight through everything around me. I had an acute awareness that my body was just a shell, that the grass was nice and green, and that I liked my outdoor life. In my garage-TV-watching, beer drinking, line snorting bubble, I liked everything. I was invincible, and then suddenly the vortex which had consumed me subsided.

Instantaneously, I found it rather lame to be drinking warm beer and watching *Jackass*. My mind needed to be stretched and yet in an instant, it was folded, folded into an origami box of discontent. I was in the mood for a dark room and slow music, but I was in a screaming haze of adult men running around in diapers.

At some point, in the middle of the night, Cody decided it was a good time to clean the boat out. And so, on the moonlit street, with the neighbours fast asleep, we stood bent over on the boat, rustling around the rubbish, dividing it into bin bags and recycling containers.

"I think you're kind", I announced, breaking the silence as I tied a sloppy knot in a bag and passed it to Cody.

"Why?" he chuckled.

"Because you help me, and I like helping you. I've never seen a guy help out like that."

"Well, it's what you should expect and what you deserve."

"I'll remember that."

I started to crave sleep, but it wasn't until the early hours that I crawled into bed, leaving Cody in the garage. It took me ages to finally fall asleep, and once I had managed to drift into unconsciousness, Cody got into bed.

"Are you awake?" He whispered, nestling towards me and putting his arms around my cosy body.

"Maybe" I murmured.

"Are you awake enough to remember what I'm about to say?"

"Maybe" I murmured again, his voice merging into my dream.

He rubbed my back, his hands getting caught on the folds of my fat as they often did. I had forgotten I used to hold my breath when that happened, in fear or embarrassment but now I'd relax into it, leaning back into him, soothed.

"I really like you", he whispered, "I'm excited for a future with you. When you're back from summer camp we'll be together."

I wish I had responded now but I don't think I did. I smiled in the dark with my eyes shut and drifted back into the calmness of the night and into a dream I wished would last forever, before Monday morning and Camp Sunshine.

But Monday rudely came around as it always did and Cody got dressed for work. I stayed in bed, burying my head under the pillow in a futile effort to block out time. Cody took longer than usual. He kept pottering around, and finally, I snapped my head up from under my pillow, "Can you leave now? I'm getting upset."

"Don't cry", he said approaching the bed "Same rule in the basement as on the boat, no crying and no falling over."

"Okay."

He looked at me one last time, before heading up the stairs and out the door into his truck and to whatever construction site awaited. And I sat quite still for some time, taking in the silence of the room, before hauling myself out of bed, and pulling on my clothes, feeling nothing but numb.

***

The journey to Camp Sunshine was terrible. As soon as I touched down in New York City, I was in a nightmare of subways and trains, hauling luggage and dropping bags. The whole way I wanted to turn back. I wasn't ready to be thrust into the world of summer camp staff and kids. My nose kept sporadically bleeding, and my comedown clung onto my face in a thick sickly hue.

I got to the camp in the early evening and tried not to cry into my plate of undercooked food, or in the tiny shower or cold cabin. I tried to introduce myself to my cabin mates with a smile and tried to act excited as they chatted about where they'd come from and what they were going to be doing all summer. But I drew further into myself as the slow hours ticked by and come the night I was ready to plot my escape.

I lay in a weight of dread, twitching with the irritable craving of nicotine and my throat tight with repressed tears. I hated my existence and the prospect of being in that hell hole for seven weeks. God, I cursed Cody. That's how I knew I loved him, I was prepared to trade seven weeks of freedom, of Hydes and smoke, of fun and friends, of adventure, to be stuck in a culty camp to have another grace period, another stretch of days if he were willing, until a doomed airport parting.

I didn't feel this panicked, heartbroken and anxious when Owen said his goodbye. I was excited and happy, and perhaps I was nervous, but it wasn't like this, it wasn't claustrophobic, counting down the seconds of the day, heart in mouth nervous. I wondered if this was how Owen had felt when I left, and I felt bad. I felt bad for how I had abandoned him, how I'd shaken him off me and stamped him while he was down. I was an asshole.

I phoned my Mum, waking her up, telling her my rushed ploy to quit tomorrow. I told Cody too. I sent him a mass paragraph of how I loved him and I couldn't bear it here, how I needed to leave, even if leaving meant being back in the U.K.

I was trapped, if I left, I'd have to get on a plane home. And I wanted to, my God I was ready now to get back to Cornwall, but I wanted more time with Cody. Why the fuck did I have to meet him? Why did I have to fall in love? If I hated every day of the camp as much as I despised that first night, then I guess it would be justice. It would be my prison sentence, seven weeks of torture for leaving Owen, for being determined, ambitious, driven — being everything every man has told me I shouldn't be. And, if Cody did leave in those ghastly seven weeks which hung over my head, then that would be karma too.

When the morning came around, I ploughed through the day. I did my specialist orientation in videography, made small talk with the nurses at lunch and forced myself to appear happy as I miserably took part in team-building exercises. The only thing I liked about the place was the chipmunks, but even then, they weren't cute enough to convince me to stay.

I had had the shakes all day. I was a hardcore Hyde addict on a coke comedown, and when I showed my film to the owner and Frank -the IT guy— their faces said it all.

"Ummm, we'll order you a Steadicam, we can get her a Steadicam, right?" Frank asked the owner, who had nodded, "I suffer from really bad vertigo, and that's making me feel seasick."

Well, I thought to myself, seems like a silly rule now doesn't it, no vaping? I arrived at the camp on Monday and come Wednesday I quit. I was told I had ten minutes to pack my bags and they dropped me at the train station without time to book transport to New York City, or to book a way back to Rochester. But I was glad, and I made it back to the city anyway.

I booked myself a night in a hostel and called Cody. I told him I had until Monday to leave the States, my journey had come to an end. He told me to come to Rochester and stay with him until I had to go home, so I purchased a bus ticket for Thursday morning and then took myself off to the park.

I told myself not to ever lose my voice, that morning I had been at Camp Sunshine, wanting to pull out my hair and consumed with the angst of feeling stuck, as if I had no escape. And now, the evening sun shone on me as I sat writing on a bench in Central Park, sucking on a Hyde and drinking a Coke Zero. It's incredible how much free will we have.

We often forget how we can just up and leave and exit a scenario that doesn't serve us. Sure, when I woke up, I thought I had until September in the States and now I had merely four days until I'd be on that plane. But I was ready to go home. I knew I'd find it boring and perhaps question my decision, but at the end of the day, I didn't want to be at a camp all summer and because I used my voice, I was going to be free.

I'd come a long way, from coming to America in a relationship I felt for years I couldn't leave, coming with baggage and a tiny voice, with a fear of authority and a lack of sense of self. And now, sitting in the June breeze, I had shifted into someone I was comfortable being.

I learnt that letting go of someone you love is hard but holding onto them when your heart isn't in it is selfish. I learnt that there are more good people in the world than bad and that actions speak louder than words. I learnt that people don't belong to each other and that loving someone is a gift that does not demand a return on investment. I learnt that it's okay to quit, to evaluate, to change your mind, to roam freely and to stray from paths.

I learnt that those who are meant to be in your life stay, and the rest are passing through. I learnt that no one owes anyone anything, and the strongest love of them all is love from your mother. It's the thankless, tireless, aching love that never breaks. If someone is important to you, tell them, show them, and wear your heart on your sleeve. You've got to live like there's no tomorrow, and not worry too much about the future. If you have a goal, go for it and if you don't, it doesn't matter, you'll figure it out.

If anything, the one takeaway is that we're all ghosts in the wind. People, places, and time are all passing wisps of ethereal wonder that you have in the palm of your hand in one moment, only to lose it in the next. Good things come by often, bad things drag, great things are to be appreciated, and those ghosts that touch your heart, may or may not come back with the next gust of wind. But don't hold your breath, life's for breathing. The greatest gift anyone can give you, and the penultimate test of love, is time.

***

I headed back up to Rochester on the Greyhound. The journey wasn't as sombre as it seemed before. I was relieved to be traveling Upstate, it felt like home. Cody met me when I got off the bus, and we grinned at each other.

"Well, I'm back", I announced as I got into the truck.

"That you are", he smiled, "I missed you."

"I missed you too", I said, shaking myself free of my coat. It had been raining in New York City, but the sun was out in Rochester, a warm greeting.

I stayed with Cody for four days, the final stretch of my American adventure. We didn't do anything, no fishing trips, no lake days. Cody sat hunched at his computer playing video games, and I drew. I felt discontent at first, fretting about his feelings as I always would. I was confused at his lack of motivation, but I was glad to be with him, anywhere but Camp Sunshine.

We only left the basement once and that was to get drugs. I hoped Cody wouldn't make a habit out of it, but then he always made a habit out of everything until he didn't. I wrote it off as another phase. We got high and it wedged a greater distance between us. Cody retreated further into his screen, and I allowed pen and paper to absorb me, into mandala daydreams and shaky scribbles.

There was a certain midnight magic which rained down, stardust ashes of red, white, and blue. Catherine's wheels explode, spiralling electrified cries. Whistles and whirs and catalytic bangs of blue lakes and orange suns. Ash of grey roads and yellow lines, brown squirrels and gold sand. White flying grit of Miami heat dazzled, and pink hearts exploded across the black sky. The moon became home to bud lights and burgers, snow boots, canteen food and far-away friends. And, as I sat with sweat running out of my pores, my clammy face blotting pink, I marvelled at my life. A bolt of lightning seared through the stars and struck me down.

I was celebrating youth and tight-skinned freedom. I was partying to the ways of the world, of the roaming journey of the *mad mad mad.* I applauded wide-eyed monsters of love and cold creatures of chaos. I gathered the weeds and turned them red, sewing fields of poppies and primroses, of petals and pearls, of boisterous yearning and forgotten grieving.

I set my cold chill alight with a single match, I bathed my body in flames. I drowned the embers in bath water and snot. I ventured everywhere and beyond, I ventured far into the East to forests and rivers. I hiked to the sunset, to pink and yellow clouds, I swam to jukeboxes and peanuts, to hills and houses. I paddled to Queens and crawled to Brooklyn, I ran to Redondo and escaped to the Everglades. I jumped off the Empire State Building and climbed bottles of water and cans of Coke, I slid down the mountain of shadows, and into the stream of dreams.

It was June 16th 2022, a year to the day that my Grandpa passed away. It was funny, I hadn't realised in all the daily chaos. The day before, when I'd been sitting under that leafy tree in Central Park, I had said "Hello Grandpa", as I felt his warmth in the sun, perhaps he was there after all.

***

Real life was calling, and I was floating further and further away, into a gargantuan galaxy of infinite days. America would slip into memories and fade into photos, into words. It would be stored in a spongy safe amid my brain and loaded onto the back of a getaway train.

I'd fallen asleep at some point and woke up with the realisation that my adventure was over. Cody picked up my bags, his movements slow and heavy as if every step carried the weight of a thousand unspoken words. He trudged up the stairs, then stood there, staring out of the garage at the empty street, the silence between us growing thick. We waited for the Uber to pull up.

"This is wild", he sighed.

"What is?"

"Today', he said, "This situation, the scenario", he trailed off, his voice strained.

"Yeah," I replied, my words hollow, empty with the finality of it all.

The Uber came and I wrapped my arms around him one last time, the tight squeeze of a strained goodbye.

"I don't want you to go", Cody uttered, "I love you."

Words escaped me. I swallowed. I was choked. The hands in my throat throttled my neck and snatched my tongue.

"I love you", he said again.

"I love you too," I managed to whisper.

I was bundled into the Uber, the door slammed shut.

"Thank you," I said, leaning out of the window, my voice thin, trying to hold onto something that was slipping through my fingers.

"No", Cody replied, his voice cracking, "Thank *you...* for everything."

And then, I drove away. I watched him disappear into the road, into Rochester, into New York. I watched him disappear all the way home in the quiet grief of something lost, something that was never meant to last.

JULY 2022

The summer was long and dreadful. The realisation I had left America dawned, and with it, the world collapsed. I was constantly drowning. Gasping for air as I slept, my lungs imploding, my heart leaking, forever sinking. Cody had given me some glimmer of hope for a couple of short weeks, telling me he missed me, that he loved me, that he wanted me to come back.

The phone rang twice before he answered. For a moment, neither of us said anything. The silence was full, heavy with everything we wanted to say but didn't know how to start.

"I miss Brockport," I finally said, my voice small, almost hesitant.

"I miss your voice," he replied, his tone soft but steady. "I miss your energy."

A lump formed in my throat. "I miss driving around with you," I admitted, my chest tightening as I spoke.

"I miss adventures with you," his voice catching on the last word.

The pause that followed stretched long. I could hear him breathing, steady and warm on the other end, and for a moment, I just let myself hold onto that.

"I was thinking about South Wedge earlier," I said.

"Oh?" he asked, his curiosity gentle.

"I was sad all the time back then," I admitted. "Anxious and lonely. It meant a lot to me that you kept coming to spend time with me, even when I didn't know how to ask for it."

"It was my favourite time with you," he said quietly. "I saw us having a family because of those days. It felt... possible."

"South Wedge was the closest I got to feeling like I had something tangible," I agreed, my voice trembling. "Like maybe I wasn't completely falling apart."

"What I've always tried to tell you," he said carefully, "is that I'm holding out for those days—until we can have them again."

His words settled into me, filling the hole that had only been stretching bigger through the summer.

"I love you," My voice breaking despite my best effort to hold it steady.

"I've never missed anyone like this," he said. His voice cracked, raw and unguarded. "It's fucking terrible."

"I want to come back."

"I know, honey," he said, his voice so tender it made my chest ache. "I'm going to marry you one day."

"Yes, please," I let out a shaky laugh.

"I never knew what love was until you," His words were quiet, but they hit me like a wave, overwhelming and undeniable, "I went out to the river today. The one where I took you fishing the first time. I was thinking of you."

"I think of you all the time," I said. "I've been going on little adventures every day because... that's when I feel closest to you."

"How long until you come back?"

"If I get into Buffalo State and find the funding," I said, "their term starts on the 26th of August."

He didn't hesitate. "I'll fund you."

The words spilled out before he could second-guess them.

***

I filled out an application with Buffalo State, desperate to transfer my degree, and yet no way to front the money. I was half the person I was in America. And then, the lonely intuition hit and I knew something wasn't right. I messaged Cody at 2 am, and he told me he was scared I wasn't coming back and I told him I was scared there was someone else, and there was.

He'd betrayed me. My world sank before my eyes. The new girl was a thief and he was a coward. And so, I started writing again, for it was only the blank page in the midnight hours, which knew how to riddle through my pain.

I spiralled into a hazy depression, and I was stumped as to how to pull myself out of it. My heart bubbled with anger and my soul ached with sadness. I felt bruised and I couldn't believe how fast everything changed, how three weeks ago I was with Cody, and now he had a girlfriend and I was alone. The world was dark and desolate. I never had time to keep up with myself. I was inhaling poison upon poison. Poison alcohol. Poison nicotine. I was a swirling pessimist, in a period of temporary despondency. I was the 21st-century Miss Havisham.

AUGUST 2022

I missed Cody's friendship, and I felt miserable. Everywhere I looked I saw rejection. I saw it in his social media posts with her, their dozens of pictures together when he and I had none. I saw it in the acceptance to Buffalo State and the empty bank account which prohibited me from going. I saw it in the mirror, it was in every inch and fold of my being. *I hurt.* I had been forgotten, and I had to walk the path alone. I wished I could've had a chance to blink before he had swept the rug from up under my feet.

I tried to look onward to Bath, to finishing my degree and to whatever hellbent adventure I'd get swept along on next. I tried to feel mostly. That whole summer was empty and bottomless, a stretch of nothing. *Nothing. Nothing.* Miserable *nothing.* My life was one vast stretch of nothingness with glints of some things that always fizzled out along the way.

I thought of stupid things, like rest stops with Cody, eating pizza in his basement, the drives and little chores, the food dates and the norm. I rarely thought of fishing with him because that felt insignificant, it was the small moments I remembered. I struggled to accept that though he had been magic to me, I had been an exotic shag in passing. And, the worst thing about it all was that I found that if I wasn't writing about him, I'd write nothing at all. How could he have everything, and I nothing? How could he have discarded me with such ease, and how could

I have been blinded for so long? I sighed, I guess Leonard Cohen was right, that's no way to say goodbye.

August 1st 2022, at least I wasn't still at the summer camp with 4 days left to go, knowing that Cody had moved on with someone new. She repulsed me, and I hoped I wouldn't become a female misogynist, for everywhere I went women of all kinds started to repulse me too. Perhaps I repulsed myself.

SEPTEMBER 2022

Queen Elizabeth II died as the seasons changed. It seemed apt, a sadness, a nation in mourning in the modern age, it symbolised change, and a closed door to an era. The constant drone of nothingness continued rolling, on and on. The rain started falling again, and it grew dark outside, and yet most of my days had been the same. I had no choice but to move forward and yet my mind was forever spinning backwards.

I saw on Facebook that Cody was planning to take Madison to Florida with my credited flight. Not on my watch. I phoned up the company, raking up international charges, and told them I wanted to book a flight to San Francisco with my credits. A few keyboard clicks later a nauseating American accent asked me if there was anything else they could help me with today. There wasn't and I hung up. I thought of that empty plane seat flying to California, and the triumph didn't replace my bitterness.

I remembered the gift voucher I bought him for a large outdoor outlet, and I bought the most pointless things possible with it, adding a fake address in Alaska.

A couple weeks went by and since no one collected it, they sent it back and redeemed the card.

OCTOBER 2022

Cody called to tell me he was in Virginia, "I'm at my Mom's in Virginia. I still have your heart right? Don't ever let me give it away again."

He'd driven down without sleep. He said it took him longer than it should've since he kept stopping to "piss" and to buy beef jerky. His grandparents had thrown him out. He thought they'd put cameras up in his basement, and I told him that probably wasn't true.

He said he was heading for Palm Coast in the morning, and that he was gonna stay with buddies and then start up his own business. I told him he'd done the right thing, but I wasn't sure if he had. I was biased for I only knew Cody in Upstate, driving around Rochester, fishing at different lakes. Palm Coast sounded like a strange land, a picture-postcard kinda place, where old ladies sunbathed topless and busty blondes with ugly toes walked the beach. I considered showing up there, hopping on a flight from New York – I had a flight booked to collect my bag I left stowed in Brockport – but it wasn't plausible, I didn't have the money nor the time. I didn't have the energy for a haphazard adventure with a crazed American, not this time.

"Come to Palm Coast," Cody said, his voice both eager and earnest. "I want to marry you so you can chase your dreams in 'Murcia. You don't have to stay with me—I just want to be the way for you to make them come true."

"I stopped believing you all the way back in Brockport."

"Marry me, and go anywhere in America you want. The choice is yours."

"I'd be going straight to New York."

There was a long pause, I almost thought the phone had disconnected, but then he continued, "I'm going to stage my own death", the mischief in his tone unmistakable. "Is that legal?"

"No," I replied without missing a beat.

"Oh fuck," he groaned dramatically. "Now the feds heard—I can't do it."

"I'd rat you out anyway."

"You better not," he warned, "You can never do that to me. Don't break my heart, please."

"Then don't fake your death," I said firmly.

"Yes, Ma'am," he replied with exaggerated obedience. "Can I break laws ever again?"

"Depends what laws."

"What about helping someone stay in the country illegally?" Cody asked, his tone almost hopeful.

"You'd have to find a way to make that legal," I said, yawning.

"Okay, so as soon as I get divorced, will you marry me?"

***

October was slow and strange. Cody had at first quietly dissolved into a spiral of chaos and then like a drugged-up phoenix from the ashes, with a loud *BOOM*, he rose and was full-blown mad. Self-professed crazy. Neurotic. Calling me at all hours of the night, telling me that he was being watched, that the FBI were on his tail. Convinced the government were deploying men to follow him, and that his phones were being tapped. He'd disappear and then reappear more muddled and confused and desperate with each ring of the phone. He said his colleagues were looking at him, staring him down with wild eyes, and that they were going to get him arrested for being a serial killer. That Madison was a spy. He quit his job because his boss was secretly a member of the mafia.

His Mum reached out to me and his Grandmother too, asking me to calm him down, and the whole time I thought, get Madison to do it. What the hell can I do?

And then all at once he had snapped and turned on me, distrustful, distasteful, he told me he didn't trust me, that I wasn't loyal, that I didn't matter.

And he blocked me.

And then unblocked me and told me to marry him.

"The feds are listening to every word we say. They'll never let you back in unless you marry me and turn on me, right? You're supposed to be the one holding my heart, not letting anyone—especially the feds—take it from you."

I didn't understand, I had already lost him.

"I'll pay you to come to America and marry me. I love and value you so deeply that I'd sign my life away just to give you the freedom to travel and do whatever you want, no strings attached."

***

I sat in the Bath Abbey square, the sun warming the Georgian stone, the abbey's windows glinting, pigeons fluttering towards the Roman Baths. An opera singer, on her knees, hands extended to the sky, belting *Time to Say Goodbye* in dramatic vibrato. And I knew, maybe she was right. It was time to say goodbye. For it's always good to listen to a sign. And I was almost moved to tears, as a small girl with pigtails and red shoes ran across the shadow of the square, towards the light. But I decided that too many tears had been shed, and I was moved in silence, my silence, instead.

And when she left, I left. I walked around the corner, and a man with an electric guitar started singing *All Along The*

Watchtower. Someone behind me told their friend they'd seen Jimi Hendrix in America, "and we stood as close as this", he said. And an old woman in a neon pink hat joined the crowd. She started dancing.

NOVEMBER 2022

I landed back in New York on Thanksgiving Day. Too late to watch the parade, too consumed by everything else to care. New York, New York, oh beautiful New York. I was so happy to be back that I wrestled jet lag, checking into my room in Chelsea, and then emerging out again, walking the streets, past bin bags of trash, eateries and window displays.

I told Cody I had landed and he was excited. Two days in the city, and three days Upstate. The journey to retrieve the belongings I had left before summer camp, my big bag awaiting me in a Brockport basement. I could hardly believe I would be seeing Cody again, and I was only sorry I would appear during his distress. Florida hadn't worked out. He was kicked out of his friend's house and had used the gift voucher I had given him to buy a tent. I was glad then that there wasn't an invisible stranger in Alaska who snatched the belongings. That at least he had a stretch of tarpaulin above his beautiful head.

And just like everything with Cody, God hadn't stopped there. There had been a hurricane in Palm Coast, and Cody's truck was "fucked up." And the tent was destroyed. He used that flight to San Francisco to get lost in Minnesota. The flight to Minneapolis was the only one he could catch. Little did he know when he asked for the voucher code, I had sat all afternoon persuading the flight desk to change it again, from Florida to San Francisco to bloody Minneapolis.

Cody had sent an array of videos of him scootering down the street where George Floyd had died. And now he was back, in Rochester, waiting to be rescued, and from all the long phone calls with his Mum in my Chelsea Hostel room, I seemed to be the one to have to do it.

But things always change, and time always moves and I was back again. The Chelsea Hostel was nestled on a side street, with graffiti of "I love NY" sprawled on the building across and a bagel shop two doors down. All I seemed to do was walk on that first day, burning off steam, feet jittering with the pure bliss of having returned. The notion that anything was possible. I was on my way to McDonald's for a dispensed drink when I was suddenly face to face with The New School. I had started my application to join the following Fall, and I did a little wish outside the doors, to the red banners above, that that too would be possible.

***

My bus to Rochester was delayed, and I spent an hour in Port Authority station, standing impatient and bog-eyed. The invisible bat of jet lag pummelled my head, and I could think of a million other places I would've rather been. It was 6 am and we lined the bus bay like a row of roaches, waiting to scuttle onto the Trailways and nest in our seats for seven hours.

The sun stretched through the skyscrapers of Union City as we rolled out of New York and the orange glow blinded me through the window. It was time to journey through New Jersey and Pennsylvania, to crawl up Interstate 90 towards Cody, and onwards to the next brief adventure. I couldn't sleep, and spent the day looking out of the window, restlessly shuffling, hitting my vape beneath my coat, and watching the vapour waltz like ghouls across the seats in the morning sun. I sent Cody my location and he sent his too. I watched as our pinpoints slowly grew nearer, through Scranton and Binghamton, past Cornell, and up through Syracuse.

In Geneva, my excitement bubbled as we passed the vast stretch of blue, the Finger Lake, and I smiled, whispering a little, "Hello". I was weak and nervous and my stomach growled with anticipation. I painted my face with foundation and concealer, eye shadows and highlighters, sticking lashes to my sweaty eyelids as the bus jolted over the rough Upstate roads. Red barns blurred into one, and the houses grew bigger, white, blue, and yellow, with porches and pickup trucks, quad bikes and railroad crossings. We rolled on under blue skies, past stop signs and Mobils, bare trees and flat grasslands.

"I'm nervous", I messaged Cody.

"I'm more nervous than you could ever be", he replied.

I wondered if it was a good idea to see a man on a mental break, homeless and abandoned, confused and struggling and alone. And, the thought merely fluttered like a dove from the fog of my brain, off up into the trees and away. For if there was ever a time to see him, my wayward American, it was now.

Madison also fluttered into my brain, a vulture with nothing better to do than keep returning to peck and scratch and hiss. I imagined the bus ploughing straight into her, wiping her out clean, feathers and blood splattered across the windscreen, and I smirked. I was approaching, stepping into her territory, a girl from England back to steal time with Cody. But Cody wasn't anyone's man, he simply existed in a world of his own. I liked him for that. I respected his independence, his stamp on the world, his unapologetic conquest to be nothing but himself. If that made him crazy, I was glad he wasn't sane.

I finally pulled into the Rochester Bus station and stumbled out into the cold, crisp air. I was met with a wash of grey, and Cody, good old Cody in his beanie, hands in pockets, dirt-covered jeans, and windbreaker. I smiled, he did too, and we hugged.

"I'm cranky ", I said.

"Oh I know how to fix that," Cody replied, taking my bag and lifting it into the truck, "first stop Wendy's."

***

I noticed his screensaver was a picture of me on the Ferris Wheel in Bristol, which I had posted on Instagram a couple of weeks before. I wondered why he had chosen it, and what he felt when he saw it. I pretended I hadn't seen— to come to my conclusion was a far better bet than to ask. I looked up at him concentrating on the road, and my heart was full, friend or foe, lover or stranger, I accepted he didn't belong to me. I liked how the only expectation was friendship, I decided that was the true test of love, and I was glad lust had disappeared. I would never love anyone like I loved him again. I thought of Central Park all those months ago, and of my quiet epiphany that love doesn't demand a return of investment. I'd forgotten that in England, in the cold, in the dark, in my moments without him. Perhaps that had been selfish, and I hoped to be more selfless, to be like him, to be good.

He wasn't crazy, he was just sad. I couldn't determine if he was depressed, or just severely upset, but underneath the smile and the rants and the incantations and racing thoughts, was a man beaten down by life, a boy needing love. It was obvious and I was startled by everyone's obliviousness. My thoughts trailed back to his wife and I wondered what she was like. I knew she couldn't have liked me very much, but I hoped she didn't see me as I did Madison. I didn't want to be her vulture. Though Cody had nothing, he wasn't short of a band of jealous women, and I didn't blame us. Who could?

***

There had been a man watching The Red Roof Inn, illuminated by a streetlight. I had clocked him as we had left and as we returned. He was in an old-fashioned, American car, in the parking lot, outside the roach motel. He had been there in the daylight and the drizzle into the night. Perhaps Cody was being watched, by a private detective or a fed, or an FBI, or perhaps his paranoia had become mine.

"He thinks you're a prostitute", Cody pointed as he saw me looking at the stranger.

Right.

He had disappeared at some point late and was replaced with a screech a beep and a yell. Cody cracked open the door and told me to stay inside. I peered around him and saw a huge truck, with big wheels and a confederate flag. It had pulled in front of the motel, and I couldn't see them but I heard a yob of men take the stairs, and then their footsteps above. I shrunk into the bed.

"Wait here", Cody said and closed the door. I did, until I heard the shouting. The profanities, the n-word, the banging. I crept out of bed and towards the window, drawing back the curtain a fraction and sneaking a peep. The light was on in Cody's truck and he was smoking a bowl. And then suddenly the voices grew louder and the footsteps surged again and I retracted.

I waited for Cody to return and realised how sketchy all of this was becoming. When he opened the door and stepped inside he explained that, "a black dude is banging that guy's girl, she's a whore. This place is full of pimps."

***

I had been on top of the world with him, the lion and the eagle, and the bottom of the barrel, the road kill beneath the wheels of a truck going nowhere, lost in the haze of what was America, through the strangling mist of washed-up dreams.

I asked him point blank what drugs he had been taking, for everyone was in agreement that he had to be on something.

"I'm not on drugs, you asshole."

And maybe he wasn't. The jury's still out on that one. Maybe it was just the rise and fall of the American dream.

Maybe rushing off to Walmart so that he could meet a stranger in the parking lot and sell his fishing rods, was the rise and fall of the American dream. Maybe using that money to buy a McDonald's meal, and then when growing hungry again, slotting his phone in a machine that gave him quick cash for another night stay in a roach motel, was just part of the rise and fall of the American dream. Maybe taking a jar of coins and shoving them in a Coin Counter and getting a mere handful of dollars in return, to go buy a jar of peanut butter and some bread, was just the rise and fall of the American dream. What would I know?

I had thought I'd pulled the short straw by not being American, by not being able to stay, but in the end, it was Cody clutching at straws, crying at the red lights for that's all that seemed to ever shine.

There had been green lights in Brockport: *go, go, go*. But now the only colour known to man was burgundy. The red lights shone on the way to the junk store. Cody's childhood books in boxes, Harry Potter, read and reread, tossed amongst others.

"You should keep one", I told him, as tears ran down his cheeks, and his hands trembled and I didn't know where to look. The Rochester Holiday Radio felt sadistic in its jolly hum.

"Why?", he sobbed, "What good would that do?"

"So that when all this blows over, at least you have something. Choose your favourite."

He swung open his door and walked round and opened mine, wiping his nose on his dirty sleeve, "You choose."

I swallowed and looked at all the childhood memories, memories lost, piled on top of each other. I pulled out Harry Potter and the Sorcerer's Stone and slid it onto the dash.

Cody walked into the store with everything he held dear, and returned out again, "He said they were worthless. He gave me five bucks."

I didn't have much to say to that. Only that I wish the light would flicker back to green. Only that I was sorry that I would be leaving in a couple of days. Leaving him in Upstate, homeless, afraid. I hope he knew I would've stayed.

"Now let's go pawn these tools."

***

It was funny how the music had changed, the country tunes that had been blasting all spring and summer had rolled into new ones, new hits, new reruns, a new season, out with the old. We sat in the truck, passing the bowl back and forth, the harsh weed that burnt our throats, and scorched our lungs. I remembered how Owen wouldn't let me smoke weed, and when I was young and in his grasp, I was sad, thinking I never would again. I made a mental note that next time I ever felt I couldn't do something, I was most probably wrong, and with the roll of time I could do anything I wanted, and all things come back around. Just like sitting there, in the dark, the dim motel light illuminating the dashboard with the beat-up Harry Potter book and paperwork. Sitting there with Cody, in a different truck, but a truck nonetheless, in a different time but there nonetheless, with a different mix of feelings in the air, but feelings nonetheless. I'd always make my way back to the things and the people and the places I desired, for I was the captain of my boat, a boat which would ebb and flow with the changing currents, sometimes to get lost or stuck or weathered in rain and storm and passing bitterness and brokenness, with cracks in the stern, and water overboard, but I was in control. I would never lose control again, for to lose control is to lose the steer and coast of life, and life is short— we only have one.

"All Americans are enslaved bro, "Cody spluttered finally.

I'd almost forgotten he was there, and although taken aback, I was never too shocked by anything he said anymore, "Well yeah, the whole world knows that."

"This shit is wild," and he passed me the bowl again.

I took a hit, "The number of people who were like…. the fuck you want to go do your Semester Abroad there," I coughed, "Would surprise you."

"They told us since birth we were the greatest country ever."

"Again, the whole world knows that about America too."

"Yeah, but America doesn't. I need to get the fuck out of here."

I hoped Cody would make love to me, but he didn't, and that was okay, for he had his boat to put back on course too. When we finished up the bowl, and the night was old, and the truck was cold, we stumbled back inside, and onto the bed. I lay on my side, and Cody wrapped his arms around my body, and we lay there for quite some time. My chest rose and fell as his heart thudded behind my back. I took his arm and held it there. He gently pulled at the back of my sweater, I shuffled around and buried my head in the crease of his arm, my hand holding him close, and he held me close too. It was slow and the night was long, and his breaths told me to decompress, and when the stoned cuddle sufficed, we slept under the stars above the clouds, and the peace extended to the morning dew.

***

It was my last day and we were headed to Brockport. Following that road home. Just like I always said I would. But home was stark and brown, empty, and cold. The students were still gone for Thanksgiving break, and I suddenly felt glad I didn't transfer there, for Bath Spa seemed more magical than this unfamiliar place.

It was too cold to get out of the truck and I rang every Brockport number I could but none of them answered. I sent an email too, and we waited, and Cody friendzoned me, and the minutes ticked. After an hour or so, we drove up and onto Main Street, we went to U-Hots, and the town was adorned with

Christmas decorations. I didn't know how I felt about being there. When we returned to Campus, we decided to go to any office we could and ask for access to my bag.

Only my bag wasn't there. Some students had stolen it, and then it was police departments and forms and disbelief. And then it was searching the basement and the trash, and pulling out my discarded items, one by one, the invaluable crap, the empty photo albums, the pair of jeans, and my dorm blanket….. a rubber duck from 'Hooligans'.

I thought of the Bristol home videos, the shaky camera footage of Owen and I, tapes of our drunken adventures down dark Bristol alleys and the corner shop man, of running around and of kisses, of addressing the camera as our future kids. I thought of my Polaroids, of getting ready with Mel and Josie, our photos of Frat parties and quiet afternoons. I thought of my journals, of my entry of the first night, the first date with Cody, the pink bubble writing confessing my love at first sight. I thought of the pages with ink splotches and teardrops, my Broadway playbooks, my L.A. travel vlogs, my saved aeroplane tickets and doodles. My Walmart Valentine's teddy and keepsakes, my secrets and souvenirs. I thought of my camera which I had taken to Nepal, and the Adidas jacket I wore my first time in New York, and I cried.

I hunched my knees to my stomach and buried my face in my jacket, my head rattling on the window of the truck driving back to Rochester, away from Brockport. I sobbed, rasping breaths as I thought of all the good which had been robbed from me, of greedy hands snatching my belongings, of the bag that was no longer there. They had tossed me out as soon as I had left. I had treasured Brockport every day for months. I was nothing but a forgotten face in a crowd of people who come and go.

***

"Take this", Cody said, fumbling in the console and pulling out ten bucks, thrusting it towards me.

"I don't want it ", I replied, "Thank you, but no thank you."

"Just take it, I'm telling you, I want you to have it—

"I don't want it", I retorted, "You don't have anything, I'm not going to take ten dollars."

"I'm begging you", Cody cried, his voice raised, his throat tight, "I want you to have it, so you can get something to eat."

"No—"

"I literally don't have anything", Cody wailed, "I have nothing, do you know what that is like, to not be able to provide? I want you to have it."

"Fine", I mumbled and took the bill, crumpling it in my pocket, cursing his generosity, in awe of his goodness. I wanted to scoop him up and take him away.

I had found my Dean Moriarty, my American straggler, my nomad on the run from himself, and I looked through the darkness, through the headlights, through the neon signs of McDonald's and Wendy's, of fast food chains fuelling greed and making a nation fat. I struggled to look beyond my woe, for Cody's pain hurt too much. I wished to return him, to trade the unhappy boy with the sad eyes for the summer boy, the boy on the boat. I wished to squeeze his hand so tight that it would fix his whole damn broken life.

I stole a glance. His face stabbed my chest again with the sharp blow of a wasted love, and the heavy ache of not being able to save a tortured soul. Tears stained his cheeks and glinted in the passing lights, and I looked away again. Helpless. Muddled. I sighed. Cody must've heard because he extended his hand and our fingers intertwined. I didn't squeeze through, for he'd been squeezed out his whole life.

I decided I wouldn't like America anymore. I still desired it and yearned for it, and it still felt like home, but out of principle,

I resented it. I couldn't like this land anymore, not for chewing Cody up and spitting him out, for feeding his mind ideologies of wealth and money and finances, for installing the machine that took his phone, and the drive-thrus which stole his dollars and robbed his health. I couldn't possibly bear to stand America for trapping a golden boy within its States, its passport-less blue-collar men, the expired, the retired, the lives not ventured overseas.

"You'll come to England won't you?" I asked.

"I'd love to," he sniffed, "I need to get a passport though."

"Well make it a priority then."

"Yes Ma'am"

Yes Ma'am, yes Ma'am, yes Ma'am. He could've yes Ma'med me all day, and I still wouldn't have believed he ever would.

"Are you looking forward to going home?"

I looked down at my feet for the road reminded me that it was the airport we were heading towards, and not the roach motel, not a Walmart parking lot nor a 7-11. I shook my head, and the tears started falling. Rivers of salt dripped off the tip of my nose, splashing like the rain outside the window onto my scuffed-up shoes. I didn't have to look up again to know that Cody echoed my grief. I could hear him crying over the turned-up radio, the great roar of wheels through puddles, and the distracting beating of disappointed hearts. I leaned my head on his arm, cradling his hand, and watched as my tears slid into his veins and ran between his white knuckles.

"It's only goodbye if you let it be", Cody sobbed.

And I laughed, immediately wishing I hadn't, "I'll never let it be goodbye."

"I've driven this road a million times", Cody choked, "I've been picked up here, but I've never dropped anybody off."

I sat in my seat as he got up out of the truck and hauled the Marlboro bag he'd given me and my suitcase out of the back, and he came round to open my door. I walked next to him holding my breath, and then we stood facing each other, red-eyed and snotty, words all dried up.

I wiped his face with my fingers and kissed his cheek.

"I've got to go," he said.

I pulled him close as we cried into each other's necks, "I love you so much. Thank you for everything."

I stood and watched as he got back into the truck and pulled away, sucking on my Hyde as if without it I'd turn blue and die. Perhaps I would turn blue and die regardless. As he passed he slowed down and shooed me, "Go get your flight".

I simply waved and when I could see him no longer, I inhaled my watermelon poison one last time and dragged my bags into the departures lounge. My heart broke for the hundredth time, and once again I was angry at life's relentlessness in hurrying us on. It was November when I left America and December when I reached England. My hand ached from where I had clasped Cody's football jersey the three thousand miles home. The jersey over my arm and my Hyde in my pocket as I stumbled into the London air were the only pieces of evidence which proved I was ever really there. The months would trickle on, and the days would push us away, but somewhere down the line, I'd be back again, tracing that road.

I didn't sleep for three days after leaving Rochester. I woke up Wednesday morning and fell asleep on Saturday. My mind was too full, my soul too tainted and my heart too heavy to close my eyes. Insomnia had returned; perhaps that was the only constant I would ever know.

When I finally succumbed to sleep, I dreamt of sewage. Moschino bags, Hello Kitty clothes, vintage Adidas and Nike, sinking into the thick, muddy shallows. Gypsies fished them out, hooking them with long wires and into boats. I saw Owen's hoody lying on the bank of the mucky water, his phone beside it and yelled. I sloshed through the sewage, it felt like quicksand, and I couldn't get to it. I was in despair, and then he appeared, Owen with his tied-up hair and beard and wonky glasses. His boyish eyes and pale skin waded towards me. Only he represented danger, a threat.

Cody's cousin— one I didn't know he had— grabbed me and the gypsies stopped hooking their loot and used boats to barricade Owen from getting to me. I was stowed away in an underground community, of gypsies sifting through trash, dropping non-valuables in a pile to be burnt, and turning the valuables into gold. I tried to leave to return to Owen, but I couldn't. Everyone got in the way, and I cried because I knew he only wanted to talk to me, and I had abandoned him once again. Men were demanding sexual favours for having rescued me, and the women were offering me off. In the dream, I phoned Cody. I begged him to come and get me, to save me, and he said no.

When I awoke I mourned my forgotten fiancé and my friend across the pond. I grieved for my stolen baggage and wept for the two loves lost. Cody started to fall distant again within a couple of days, and I knew he was seeing Madison. His fatal flaw was the constant need for validation. He confirmed it on the phone less than a week after I saw him last, and I dabbled with the possibility of taking myself away again, withdrawing to a winter silence and only emerging when my heart would not bruise.

***

I had met Tom six days after I left Rochester, and he'd become a permanent fixture ever since.

***

Cody called me to tell me Madison had been saying how fat and ugly I was, and yet he continued to hang out with her and validate her, be intimate with her and to some degree, love her. I was angry that everybody seemed to think it okay to call me fat and ugly, and how Owen had for three years, and how even my own Dad had. I thought of the nasty boys in secondary school and the lingering taunts, "unfuckable".

I didn't trust Cody hadn't agreed with her. The world was a dark place and people bumbled along tearing the hearts of those who strayed on their path. I wasn't fat and I wasn't ugly. I was someone with a body the size of my trauma. How would she like to be beaten and raped and left for dead, only for a silly cunt to turn around and call her fat and ugly? Her soul was ugly and her problems were fat, and there were only a handful of people I've ever wished harm on. She was one of them. I wished ill on her in a great plague and hoped unhappiness would come crashing down on her like a ton of nail-probed bricks. I questioned whether I could be Cody's friend, not out of jealousy but out of principle. How could he fuck someone so unkind?

"I had a dream last night where I kept trying to cuddle her, but someone else kept getting in the way. It was uncomfortable."

"I don't get what you see in her. I really don't like her."

"Half of my energy is just wasted on this."

"Your energy is just bad news."

***

I was depressed again, and I sat and thought of Cody, in his beanie, his back turned with a hidden smile. I thought of Cody and his fishing rod and his reel, I thought of Cody against the world, another pair of headlights in Upstate New York, another foot on the trail, another man with a wish and empty pockets. Cody and his cloud of pain, Cody the man I love. Come Christmas, neither Owen nor Cody sent their well wishes and I thought of them both as I cried into my food. The walls closed in on me. As the curtain fell on 2022 and the winter darkness grew thick, the year of being twenty-one came to an end, and I left it as lonely as it had begun.

JANUARY 2023

"*H*appy Birthday.

Words feel so small right now. I worked today and all I could hear was your voice in my head, telling me, 'You need to get your positivity back.' I thought about it, and sure, positivity is great, but the truth is, I really fucking miss you.

Happy damn birthday.

Saying I owe you my life doesn't even come close. Thank you for being the light of love and positivity that kept me grounded through the most traumatic moments of my life.

Thank you for setting aside your own feelings just to be there for me when I needed it most.

You are one hell of a human being. I'm genuinely excited to see where life takes you because, if anyone has the world at their feet, it's you."

***

I remembered Los Angeles, being wistful and stupid, poetically yearning my next adventure and now I had a windfall of them, empty pockets and a backlog of assignments, and I didn't know whether my ability to be so careless made me overly pretentious or one of the soundest people I knew.

I was either reckless and stupid or a genius for fucking off to the Philippines for a month in the final semester of my final year of Uni. I decided that degrees are overhyped and I'd only ever be twenty-two and working as a photojournalist once, and degrees are mostly useless, and everyone who disapproved of me was going to disapprove of everything, and so what the hell does any of it even matter? I maxed out my credit card and booked the flights. In March I would be jetting off on another adventure, to help people, to fill that inner need to be whole, just like all those years ago when I trundled off to Nepal. March 2023: Photojournalist Internship in the Philippines. Back on track again.

***

As I listened to the folk fiddler in the square of the Abbey, and as the golden sun traced the etched buildings and carved gargoyles, and cherubs perched on their centuries-old resting place, I smiled. I was washed with the overcoming sense of loving Europe, of loving life, of loving music and the act of sitting and listening to the cold air and peeping sun. I breathed, spring was coming, and I couldn't have been happier if I tried. I loved music and art and people and history, and life oozing with whimsy and romance. A brimming sensation of thankfulness at the pure art of existing, at the nature of being: of oneness, of journeys and beginnings. I always fell in love with every musician I saw.

Never has a craft been so pure. It brings wonderful joy. It's a catching virus, a spread, a discovery, an exploration, a wonder of the world. I'd always be in a rush, frantic, hastening everything along. And now I realise how foolish that was, for one day there won't be another great adventure, another love won't come knocking, one day the friends I have now will be the best I ever had, and I'll fall asleep and won't awake, and will kick myself for rushing an existence we must prolong.

FEBRUARY 2023

I was up off again, into the air, into the vortex, into the atmosphere, jetting through the portals of heaven and earth, of life and the beckoning of a new land. I hoped Italy would inspire me. I always venture with a purpose, and as the pilot ploughed towards Pisa, I thought once again of Brockport. I thought of this day a year ago, and whatever I was doing, I didn't know I would be off a year later with new people once again, off to meet Meave, off to eat pizza and drink wine, in between wads of nicotine gum and splutters of quitters cough. Off to make memories in a world forever changing. I was departing England for a few days, leaving behind not Owen nor Cody, but a new man, a new face, Tom.

The sky was blue and the journey was short, and the sun warmed my cheek as I pressed it against the window. My eyes were heavy from a night of unrest, a 4 am sore throat and soother popping nightmare followed by a 7 am start. I always travel tired, I wondered if the whole world did: eyes sore, eyebags creasing, drowsily and clumsily entering a new border. It was Monday and I'd be back again on Friday, and I was glad that was hardly enough time to fall in love.

It was a panini trip, a pizza escapade and I looked forward to a full stomach, good friends and disappearing into the world of the Medici in Florence, just like I had devoured the historical drama on Netflix in the dark room, an escape from the claws of Owen. And I smiled, for the things I dream of, my fantasies of the

Duma, and Michaelangelo, all come true. Sometimes in the form of a "Let's go to Florence, first stop Pisa" kinda way. I was glad we flew from Bristol airport, watching it shrink beneath us was satisfying and symbolic and when we had departed I looked down and imagined a parallel universe where I was still sitting watching the Medici, in the room of horrors, and I told that version of me, that I was up in the sky, and she would soon be too.

Turbulence hit as we flew over the Alps, shaking in our seats as the plane jolted over the mountains. White tips struck up from the clouds, daring to scratch the plane, and send us all plummeting to a Swiss death. The white mountain tops, the jagged grey reminded me of a Bob Ross painting and of Everest, I thought of my brother and his snowboarding, I thought too much, and when we landed in Pisa, I was so tired and so heavy and my eyes itched so viciously, I cursed myself for having thought instead of sleep.

***

It fascinated me how willing people were to stop and take a photo of a stranger. I would never say no if someone I didn't know asked for a picture, but why is it? Because we all hurry to capture a moment and recognize the beating heart which flies by too quickly?

I got onto the train and slumped in my seat just as it pulled away from Florence and chugged onwards, towards Rome.

***

A black-cloaked creature swooped down on me and I woke Tom up by shouting, "What the fuck?"

My Fitbit told me my heart rate was 119, and then I was sick and fell asleep again.

***

"I miss you, Miss England."

***

"Remember when I told you, 'Don't get a boyfriend who'll make you stop being my friend,' and then you went and did exactly that?"

"You're the one who replaced me first."

"Fine, now I'm gonna want royalties for my story, and I'm getting a passport just to crash your life with you and Tom."

I sent Cody screenshots of my writing, of our wind-swept, rainy, fucked off day on the lake. The day we got locked out. I sent him paragraphs of us cuddling at the side of the road, of Rancho Viejo,

"So, sue me."

"You're a good writer. That's great. But why do you hate me? I'm just trying to figure my shit out whilst you're busy with your new guy"

"You're busy with Madison."

"I could sleep with six women, wake up beside all of them, and still think of you when I open my eyes because I love you."

MARCH 2023

People borrow me and I guess I borrow them too because we're not fixed to anyone. It's a life of exchange and transactions. That's why it's solidly, indisputably important, that you're comfortable with yourself, that your love affair is between your heart and your adventures, your boldness and your will. Your head and your steps towards whatever journey you're heading towards. That was my thought as Tom drove on through the night, in the rain, past blurring headlights, from Bath to London, where we'd depart for Iceland.

I asked him where his values lay and he said his car and his skills, his house. I'm always finding practical men. Men who go through the motions, I wondered if he knew he was borrowing me too. I'll always associate drives and the rain and the wind and the car and the wheel with freedom. Freedom, above all else, is what I value the most. Freedom, choices, and parting ways is if not the most painful, the most liberating freedom of them all. I was happy to trade the rain for the snow, and I hoped I would see the northern lights. If I did, I'd say hello to Grandpa. I still missed him, I always would after all.

***

Brown flats, snow peaked mountains, and suddenly they emerged a streak of green, a snake of green, a bow of light across the stars, a kiss of a wish amongst the heavens.

Green ribbons dancing in the sky; the Northern Lights.

***

The rain started falling over Victoria Park again. It had been a few days since I'd gotten back from Iceland and it felt warm, I thought of Dubai and the Philippines the following week, and though I was daunted, I was glad. The fast-paced whirlwind of chaos that had struck America had faded to a more manageable current, and I thought it apt that I would be working as a groundworker for natural disaster survivors.

It was true, what everyone said, about life moving only more and more rapidly the older we get. But, the flux was exciting, it wasn't soul-wrenching, and I had a good life. I made it. One year ago on the day that rain fell over Victoria Park, I had been in L.A. It was only in hindsight that I realised how unhappy I had been, how far from myself I had been, how lost I had become. I hadn't even looked like myself, and I was glad I had come so far. Relieved. I relinquished the rain, it cleanses, it cleans, I was in the midst of a new era, and a new woman I had become…. Cody messaged, "*I miss you.*"

"*I'm in the park writing, you always pop up at poignant times*"
He really did.

***

I tried to ground myself the last few nights before the Philippines. I was unusually anxious and felt overwhelmingly unprepared, inundated and exhausted. I closed my eyes meditating on Tom's snores, trying to drown out the wind, the howling gale whipping at the panes of my life.

I envisioned life to be that of a flip book. I saw the hands flipping the pages of a little cartoon man sprinting, until the pages ran out, and he inevitably met his maker. Life is always running and we are always flipping, and it's funny how a simple act such as falling asleep each night, brings further and further days until one day you're so far from where you started you feel as if you were hardly there at all. I thought of rewinding time, of making the little man run backwards across the pages, perhaps building such momentum that he'd fall on his heel and crack his head, and a gooey brain of love and lust and life and loss and long ago days would stain the pages pink. Not too long ago I was falling asleep with Valentina under the roof of our Brockport dorm, not too long ago I was standing in the cold, waiting for Cody to appear in the loading dock. A few more sleeps ago I was with Owen, in his ash-stained bed, bulging stomach and tired eyes.

The journey to the Philippines was daunting, I felt I'd hardly had time to recover from classes, Iceland, Germany, Italy, Christmas, New York, my Semester Abroad, my relationship, my woes and my worries, my whole twenty-two years of life. I hoped to almost close my eyes and open them to emerge there in a clammy bed, too hot to sleep to strange noises, under the Asian skies.

I remembered my first night in Kathmandu. The sticky night, the lonely night, the sick to my stomach, eyes wide, missing home night. I was so lucky to have gone so young, to have been seventeen, for there's a carefree, recklessness about being seventeen. The kind where even the most scary of things can be conquered. I yearned for the Philippines nights to be one of the same as Nepal. I hoped my Nepalese soul would come back, prising the skin and bones off this one here in Wiltshire. I hoped she'd become uncaged and that the same boldness, fearlessness and tenacity would emerge again. With all the things that had already gone wrong, I wished for the Philippines to be the one thing to go absolutely, terrifically, unexpectedly right.

***

There's a certain poetry when you leave a place, a hum in the air, a melody vibrating the soles of your feet as you walk the ground. Harmonies and symphonies as you walk away from what you know and venture into a new land. And as I sat on the bench at Temple Meads, the bench I waited for Owen to come to meet me at, the first time, all those years ago, I sat firm in the knowledge that we always come and go, and it's never too long until you're on the beaten track home.

And then after I'd finished my sandwich and dusted myself off, I got up and walked to the bus station in the rain. Turning left at the fork of the road, my back to the flat we once lived together, and I thought it quite remarkable that this time, I was heading to the Philippines and not a small room with an angry man and cigarette butts on the floor.

***

I lay down on the hard cold floor, a chill creeping from my shoulder down my arm, one of the many bodies on the 2 am airport slabs. I'd never seen so many people curled up and splayed out. I envisioned a refugee camp at first when I walked through the doors, and that felt twisted. Stansted had shut down for the night and there was nothing for anyone to do and nowhere for them to go. As I lay looking up at the white ceiling, thinking it funny how everyone else had shut down with it, I suddenly realised what I wanted to do. Not today or tomorrow or next week or even this year, but in life. Eurekas always seem obvious once you have them. I decided right there and then that I was going to work for National Geographic. I wanted to walk through the airport with a lanyard.

"She's with National Geographic", they'd say. I liked that, it had pazzazz, and the fire in my heart flickered again. First Fullbright I told myself, and then The New School. Then as a graduate, I'd do a Will Smith in the Pursuit of Happyness and land a job right there in the National Geographic office and off I'd go. Paid adventures, connections, the human story, my story against the world. No wonder I could never sleep.

I prised myself up and strolled out for a vape. Two cockneys occupied the smoking bay,

"She's fucking tasty", one said looking at his friend shone, "Oh yeah she's a bit of me", and so on and so forth.

I hoped Tom didn't speak about women like that. I was already uncomfortable that he'd be turning to porn for a month, and that's why as a woman, you should be selfish. Do what you want when you want and seize what you can, so that the men objectifying you do it from their cages as you fly free. As I walked back in, ready to kill some more time a man asked me for a lighter. "No, I vape, I'm sorry."

That was something I used to be proud of, but not anymore. I'd spent the year dodging popcorn lung, and that's another thing, call it a Nostradamus prophecy, but vaping is far worse.

***

Where I once was so unfathomably uncomfortable with being alone, I now enjoyed it. The quiet, the certainty, the confidence to know who you are and where you're going. I was a friend, a daughter, a stranger, a filmmaker, a photographer, a writer. I had fallen asleep and had woken up in Dubai, a stranger in the Middle East. I was going to the Burj Khalifa, on the metro red line, somewhere between Centerpoint and Expo 2020.

***

The flight from Manila to Tacloban reminded me of that flight so long ago from Delhi to Kathmandu. A rickety little plane, one so rickety you think that with a hard land, your seat would fall right through the floor and onto the runway for a speedy departure. I was the only Westerner on the flight, the same was said for Kathmandu. I wondered how much likeness I would see between Nepal and the Philippines, for they were thousands of miles apart, but perhaps those Himalayan days were the only thing I could compare it to, for until now that had been my biggest leap into the unknown. As long as I could vape, I wasn't worried, and that really shows how much an addiction can impact things. Manila wasn't a good start, *strictly no smoking* plastered in bold red, a firm fixture of the airport decor. However, I did find a vaper's lounge, so that gave me a twinge of promise. I needed some sort of vice.

As I was boarding a Filipino man said to who I can only presume was his daughter, "If it gets rough at least give it a go."

I was curious about the context but nonetheless applied it to myself. If it gets rough, at least give it a go.

***

My world sleeps whilst this world awakes. The weekend had been slow and strange. On Sunday my homestay sister, Hana, took me to church.

***

Every day was Groundhog Day. *Beep. Beep. Beep.* My alarm would go off and I'd awake to the whir of the fan, the bark of the dog, the smell of breakfast rising up the stairs, and the sheet snaked around my body. I'd blink a couple of times, groggy, three blinks before the realisation would dawn, yes, I'm still here. Another day in the Philippines, another day in the Asian heat, another breakfast of eggs and hot dogs, of bread and rice cakes, of mangos and tea with creamer. One cup of tea a day, with half a sachet of creamer, that's how I'd start my morning, and oftentimes I'd be too tired to really relish it. Though, I was appreciative of it nonetheless.

Getting dressed before going downstairs was the worst part, being damp from a night of sweat, pulling on a bra and pants and a T-shirt and trousers or a dress, whichever it would be, would exert more effort than you'd think. I'd head to the office and see where

I'd be assigned for the day. Oftentimes it would be the Nutrition Centre, either at Bliss, Santo Nino or Cangumbang. Bliss was the main centre, the little one on my homestay alley. A one-minute walk and usually a quiet shift, time to play with the children and talk amongst the adults in between spoons of rice and camera clicks. Santo Nino and Cangumbang were more of a trek, a motor cab and a couple of jeepneys away. These centres would involve stops at the market to source ingredients, some of which we have in the U.K.: onions and rice and tuna or chicken, sometimes pork, others more exotic. Vegetables with names I couldn't pronounce and seasonings which smelt familiar but which I couldn't put my finger on. I'd take photos at the placements, Santo Nino being my favourite for the children were always smiling and happy and walked with a bounce in their step, except for when they'd swing the resident cat by the tale as it meowed in pain and terror, and then I'd have to wag and finger and tell them off.

Cangumbang was nestled between rice fields and makeshift houses of cast iron and bamboo, the centre was raised so that if a typhoon were to hit it'd act as a safety centre. The heat in Cangumbang was unforgiving, and although that benefited the grains of rice scattered to dry on hot tarpaulin, the children sometimes wouldn't show up for lunch, too hot to leave their houses, the weather slowly sucking at their souls. The journeys to Santo Nino and Cangumbang would make me irritable. The jeepneys were manageable although crowded, it was the motorcabs I didn't like. Sat hunched, head banging hard metal with every bump, knuckles white from gripping on, grit and dust lashing the eyes and cheeks. I'd always curse in my head when sitting at the back of a motor cab and wonder how much more of the journey was left.

The afternoon and evenings would drag, they'd be my quiet hours in my bedroom, lying under the blue canopy of the mosquito net, listening to the rhythm of the whir of the fan.

Sometimes I would walk to Robinsons for various items I tricked myself into needing, but more so the walk killed time, and the air con deceived me into thinking I was someplace cool again. Like Iceland with the mountains and the bitter wind, the -25 degrees and frozen eyelashes. Between two and six were my waiting hours. I'd wait for dinner for after dinner would be my half an hour call with Tom and then I'd be asleep by 8. At least I was tired enough to sleep here, I couldn't imagine being up past midnight let alone until 5 or 6 am like sometimes in England. Insomnia didn't exist in that small house in Tacloban.

My host mama Renee always had a different meal on the table each night: fish, sometimes fillets, sometimes whole with the eyes and the head and the tail and the scales and unhappy faces. Chicken, pork, lentils, rice (always rice), vegetables, mangos, spring rolls, squash. At least I ate well, but I'd always catch glimpses of myself in the mirror and feel fat again. I wasn't sure if it was because everyone else was so small, or if I was actually getting bigger. If I was wrong and was in fact waning smaller, I must've started off rounder than I originally thought. I wasn't sure and I wasn't ready to weigh myself again when I'd finally end up back in Bath. I'd lost four stone since Brockport, and I felt like I was gaining it back again.

Everything was hard to judge with no mirrors and bucket baths and clothes I wouldn't usually wear, bare-faced and hair pulled back. I felt like a version of myself that I wasn't comfortable being, from extensions and nails and lashes and fakery in Brockport a year earlier to wild brows and frizzy hair, bug bites and hairy armpits, basic t-shirts and pull-on trousers. I missed my hair straighteners. I was glad to be going to Kuala Lumpur for Easter, for I needed a shower, a shave and a night's sleep in a cool room. Life's hard to navigate when you feel disconnected from yourself.

APRIL 2023

My Nanay sent me off to the airport with a warm egg salad sandwich wrapped in tissue. She had ushered me into a car and rode in the back, *ahhhing* in sweet relief at the air conditioning.

Tacloban airport was small and full of locals as to be expected. Perhaps they craved the same sense of freedom as I after one too many nights in a cramped hot slum, or perhaps they had work to do, or family to see. I felt ashamed to make presumptions. It's funny how easily writing comes the moment I'm removed from a situation. I proceeded to the waiting area, which was outside and sweaty, with flies buzzing from one ear to the next, swatted away with fans and angry noises. There was another Westerner, and I felt for a moment we could relate in our fleeting glance, but he manoeuvred over to a Filipino woman and sat beside her, wrapping his arm around her shoulders. That's another thing. If you see a Western man in this part of the world, if he's without a backpack and scruffy hair, with a brown tan and a goofy grin, he tends to be older and wider and with a local woman younger and thinner.

Everyone looked hot and bored and tired, and after I'd eaten my sandwich the bread and egg sticking to the roof of my mouth, and swigged it down with coke, I was hot and bored and tired too. I wanted to get up and go for a vape, but the seats were minimal and hungry eyes were already devouring my table. To get up would be to sacrifice a chair in the shade and I thought I'd wait it out as long as my addiction allowed me to. It was a good time to reflect on the previous week. Eleven days. I had been in the Philippines eleven days and yet it felt shy of a week and a million years all at the same time. I wiped the sweat from the back of my neck as I thought of the three weeks I had left. Time moved fast in the Philippines, my host mama called it "Asian Time", I seemed to agree with her, for the hours pushed on by, the hands whizzing around the clocks, if there were any clocks. Yet, the weeks seemed long, it was hard to explain. I thought back to my hazy days in Nepal, and seemed to remember having been there a lifetime, though when you're reminiscing something that happened a lifetime ago, your judgement calls for questioning. One day the Philippines would seem like a lifetime ago too, and I don't think I'd be too sad about that. I only wish I had written more, but the words seems to flow, as I said, once removed from the four walls and the dog barks and bucket baths and echoes of foreign chatter. I thought of the *pit pat pitting* of flip flops on hot slabs, the smell of faeces and the narrow alleys connecting blocks of squat houses with iron gates and barred windows. I thought of the teens playing basketball in the square of the plaza and the sound of karaoke through the walls. It all sounded rather whimsical, though an hour ago I was there and sticky, my black trousers permanently damp and hair permanently itching and the sun forever sunning.

I couldn't really even sit and enjoy the moment I had been accepted into The New School, for one I had woken up for a 5 am wee, something that by now had become a daily occurrence, the kind of rude awakening of an aching stomach and the forbidding trickle of a urine escape— too much water at bedtime! And for two, it was too hot and sticky and tiresome to be particularly overjoyed about anything. I had been in a permanent state of autopilot and perhaps that's why I don't write, for who would want to read a book written in autopilot, one written by a chaotic pilot with multiple personalities trying to land a burning plane is effort enough. Though, I was proud of that. The New School, the glossy red flags of The New School in Greenwich Village awaited. And as my professor had put, so did the ghostly shadows of Jack Kerouac, James Baldwin, Harry Belafonte and Tennessee Williams. It was funny, for all the times I had heard the cry, "Stellaaaa", and the time I had bought a Streetcar Named Desire starring Marlon Brando, I never knew I would be admitted to the same school that nursed them. And for all the times I read On the Road by Jack Kerouac, I was proud I received the same sort of acceptance letter that he would've done all those years ago, from perhaps the time when The New School was actually— new.

The previous night, I had a dream of New York. I was in Brooklyn and had found myself a restaurant owner with dark hair. We were entwined in some sort of romance, back of the motorcycle, coffees and sandwiches kinda hazy love. I don't even drink coffee but I seemed to enjoy it. I remember in the dream, I was already a student of The New School and kept promising myself I'd go to Times Square but as a fake New Yorker it didn't hold the same allure and I never went. I woke up angry at my need for a 5 am wee for it was a dream I wanted to hold onto, I felt loved and valued and Western. And I hoped Tom wasn't having dreams about far-away American romances too, and if he did I wished he didn't have the same longing to hold onto it as I did.

Anyway, the addiction has won and my vape is calling, and in a few hours Manila will be calling too. In Manila, I had been shouted at for vaping in a car park disconnected from the terminal and ushered away. In Tacloban, I was side-eyed for asking a security guard where the smoking area was, "Smoke wherever you want."

Just another difference between the two cities. Tacloban had its charm, I suppose you could call it that, but it was a place even the locals said no one wanted to be. I wondered how much culture shock a native Filipino would get if they'd never left the country and found themselves in London. Would it be the same mixture of thrill and ache I found myself sat with?

***

Your time, my time. Your time. My time.
"What time do you leave your time?"
"I start work tomorrow at seven my time."
Your time, my time.
"What time is it your time?"
"It's eight o o'clock my time."
Your time , my time. Everybody's fucking time. My flight to Malaysia was cancelled, I spent eight hours in Manila airport seething and crying and back to seething again. That was my time, what about your time?

***

The Philippines taught me the gift of patience. I learnt on my second to last night, that all things pass, the good and the bad , the longest days and longest weeks. I was always so focused on clinging onto things and fiercely not wanting to let go. I spent many days in the Philippines doing the opposite, wanting time to hurry along, wanting to come back home. But as the chapter closed I found myself sad, I had grown to love my homestay and my friends, and my little routine and the familiar faces and children's chant of "Ayte." I learnt that had I been patient I would've made the most of it all, rather than wishing it to end. Sometimes you've just got to trust that you'll be heading home and know that all those you love are waiting with open arms, and wishing that day to come soon, only taints the days you have to soak in an experience. Days aren't long, not in the scheme of things. Months are long, years longer, but days, there's no reason in grumbling about days. Though that's always easier to say at the end.

***

I felt the heavy silence of a dying dream, a heart quivering beneath the ashes of what could've been. Black and grey soot, charcoal against the grain of yellows, hues of mornings stretching beyond the blue. Sunlight, sun rays, skin salted and seared and then soothed. The same old ebb, the same old ache, the promise parting once again. Life, endless and vast, a dog bounding through meadows of green and yellows, and then caught and caged. Back up, hunched, feral, crying, simpering, barking, yelling. Only someone above, he who controls when the earth quakes, can answer the cries of birds and blood in the trees of the evening.

And just as it had rolled into the lap of my life, it rolled away again, outwards and outwards, bobbing in turquoise shimmers, snippets of heaven passed the clouds. Friends lighting fires somewhere along the shore. Nothing made sense, other than heavy eyes and stress lines, other than a head on a pillow under the Malaysian heat or Philippines dusk, or Dubai stars. I was imagining all the people, in bed, weary and woeful, thought clouds rising from their soft minds, of loved ones, of a fadeaway gleam of life somewhere better and bolder, and burning. Flickers of fortune and gold.

We all harbour different gold, blocks and chains, wasted and worn. And I was back again in a dead space, looking at a blank wall, and not knowing whether to smash my head against the blocks, or to draw with great sadness a mural of nothingness. I picked up a brush and splattered Brooklyn in the spring, pink buds and blossoms twirling around the branches of the trees lining the streets. I sketched the mountains of the Himalayas, smudged peaks and grey sunsets, shadowy figures with baskets on their heads and cows scuffing hooves in dry grass. I crayoned a midday bike ride along the California coast, blue jackets billowing in the whizzing air, tires flying past the sand. I painted the aqua waters of Kalanggaman island, and the motorcabs in the rain. I scratched the pillars of the colosseum and printed wanted pictures of Pisa. Inky drips of the empire state and collages of the Brandenburg Gate. And then I doused the wall in great sloshes of gasoline, and set it alight. For what did a life in colour matter, if I was always crawling back to the dark? Why keep on, when the desired drifts further away?

I was tired. My life was a course of forgetting what was left behind. And I wanted to be on a beach somewhere, somewhere alone and desolate, with a blanket of flickering stars, a shroud of midnight blue. I wanted my chest to rise and fall with the coming tide, to know what it feels to be content, to bid goodbye to a dream. To let go of the fuel to the fire, the beat between the breaths, the heart pumping, brain catching, feet pattering dream. The dream within reach , with slipping hands. I had so many things to do, so many responsibilities and requirements, pressures and commitments, that I don't think I could've found peace anywhere. It's once you've recovered from jet lag and have had the time to sit alone in the quiet of your own thoughts, that you suddenly realise that everything is terrible.

MAY 2023

I wrestled with the idea that you can lose someone and love someone else. To move on, and to a close door which always seemed to have a foot in it, I had to brand Cody as dead. It was the only way I could see clearly and run into adventure, and a life of exploration exploding across the skies, a life I wanted to live. Yet I was still stuck, for I couldn't love Tom the way he deserved to be loved, for I had it ingrained , in the very etches of my soul, that true love doesn't allow you to love anyone else. No matter how dead, or frozen, or forgotten, or broken that true love may have become with every tick of a damned clock. Just like how I had to pretend Owen was dead too for me to flit to Cody. It didn't matter how bad Owen was, because truth be told, a lot of him, most of him, was rotten. And he was dead, and so I was grieving, and in all my mourning, I still couldn't bring myself to love another, even if they were good. My dead fiancé. My dead best friend. My dead abuser. My dead nothing.

My dead Cody, his body still warm, washed up somewhere on some lake shore. I knew I could resuscitate him, any time I chose, the temptation was always there. Unlike Owen, cold and cracked.

The funny thing with Tom was, I knew I'd never have to kill him off, I could simply walk away and watch him live. With Cody that release wasn't so simple, I'd have to pray the jealousy away.

***

I had exhausted all my options. My credit score was too fucked for any bank to loan me money. I didn't have an American guarantor, so I couldn't get college-backed funding. I didn't have a house to offer the banks, nor did I have any savings. I requested to defer my place at The New School, but they replied stating that my position was so competitive that they didn't offer deferrals. So with a sudden blow and permanent sadness, I declined my space. Just like that, with a click of the mouse, and the closing of a tab, I was no longer going to be a New School alumni. My inner child, who had plotted that place for ten years, died.

"When are you coming?"

"I'm not. I had to let go of my spot, I just couldn't afford it."

"Well, that's just perfect."

"Are you upset?"

"Honestly, I don't think you'll even remember me in a year, let alone two. I was holding on to the thought of you being in NYC, so maybe I could see you. But I know how this goes. I'll just become another face in the crowd, someone you won't even think of anymore."

JUNE 2023

I sat on the train and watched the digital letters roll in a constant loop of orange, *This is a Great Western Railway service to Wiltshire.*

It was 11.30 pm, and I'd been working 7 am start shifts back to back, with another the following morning. And yet, off I was, going to Wiltshire for weed and Tom. I was fleeing again, to return groggy and baggy-eyed and sad when the dawn would break. My life was a series of fleeing. Small flees and big flees and crying out flees and screaming flees and wretched waking day and night flees. All the flees you could think of, plus some more.

I was disappointed I was without money. For some reason, it struck me all of a sudden on that train, that to live you need money and to need money you need to work, and if you work, you're not living. And I don't know why it took me twenty-two years to realise that I, myself, was not immune to the system and that my life would be a series of working to make money. No matter how much I disagreed with it. The daft thing about it all was that I was paying £5000 to work for free, just to work in New York. In October I would be a New York City intern for six months, chasing that Brockport dream. Working doesn't feel like working when it's abroad. I worked for free in Nepal and the Philippines after all. But this time was different, they were trying to place me in New Jersey. Fucking Jersey City. I couldn't see any good reason to go to Jersey City, let alone pay a small fortune to do so, to work full-time for free. It was all probably a terrible idea. But, all my ideas seemed terrible until they weren't.

Perhaps it's at 11.34 pm, when you've been working 7 am shifts back to back, and leaving the city where you work to travel 40 minutes away to smoke weed for an hour before going to bed, that everything seems terrible.

I dropped £20 on two train tickets. So two hours would be spent the following day earning it back, and the next few years of work would be spent earning back all the vapes, all the pointless, poisonous nicotine. It's no fun being an addict. And as my belly rumbled, day two of dieting again, I was glad I was at least in control of something. I was tired, so so so completely tired.

***

I saw life for now, not so much for later. But the later trailed after me, the hiker behind the Sherpa, and it never once lost course. I wondered if that was the call to life, the climb to the summit, after all they say it's the journey that matters, not the destination. Some plummet to pearly white deaths, half smothered by snow.

I was tired and as the hot sun hit my discoloured skin, I struggled to think of a time when I wasn't worn down, and creased and collapsed by this whole thing called life.

I always felt better when I was moving. Crawling into some other destination, not even necessarily abroad, but in the U.K. too. I get restless and I have to move. Buses and trains and cars, and journeys. Sometimes I couldn't think of anything worse than being still.

JULY 2023

I lay and looked up and the oak tree and the green leaves being soaked by the July sun. And I realised, I was starting to forget about him. I wasn't sure if my gooey mass of brain was doing that thing, the thing where it blocks out the bad stuff, with a great thick wet squelching black marker. Just like Stuttgart. But, Owen was fading. And I thought about one of the last times I saw Owen in Wales and strained my memory. We had gone to a beach at golden hour, and I couldn't even remember which, only that it was near Holyhead, the day we'd seen the lighthouse. We were waist deep I think, clothed, in the sea, and I was looking out thinking about America. Owen told me we had to be together again, and I told him I didn't want to, and he cried, in that sea. And now his tears had been washed with the tide, and the tide had now too taken him away. And I couldn't have ever been more fine about it, and more glad, than right then, under that oak tree.

I was living in a Groundhog Day of being an Activity Leader. Six days a week, 52-hour weeks. Palestinians, Italians, Spanish, Israelis, French, kids who didn't want to be there. And as someone who fundamentally disagrees with working, and someone who hates unnecessary socialising, and didn't want to be there either, I was glad I had food poisoning. It meant I could look at this tree, instead of blowing a whistle at a football match or checking dinner cards at the canteen. Oh six weeks, please hurry. I'm always talking about slowing time but sometimes time running out ain't a bad thing when you're trapped.

"Do you have rhubarb in your garden?"

One woman asked another as they walked past in sundresses and oversized hats.

"I think so but I haven't harvested it."

The other replied and then their voices trailed off.

I hoped she'd get to have her rhubarb and make a big ol' pie with it, and invite me over to her big Bath house, so I could take a slice and run away. I'd eat it under the tree, purple smeared across my face. Oh, to be old and rich and happy.

I didn't really mind that I wouldn't be attending The New School anymore in the Fall. I'd achieved that dream without the $100,000 price tag, without having to follow through. I could write anywhere, any time, about whatever the fuck I wanted, with as many or little profanities as possible, because I'd been accepted. Just like Jack Kerouac. Just like J. D Salinger. Just like Tenessee Williams. I'd still get to go to New York, I'd get to do an internship and hell, I could write a whole book about it in Central Park in the evenings, or not. I think I was done trying to prove myself, often it's the people with something to say who don't get the platform to say it. The people I love are the things that matter, but hey, I'll still print out the acceptance letter, it can collect dust in a frame.

***

I lay in bed not feeling sure about how I felt anymore. My eyes always felt tight and my legs always ached and I couldn't process that it was all temporary. The constant onward spiral of activity leading, sent me whirling in a vortex of football, basketball, volleyball, canteen food and a constant buzz of WhatsApp messages. I didn't know why I hadn't learnt from Camp Sunshine, I guess after a while all our lessons fade. Meave loved it like I knew she would, and I felt alone in my bitterness. She told me I was an introvert because I charged my battery by spending time alone, and she was right. I couldn't believe I once hated being by myself, for now, I couldn't think of anything more blissful. I couldn't understand why anyone wouldn't want to be on their own.

I needed to scheme a way to live without work, which would mean living without money. Or, I needed easy money. I felt it ridiculously unfair that we had to work to make a living, we had to be somewhere we didn't want to be with people we didn't want to know to survive. It's such a fucked up system. I was disgruntled that now I had finished University, work was to to replace it until I was sixty or older, or whenever the age of retirement was. I didn't want a pension scheme to be taxed, or to retire for I didn't want to work at all. And yet, I was paying thousands of pounds to work in America, in an unpaid internship, and I didn't even know what for anymore. At least I won the fight and I was going to be working in Brooklyn, not New Jersey. God, they would've been crooks if they placed me there.

Lost and ambitious. I decided to go to sleep and I hoped I would dream, amongst the stars, or the sea, amongst something vast and foreign and magical. I wanted to astral project again, but that seemed to have vanished with childhood and teenage years and angst, and my whole life was vanishing. I was getting old, and yet I was young, with years and years stretching in front of me, and no way of knowing how to untangle them.

***

I received the news that my friend had died. They'd killed themselves. Bled out in my hometown. I felt too empty to write too much about it, only that I never knew you could feel such pain and guilt for someone you no longer knew, nor that death could show up one morning in such distaste. I flew out of the house and into the park and wept.

I was invited to the funeral, although I hadn't expected to be, and I went. It was the same crematorium where my Grandpa's service was held. It's all about tricking yourself until tomorrow. Broken dreams break people, and there I was, red-eyed and heartbreaking, muffling my sobs as I stared at the wooden box which held my friend. And, I wished her dream had come true, for if it had, she wouldn't be buried at twenty-one.

The funeral took place in front of a large window, overlooking a meadow. A poem was read, and a deer stepped out into the green. A young doe stood.

Everyone noticed in their grief, and for a moment the sadness ceased to swell, for she had returned to say goodbye.

***

The sadder you are the sadder your accidental manifestations become. Things break, and tear, and arguments come in roaring waves, friendships splinter and the days roll bleeker. And, the happier you become, the better the days flow and the more connections you make. I'd been depressed for two weeks, and everything went wrong—the funeral of a friend gone too fast, a broken phone, the first few breakdowns of my relationship with Tom, a wedge between me and Meave, nights upon nights of terrors and monsters unknown. Dragging my feet to work, not a second to think, only wave after wave of lonely heartache.

And then, on a random Sunday, I sprung out of bed and saw that suddenly everything wasn't so bad, or at least tricked myself into thinking so. I'm like a boomerang, I hurtle from pain to significantly less pain at a speed some would call manic-depressive. Self-diagnosed of course, so take it with a pinch of salt. Anyway, there I was walking down the drive in the July rain, my shoes squeaking when I heard a beep.

The bus driver for the Cardiff excursion. The doors opened, "Get on in."

I couldn't understand much of what he said afterwards. His West Country accent was thicker than a stale loaf of bread. And, that's coming from a Cornish maid. I thanked him though,

"For all these weeks I've been waking up and down this drive—

"No one stopped?" he interjected.

"No one stopped."

"Pah", he exclaimed, "People."

And as soon as I got off I knew I probably would forget our encounter over time. So perhaps in aid of not doing so, I write this now. He worked for National Express for eight years, and now Berkeley's for four.

"Which do you prefer?" I asked.

"This job. National Express was the same thing every day for eight years."

"That can't be fun," I said, as I got off to complete my own Groundhog Day.

***

I started a bad habit of muttering to myself down the street. I wondered if people thought I was crazy and then I was soothed in smug defiance. I hoped people did think I was crazy, maybe then they'd leave me the fuck alone. Cody had resurfaced, only to rub Madison in my face, and I shouldn't have allowed him to anger me but he succeeded, and America could've almost felt like a dirty word, *America*, a curse word. *America, America, America. Fuck, fuck, fuck, fuckity fuck.* If you read it over enough times it has the same feel, the same flare, or maybe it doesn't.

***

It was the cigarette stage of the night. Tom was showing me his suit for my graduation. Sleeves down or rolled up was the debate.

"I like the rolled-up sleeve look," I said, "Very 50s… Marlon Brando."

I paused. My heart sank. The New School. I was met with memories of the 1950s New School, the images, the words, the nostalgia. My childhood of browsing the website and googling the alumni, walking down the streets of New York in my dreams. And it not only sunk but broke, for I had blocked out the most important part. In my angst of having to say goodbye to the notoriety, I had forgotten the little girl with the burning dream, her late-night imagination, her consumed life of the future and the Academy Awards. I had successfully painted the picture of my life, I had manifested it perfectly. I had gotten in, and it had to be let go. I had achieved and I couldn't have it anyway.

***

The wind pushed the rain across the train window, droplets racing in wet streaks. As a child I used to watch as rain rolled on by, placing bets on which droplet would trail the fastest and the longest. I liked the rain, I had always liked it.

I was tired, my feet ached and my eyes felt heavy, but it was my first day out of the job. My first day free from summer school, and I couldn't quite believe I had made it. From fleeing Camp Sunshine the previous year, to persevering through six gruelling weeks of the same old shit this year. I had grown. I enjoyed the kick out of knowing I had completed something difficult, I relished in punishing myself. I guess that's what the Philippines, America and Nepal all were too, fragments of self-hate, piercing the veil of a whirlwind of a journey. That's the best combination of love and hate. However, I never did once love the Summer School and certainly not Camp Sunshine either. Some things are just a test of resilience.

I was on the train travelling back from Wiltshire, Tom had rescued me the previous night, whizzing to campus in the dark, picking me up and stealing me away. My freedom ride. We played the car music loud and got home and got stoned and fucked around. Getting stoned and fucking around had become a dangerous habit for me. Sometimes it was all I ever wanted to do.

I was moving out of Bath. I had to get the train back to pack up my life, to clear out my room, to transform a haven of photos and memories and keepsakes and mess and empty coke bottles and dead vapes into a stark empty room of nothingness. To wipe the slate clean. Meave was going to be packing up too. We'd both be shoving things into bags and hoovering and wiping and sighing. Meave my through-the-wall companion, I'd spent so many nights hearing her giggling into the phone and then receiving a *ping* and listening, our texting and door knocking and my snoring and her alarm ringing. Since Brockport, Meave had become more than a friend, she'd become a sister. And I kicked myself for not having written more about her whilst I was in America.

I couldn't sleep. I wasn't sleeping much, if at all. My nights were plagued with excited overthinking, of happy spirals of New York City, of Mexico, of reuniting. When I did drift off, it would be into ugly dreams, dreams of Owen, of his cruel fist. Tom's kindness, patience, loving hand, and dedicated soul, ripped me apart, for it only made me realise how abusive Owen had been. It wasn't the shouting, it was the snapping, slapping, seething, snaring and threatening that did it. It wasn't Owen's obsession and coercion and control that made me conclude that I was no more than a punching bag, a lowly possession. It was Tom's inability to be cruel that killed me, for it proved that Owen never did love me, he loathed me. I felt sad that Tom wasn't subject to my writing, that I didn't have a whole book on him, for if anyone deserved one it was that blue-eyed bearded creature, the only one who I believe has ever properly cared for me. You see, we don't write about what makes us happy.

Happy people don't write. And so, there are big blanks, huge blanks, gaps of love and laughter and understanding, of healing, that haven't been archived, that have simply escaped the pages. But, my dear Tom, that undoubtedly in all its juxtaposition, proves your worth. You are too good, too kind, and too beautiful, to be reduced to words. You don't belong in my book, for you aren't a story, you aren't a passing moment, a character, a quip, an anecdote. You are a person, who has come into my world and lifted me, and I love you so dearly, that there is no confusion, there is no muddle, no questioning, and so, there are no chapters.

Our moments are private, they're not reported, they're intimate, they're for me and you, and whether you go or stay, you're far too good, to be a subject on a page, and my words are stunted, for with you, I don't write, I let go and live. I had hardly written at all in 2023, with all my countries and all my pursuits, I thought I hadn't had the time, but in truth, at twenty-two, I was the happiest I had ever been and my life was the healthiest I had ever experienced, and although it is a great shame humans are drawn to expressions of darkness for art rarely encapsulate the light, a lack of writing was a good thing, for it symbolised a lack of helpless dying. For the first time in my two decades, I was wholeheartedly alive.

SEPTEMBER 2023

Meave and I took off for Mexico. Two weeks: Cancun, Chichen Itza, Isla Mujeres and Mexico City. Maybe one day it'll get a book of its own. I had too much fun to write anything about it at all— except that all the best bromances are Mexican. I also reunited with my Dad's family in Spain and Gibraltar. I stayed in my cousin's flat in the heart of the birth town of my grandmother and her mother too. A whole month of moments like September don't come often, but when they do, you take a moment to look around, feel the air in your lungs, the past behind you, and let out a long old sigh of relief. There's beauty if you know where to look for it. Everything beautiful this year had been extraordinarily un-American.

***

I got completely drunk. Blind drunk, the kind when the world spins and truth flies out of your mouth, and the next day you shrink away,

"I wish you loved me."

"How can you be sure I don't?"

"Because Madison."

He didn't reply to that and I was too far gone to let him fade away again, to disappear and to retreat,

"Tom doesn't want me to go to America."

"I never wanted you to leave."

***

I was fearful of returning to New York and having been at home in Cornwall for a week, I thought it a shame to leave. To leave the coast, the kitchen, the aqua pools and the rolling waves. I would be trading rugged cliffs and flagstones, fire pits and places, my friends and my family, to be in a concrete jungle. To be another nobody craving to be somebody in a city vast yet empty, exciting yet cold. The more I thought about it, the sicker I felt.

I sat writing in the kitchen, the flagstones cool against my feet, petals, pink and yellow, strewn across the table, from where the bouquet still stood but had withered and drooped, in the beautiful wilderness. The blue walls and white cabinets felt Cornish, and rustic, my pasta boiling on a gas stove. The radio, small and compact, smug for being cool, rescued from my grandparent's attic, played live Reading and Leeds. Lush foliage, green leaves wild roses with thorns, a magnolia tree with a string of fairy lights and a mowed lawn. Why would I trade the coast life, Cornish life and middle-class bo-ho, for America, and its dark skies and buildings and blow-ups and ribbons of racism and tassels of woe?

I travelled to every corner of the world to find peace and never did lay my hand on it, for I was always at war with myself, and all the ghosts that dared trail behind.

OCTOBER 2023

I moved to Brooklyn on a random Wednesday evening, with the sun stretching yellow across the fire escapes, and the brown Brooklyn building sprawling from the streets, like branches. I woke up to messages from dozens of people, people who I'd touched and who had touched me across all stages of life. I felt like crying, for no other reason than gratitude. For, I didn't know the impact I had. I didn't know that I had friends from across the globe, current friends, friends from months ago, flitting friends and friends from childhood, rooting for me, supporting my journey. I never knew I was that significant. I wasn't nervous nor excited to be back in New York City, the city of dreams, which cradled me, my dream, the apple of my eye. Lady Liberty was raising her torch, a green lantern of everything that was meant to be, and I was right where I had always hoped I would end up. And on my first day back in the city, so many miles away, I was glad I chased my dream for already it showed me how loved I was, and how loved I didn't know I would be. All the good people I had left behind, were the people I never knew were missing, the people who would never go anywhere. That was a comforting thing indeed.

I thought of all those cold winters with Owen, all those nights in his arms yet nights rotting alone. Oh how wrong he was, that I was nothing, that I meant nothing, that no one loved me. I'd call it careless but it was fate, for I will spend a lifetime proving him wrong, and with every step I take on American soil, every breath of Brooklyn air swept down my lungs and all the New York grit pumping my heart, is a step towards never letting anyone tear me apart. I don't regret having lived in the dark for so long, for my blind eyes had opened and now I knew how to dance in the light.

***

It hadn't stopped raining and I hadn't a coat, and after locking myself in my room for the morning, I decided to go out. Mission objectives, cigarettes, Target and a rush of fresh air. I hopped on the 3 train. I found the subway in New York easy. Yet the underground in London was a one-way ticket to pissing me off. I guess that's why I was in New York and not my capital. The screech of the subway seared through my skull, splitting my head in half, and I hoped it would fall off into my lap, stick out a tongue and voraciously cry. I spent a lot of time hoping for outlandish things, landing on my feet, and I wasn't going to stop now. I was off to the World Trade Center, to pick up a target order, but more important to fuel my sense of solace. I wanted cigarettes and nowhere seemed to sell them in New York. It's not like the '70s movies or the '80s or '90s or 2000s out here, sometimes I think New York its modern age and has lost its flair, cigarettes are not stacked on shelves, here in New York City, who would've thought?

The screeching only intensified with every passing stop, women jabbing fingers in their ears, others with headphones to drown it out. I was glad I was half deaf, and if I wasn't, I would be now.

"Wall Street."

I wish.

I spent the day in the torrential rain instead, looping laps around the World Trade Centre Memorial. I was in a foul mood, and I wasn't sure if it was because I hadn't slept enough or eaten enough or done enough, or if I was doing too much. New York was grey. The sky was grey. The world today was grey, but tomorrow I hoped it would be yellow. A sunny day of blossoming futures, a warm day, a hug. But it wouldn't be, I had checked the forecast and the heavens were due to be open again. A "Free Palestine" protest marched down the street, and I was glad at least I had witnessed that.

It was a nothing day, a write-off, an expensive one too, for I bought a flat iron and a coat and some socks and some cigarettes and a Chick-fil-A, a lighter and the subways. Breathing is money here, breathing is money, but money never breathes. Soaked and pale and alone I headed back to 856 Nostrand Ave, with a hole in my heart. I felt out of depth financially but told myself I'd be okay, for finances are a made-up concept, and you can't put a price on a dream, and those who go against the grain, who keep on fighting, keep on persisting and gamble and risk and believe, are the ones with kind of bank accounts that one day, I'll have to, and in all my riches, I'll thank this broke damned self. My writing was rusty and I was weary but with only the weekend between now and my new job starting, I was ready to seize life by the balls.

***

Cody wasn't speaking to me, not really, nor did he seem to care that I was in his country, down the road. My own boyfriend seemed not to care that I had left, and I wasn't really sure what it was I did wrong. Perhaps I was just a victim of time moving on, and with time humans too shuffle along. I was never much good at goodbyes, I was always holding on, holding that door ajar, perhaps I was stupid to think others felt the same.

I had been in New York for five days, time moved slowly here. It trickled. In the Philippines time moved fast, they called it Filipino time. New York time was stretched thin, the hours dragged, it was quite incredible, the buckets of time I had here.

In five days, I had gone to Times Square, The World Trade Centre Memorial, and the Social Security office and been followed by a man with nunchucks. I had done an intern excursion to the Whitney Museum of American Art and trundled with them all through Chelsea, up the high line and around Little Island. They were rich kids. The elite of the elite, in head-to-toe Armani, millionaires. I think they sniffed the poverty on me, me with my rationed pasta. Eating cold pasta sauce out of the jar, feeding that growl, feeding that emptiness, one raw teaspoon at a time. In five days I had ridden the subway, from Brooklyn to Manhattan so many times I had it memorised. The 3 train, from Nostrand Ave to 96 street. I had had an orientation in a coffee shop around the corner from Penn Station, gone to Central Park in the dark, and looked, numb at the skyline, the penthouses with their yellow squares of wonder— what did lie behind those glowing windows? Fortunes? Riches? Sex? Loneliness? Suicide? Contempt?

I had gotten Starbucks with Rodrigo and Takumi, a Columbian in his late twenties, living out in the New Jersey sticks, walking in the world of the rich. Takumi, from Tokyo, announced $100,000 for The New School was not a problem, paying $2600 a month for accommodation in the Upper West Side. The three of us discussed Gaza Hamas and New York terrorist attacks. In five days, I had met the most beautiful souls. My Brooklyn roommates are Jamaican women, beautiful women. Radiating women, women who made me want to be a better woman. They gave me candy and flowers and wine, jerk pork and avocados. They gave me eucalyptus and turmeric soap, they gave me lavender body butter and shampoo and conditioner for my black hair, my mixed hair, my broken hair.

In five days, I had started my job. Video Editor for Whizz Media. Whizz Media sprawled in countless Forbes articles. I read in 2021 they turned over $500,000 in one year. I wondered with 2024 on the brink, how many thousands they were rolling in now. I was on $100 a week, and that for me, was more than I had had for a while. I was working in the office of the CEO and she announced that on Thursday we would go to an exclusive members-only club, Soho House for lunch, as a welcome to the company. Leonardo DiCaprio was a member. Perhaps that's how I knew I was moving in the right direction. Yet, I couldn't help but feel like an imposter, walking amongst peers who would've been able to pay for The New School, who would've been able to do everything that money limited me from doing, and yet, because I had a mother who believed in me, with a generous heart and beautiful soul, I had the same opportunity as them. And, that itself, was no small feat.

In five days, I had dreamt of Cody, and I had missed Upstate in five days I hadn't felt like I was in America, for my America was red white and blue, it was yellow-lined roads and pickup trucks, it was fishing and hiking and tall trees and small saloons, it was snow and nasally accents. It was northern, and I was south. In five days I felt homesick for Brockport, realised why New Yorkers avoid midtown Manhattan, and unlocked a new love for Brooklyn.

I was listening to Leonard Cohen, in Biggie Smalls' neighbourhood, a ten-minute walk from his childhood home. I was sad and yet I was happy, I was empty and yet full. I felt the weight of pressure and the billow of freedom. A lot can happen in five days, see, New York time. Six months in New York is a lifetime elsewhere and for that, I was glad, for who wouldn't want to live forever?

I had kept waiting for that sudden excitement, that sudden realisation that I was back in New York. That desire to go, "Yoo-hoo", and go off the rails, celebrate, look around in awe and lust and wonder and yet it never came. It felt strange how familiar New York was, how normal, how placid. I had lay at night and contemplated that I had been here before. Not last year, but before, before I could remember before I was me before I had fingers and toes and woes. For, it's a peculiar thing that a child from rural Cornwall, a village without a shop, would know of New York, would desire it, would pave the slabs towards it, one heavy thud at a time, chisel after chisel, for years, half a lifetime, to get there and feel nothing but normalcy. The only abnormal things were the interns, the Fortune 500 companies, university students or graduates with a budget which would make our annual salary appear small. Hell, I didn't even have an annual salary.

I was leading an impressive life. 2023, 12 countries, two internships, and an acceptance to one of the most prestigious liberal arts colleges in the world, although that's not where I ended up. And now my life was yellow taxis and millionaires. Yet I was always on the outskirts looking in. A participating voyeur. A broken New York poet by night, a young intern getting whipped into shape by day, a communist in the dark and a rat in the race at dawn. A double life. Lunches at SoHo House, and dinners in Brooklyn, two boiled eggs on the hob.

***

Crisp and sunny, shadow and light, autumn rolled around with a soft delight, and we headed towards winter again. My writing was stunted, the words didn't flow like they used to, they didn't ebb and weave and I felt as though I had nothing left to say. It became clear that I was no longer meant to continue this story for the era had ended, it ended on my flight from London to JFK. For you see, this book has been a tale of struggles, of determination, of a beating heart daring to go further, daring to seek beyond. Daring to return to America, and now I was there, in the early hours under an invisible moon, and my web had been spun, my tale told. The girl from Brockport was the ghost, and the woman in New York, with lunches at Soho House and meetings in Manhattan and dreams of Dumbo, followed the wind.

Yet, I suddenly felt very sad, and worn out and ill all at once. The days were rolling on, as if time didn't exist at all. Tired and aching and worn and done. It had been a while since I had felt sad enough to write, for it was always misery that compelled me.

I cried after a night at an exclusive rooftop in New York City for Rodrigo's birthday. I saw the Empire State Building lit up — dazzling lights. We ate $50 steak in an igloo, with a fake blossom tree in the middle and an old English lady, barking for free red wine, because her steak was too cold. Mine was cold too, I wish I had gotten free wine.

I cried because I missed my Dad. He was all around me in Brooklyn, everywhere I turned, he was in the African art in the apartment, in Peter's locs, in Emmanuel's eyes and in the strangers who would pass. I looked through my archived photos of him, where he was young, dreadlocked when he had fewer tattoos and a wrinkle-free face. In all the pictures before I was born, in the pictures of me as a baby, I had years, if not a decade of photos where I didn't exist. Where I was on this planet, but oh so far away. All the missed birthdays, the absent Christmases. The graduation. The funerals. The prom. The school plays. Where was my Dad? Daddy was always gone, even when he was there. And what hurt the most, was the shock, the surprise, the sheer disbelief that I had a black Dad, the fleeting comments "You don't look like him", "I can't see it", "*That's* your Dad?"

If I didn't look like him, he wasn't mine. If I didn't look like him, I was even more estranged, shunted, pushed away. I was even more disconnected, and I was already as disconnected and desperate as a daughter could get. I cried for the cousins I didn't get to grow up with, the Aunty who didn't know me until I was twenty-two. The family I needed was torn apart. I cried for the lost time, for time is fleeting, and I didn't know whether I would see him again. I cried because I loved him. I cried because I loved him more than I dared let my heart believe, for if it realised, it would break, far more than any other man had broken it before. I cried because I had tried, and I knew no amount of trying would ever change anything. I cried because when he died, I wouldn't know him any more than he knew me. I cried because he was there, I cried because knowing we had him temporarily and then not at all, was worse than having never known him at all because, for years, I've been slowly grieving the Father who died, but who was still alive. I cried because I thought about him every day, and the older I became the more harrowing the story.

I cried because I loved my parents. I hated the thought of them growing old, I hated the thought that they would die. I hated the thought of life without them, for it would be a life in the gutter.

***

Outside looking in, not knowing where to fit, to mould, to bend, foreign accents petrifying, ballooning, beginning again.

I was a fraud on the outside. Millionaires at day, boat cruises, museums, lunches I couldn't afford, half-drunk drinks poured down the sink and memories within. I was poor, in Brooklyn, with my black friends, a social commentary, a slice of life, a reckoning. I miss my Dad. A fad, a beckoning.

An insider on the outside and outsider on the inside, a nothing and an everything, a dark Brooklyn night and a promising.

Growing, budding, becoming light. I hated and loved and reckoned and doubted and cried and spouted. Who was I? A woman in a dive bar? Is a woman making sense?

Cody invited me to Thanksgiving in Virginia with his family. I said I would go but hadn't informed Tom and was quite frankly out of my mind. Cecelia had given me edibles and they made me anxious, thinking, oh unruly thinking until I turned to drink, and even then I was in the dark.

I felt like everything I wrote was stupid. I was sinking. My Dad was sinking. Black was sinking. I knew nowhere else I was meant to be.

I didn't like myself so writing about New York didn't come easily. It felt like a constraint and I desired freedom. I didn't feel like I owed anyone anything. So I rebelled against writing. Perhaps when I'm drunk and alone and writing into the night, I think it will make me feel something I don't. Who knows. All I know is I love my Father and I love my Mother. White and black, beautiful and ethereal.

I stared down tequila bottles and they stared back. I couldn't tell if I was poor or privileged, and that felt worse than knowing. I was both, just like I was black and white and no one understood. I guess in their eyes I didn't exist.

I wondered if Cody had stayed the same or shifted into something completely different. I wondered if it mattered.

I had to escape. It was 3.20 am and everyone was in the midst of a tipping debate, the race war became too escalated and I craved a simple life. I'm a stranger to balance, I know no such thing. I was retreating inside the walls of my head, outside was too loud, too clumsy, and I was too enveloped in a whimsy. What to give, what to not? I always choose to give. I felt upset and offered to pay, although I had nothing to my name.

NOVEMBER 2023

There I was, an English girl, walking the stairs of a great big house in Virginia, the storybook kind. Smoking cigarettes on the white veranda, nestled on a settee set. Watching television next to ancient Memaw, insisting I didn't need to share her blanket, yet insulting her if I hadn't. We were cosy in an impressive living room with a sculpted ceiling, a fireplace, and a 1920s awning. Yawning and retiring to vast bedrooms with ceiling fans and shuttered windows. Wooden doors and floorboards, a dining room, a kitchen, a red barn and chickens.

After a 12-hour bus ride, stifling, sticky and squashed from New York, snaking through New Jersey, and trundling through Pennsylvania, stopping in Delaware and Baltimore, traffic jammed in DC and crawling through Richmond, I was there in Virginia. Waving "Hello" to Nonna and smiling at Grandpap, greeting Cody's Mum—Betty Lou—and East Coast Southern accents.

I lay on my bed curiously hitting my Hyde, and adjusted to the fact that I had left New York, opened a door and was suddenly slapped across the face with a sudden *thwack*. I was that Brockport girl again. I was in my dorm room, where New York City felt far away as if it hadn't happened yet, and I had that sparking hope and wistful demise of daring to dance with the boy in the sky. The wind swept past the window so loud and so low, so harmonious in its country groans. Oh to go from Cecelia, and stewed apples on the stove, weed aromas, Afro portraits and locking doors, from Brooklyn, my bustling ball of hood and joy, to this red brick house which creaked with character and told stories of its own. The farmlands, the rural, the red white and blue.

Cody arrived, texting me, "I see yew", and I already knew he had before he had sent it. I didn't look out of the window, into the darkness. I became retracted, I drew shy. I stepped outside and he threw his arms out wide. He was a silhouetted scarecrow and I looked at the ground as I approached him, hugging him briefly. I hadn't expected to see him, and now that I had I was struck by how little it moved me. How the protagonist was just a man. He was ecstatic to see me and kept grinning and talking excitedly. I met his cousin too, he was kind-eyed and tattooed, bearded, and he resembled Owen and that was striking. Like all good family occasions, I was invited to slink off with the cousins, upstairs, to a bedroom. Where they pulled out a bag of weed and started rolling. His cousin, CJ, asked me everything about the U.K., about what we smoke there, miffed that weed was illegal. He said he wanted to go to London. All Americans do.

When the blunt was ready, Cody came over and grabbed my toes, brushing his hand up my leg and I retracted. I had a boyfriend. That's the thing about Cody, the last time he saw me he friendzoned me, and now he had spent the evening stealing glances, touching me in passing, wanting to share a bedroom, a bed, a body.

"Don't touch me", I said it in jest but the spark in his eyes dulled, and he never said much else that evening. He announced although he had been bubbly and bouncing and gleeful, that he was suddenly tired. And as we walked upstairs again, stoned and estranged, my heart was like ice. While he was wounded.

Cody turned around, "You know they'd put us in one bedroom if we asked."

"That would just mean one on the bed and one on the floor", I replied.

"One on the bed and one on the floor", he scoffed yet I caught his blink and his shielding of surprise.

***

Virginia was a whirlwind, it left as fast as it had arrived. Brown trees and a white jeep, chickens running loose, and the constant southern reminder from Betty-Lou that, some some time ago, had been stolen by a hawk. Memaw teaching me solitaire and on the same night forgetting she ever had, looking at me confused, pondering the rules, tentatively drawing another card:

"Who's that beautiful gal next to me?"

"Are you behaving yourself?"

"No cheating now."

"Is that boy next to you good?"

"Is there anything I can do for you?"

"Hell, no one's as old as me."

"Care to give us your company, we'll love you all the same?"

And Nonna and Grandpap scrapping, Betty- Lou and Cody hollering, cats hidden on the backs of sofas and under chairs, creaky beds and hardwood floors. Shops on Strawberry Street, and cotton fields rolling white, ones that Cody's stepfather had planted, the hard worker, the quiet, the stoic. Dolly Parton at the Thanksgiving halftime show. Biscuits and gravy, sausages with maple syrup, Nonna's sauce, meatballs and blunts out on the veranda. A hike at dusk, with Cody and CJ, hunters shots and snapping twigs, and farm tracks and dusty lanes. Late nights drugs and forbidden sex. Snoring and yapping and laughing and driving. A "You're part of the family now", and "You'll come again won't you?"

Grandpap the Vietnam veteran, offering Christmas presents with his bark and frown and Nonna interjects "We get a military discount wherever we go."

I told him my brother was a Marine, whenever I told anyone that my brother was a Marine, I'd say how he was only twenty, earning the green beret at seventeen. I was proud of him. I loved my brother, though I couldn't remember the last time I'd told him that. Virginia was beautiful, as were Cody's family, and I caught myself moved by their kindness.

***

A slow, steady sadness, the kind that is sure of itself and never creeps away, only forward and into and around, clinging to my chest as the week dawdled on. Virginia was vast, and I imagined a yellow moon hanging in a starry sky, with a picture-book shooting star every night, before the morning calls the rooster wakes, the floorboards creak, and breakfast sizzles, a cat paws pad the dew on the morning blade. Surrounded by the voices, the walls, the red barn and the changing leaves. Cody too had shed his leaves, the blossoming boy with the colourful buds, had wilted and withered and dropped to the ground in auburn folds, and now his leaves had turned to dust. Was it his soul or mine that had changed?

Some time back, he gutted me and I'd spilt my secrets, and now I was stuffed with wool, and cotton from the fields his stepfather picked. I thought of how easy it would be to venture back to New York, hoist myself up the rungs of the Manhattan bridge, and let myself fall below in a sad splash and a sad sink and a sad death, and emerge like a siren with long hair and a seashell bra, back across the Atlantic, soft and feminine and ethereal, yet carved into wood, into something heavy and phallic and solid, something tough and splintered and foreign, a hollowed out version of someone else's ideal.

I wanted to be on the move again. I felt restless, and if I hadn't had any need for anything at all, I probably wouldn't have returned to New York. I would've gotten on a bus someplace else, further West. I would've felt the wind in my hair and the laughter of a good friend by my side, I would've been Bonnie and Clyde or Thelma and Louise. Or perhaps I would've been nothing at all, but a tale on a tongue or a firm wag of a finger, a clue to a treasure chest, a fable, a story, a faceless name. It started with nothing better to do than succumb to a half-hearted adventure, until one day I woke up in some strange way, and the whole world would stop revolving if one foot strayed off the wayward path. Once you venture far enough, wide enough, across the globe and back, you never really can stop, for there's no other place to go. Other than on, and on and on, and on, into the abyss and beyond, into the unknown until it becomes so well trod, so well known, so mundane, that you have to pack up your bags and do it again.

Thanksgiving was long and full and happy and sad and empty, with biscuits and gravy for breakfast, the live Macy's Thanksgiving parade, and NFL and college sports. Turkey, macaroni cheese, mashed potatoes, green bean casseroles, pumpkin pie, sweet potato pie, apple crisp and charcuterie boards. Smokes on the veranda and feeling alone. Cody spent the day avoiding me, silent, unable to tell what he was thinking or if he was thinking at all. I had forgotten I felt this way around him—unsure of myself.

***

From Virginia, the country roads were taking me home, all the way to Maryland, and then onto New York. Back to the grind, to Cecelia and Daniela and Emmanuel too. Back to Brooklyn and the noise. Back to responsibilities far away from Cody and Betty-Lou and Nonna and Grandpap and Memaw and CJ, from the red barn and the crisp trees and the Hershey's.

On the way home I fell asleep in the warm car, legs squished, feet cramping, Sonny and Cher bleating, early morning mumbles, darkness succumbing to day, quiet roads and hazy nicotine, wrinkled eyes, heavy sighs, moments, moments, always fleeting. Cody ran his hand down my neck and massaged my shoulders, thumbing the silver ribbon of my necklace. I leant back into his palm. Dozing there, into his calloused skin, before being flung back to New York City. Cody was confusing. Stepping back and stained with change, I could see who he was. I had moved on in the year since I'd seen him last, more than either of us anticipated.

I didn't trust him, and I wasn't sure he was entirely good. I was upset, but he too was upset with me, never knowing how to connect. It seemed my hatred of Madison was one I never did shake, for it tainted my view of him. It came in a drowsy sadness, the knowingness that there was nothing left.

We had bundled into the car at 6 am. Cody told me he didn't like saying goodbye to me, that he was sad, and I believed him, as much as I could, for I was always prising truth from fiction, meaningful words from a smooth mouth. At least he wasn't cruel. I still saw the quiet kindness which ebbed through his bones. It was only on our last day that the coldness between us had begun to thaw, and I was sorry for my part in building the walls. He hadn't shaken the "Don't touch me comment" from the first night when he playfully grabbed my toes. The days that had ensued were a game of avoiding each other, and I thought that a shame, and a waste, and how old Cody and old me, would've been disappointed we did such a thing. Perhaps old Cody was this Cody, and I was the one who'd shifted into someone else. Perhaps that was the cause for his despondency.

He'd swallowed his rejection and had come creeping into my room the night after that.

"I was about ready to sleep in CJ's room, I didn't want to be alone after you said that", he told me, "You said it in front of him."

"I'm sorry."

He had rubbed my stomach, holding the folds. I wondered if he had noticed I had shrunk, or if hadn't noticed at all. Perhaps he preferred the girl before. I had changed, and she was the ghost on his tongue, just as my ghost was his name. He was warm and I silently loved him the only way I knew how, but his face on my neck and the delicate kisses he planted, and his hands rubbing the crease of my thigh were damaged now. He was a constant drizzle, a cloud in the sky.

"You know I'm divorced now right?"

"I know."

"If they don't let you stay I'm gonna make you stay", with a "*Ranggg*", he added, clarifying that I didn't breathe or move nor nudge, nor significantly care.

"I've been hearing that story for two years now"

He didn't have much to say to that and so pulled me closer instead. I thought of Tom. Every time Cody touched me, I thought of Tom like a whip to the face. How easy for Cody I thought, how easily he cheats. I was taken and yet I despised him for having loved Madison, for touching my body so soon after hers. She was hot on his skin. He was going back to Rochester to whisper into her ear, and I was back to New York with my conscience whispering into mine. I was disgusted with myself.

"You're sexy."

And yet I didn't feel as if I was, "Mhm."

"Did you hear me?"

"Mhm."

"You don't like-like me anymore", he said, sadness lacing his tone.

I shrugged, "You don't like me anymore."

"No", he defended himself, crossing his arms, a look I couldn't read on his freckled face, "You're special."

I could tell his heart was bruised for he was bruising mine.

If one thing Cody and I had in common, it was that we spent too long wrestling ourselves. So much so that the only thing we now seemed to know was wrestling each other, with dry tones and harsh words and his willingness and my turning away.

I spent the past few days on edge. There was always a lot I wanted to say, gestures I withdrew, a touch I craved and yet a hand I couldn't dare to raise. Cody was my definition of "a cat caught your tongue", for he clawed my tongue until saying anything at all was to choke on blood. And, anytime he opened his arms, asked for a hug or drew me in, I declined, I refused, I retorted, I jabbed and I jibed. I struggled to even be in his aurora, for it wasn't one I understood. I felt so uncomfortably nervous to be in his presence, so embarrassingly outwardly awkward, that he started ignoring me. I stepped onto the veranda and he stepped inside, I anxiously craved his space again, telling myself that this time I would be warm, he would feel that there was anything, something, a thread of feeling left. And, every time I only pushed him further away. I wanted to be his friend by day, and yet he only enveloped me in a selfish greed deep into the night. I was more alone than ever.

And then in the car with only an hour left, with daylight pouring in, the sun brought reassurances of the soft hand, the caress, the palm on my neck at 7 am to the 60s radio, driving into Maryland, with a fog in the throat and in the air. I could feel his eyes trace my face and leant back into his hand once again. The hand that fed me was the hand that hurt me.

I thought of Nepal. Everything always seemed to lead back to 2018, and my colourful life in the Himalayas.

"Don't marry someone you love", Sunita had said, "Marry someone nice."

Tom was nice. Tom was safe.

Cody had run his hand across my shoulder and down my arm, as we had passed each other in the living room the previous night, breaking our silent truce, he had touched my hair, "You're so beautiful, your skin is caramel."

I didn't know what it was, to feel beautiful, let alone be such.

"Do you have my vape?"

"No, I don't touch things that don't belong to me." He replied, a smug smile sprawled.

I tried not to be sad when we said goodbye. But it forever was. Strange goodbyes.

"Let us know when you get on the bus", Nonna said, handing me a carrier bag of assorted chips and a ten dollar note, which I politely refused and she impolitely insisted.

"Call us when you get to Brooklyn", Grandpap barked from the front seat, "Every week."

"I will", I chimed, knowing I wouldn't. I wish I had though, they were some of the nicest people I ever knew.

"Oh don't worry, she'll be texting me the whole ride back. Telling me she misses me, won't you Miss?"

I looked away from Cody, it was all I seemed to ever do.

"Oh she'll miss you", CJ laughed, "She's definitely gonna miss my cousin. I know she will."

I liked CJ, but I didn't like his jest, "I'm not gonna message at all now you've said that."

"That's mean, you hear that cousin? She said she's not gonna message you."

"Oh that's the thing with Miss", Cody replied in his drawl, "She's all there one minute and then…" —He scrunched up his fist and suddenly splayed his fingers —"*Poof* she's gone."

He stepped around the car, "Gimme a big hug."

I hugged him as tight as I could for as short as I could, and I hoped he wasn't disappointed in me, in seeing me, in knowing me. I was only disappointed in what he was, and not who he was.

"See you in another year," I said.

"Naww," he shrugged, "It'll be sooner than that.

I wheeled my suitcase to the front of Walmart, lit a cigarette from the pack CJ had bought me, and watched as they drove away, with my phone on the roof of the car. Salisbury, Maryland, phoneless, empty, cold and alone. By the time I had scoured the parking lot twice for my phone, fearing it had dropped off, asked Customer Service if they'd received a handed-in phone, bought a Sprite, squatted by the big style American mobility scooters, unplugged one and charged my laptop, created an account to connect to the wifi and opened up FindMyIphone, it was In Greenwood, Delaware.

I phoned Cody.

"Hey?"

"Hi."

"What's up?"

"Are you in Greenwood, Delaware?"

"Uhhh yeah?"

"My phone's on the car roof."

"What?", Nonna yelled out, and then chaos ensued, and an argument broke out,

"We need to turn back—

"I'm not turning back—

"She doesn't have her phone—

"Well she's managed to call you somehow—

"Yeah on her laptop Nonna, we need to go back and give it to her—

"You don't have to, you can mail it", I interjected but wasn't heard.

"WE'RE NOT GOING BACK"

"YOU HAVE TO."

"NOW I'M GOING THE WRONG WAY"

I hung up and texted Cody my address, and he said he was sorry and if it was up to him he'd return it, and I said I was sorry for creating a row.

"That's hilarious it stayed on the roof, all the way to Delaware", he messaged, followed by *"I wish we were closer"* and a sad-faced emoji.

Closer to where? Salisbury? Rochester? You and them? Me and you? Closer geographically, closing the bridge from Rochester to New York City. Or closer mentally? Spiritually?

I waited in the rain for the bus, cigarettes staining my fingertips, engulfing me in a stale aroma. I sat in the only free seat, in front of the toilet, old urine and upset tummies filling my nostrils with putrid air. My ID and debit card were with my phone, and once back in New York, I would have to jump the subway barriers and guess my way home. I'd have to try and forget about Cody again before he forgot about me.

"Remember when we had a spark?" He had asked me In the Norfolk Mall, coy and cold and callous.

I was tired of remembering and incapable of forgetting, and it was time to get lost down a different road, towards a better dawn or a thicker blanket of heavenly darkness, to wake with the departed and bid goodbye to the brokenhearted. He wasn't the one and my heart broke for the girl who had once hoped he was. I was startled at how beat down, how unhappy I must've been, to beg a cold shoulder to stay. How hollow his heart, how sorrowful mine.

I still didn't love myself, but I knew myself enough to know that Cody was a sex addict with a complex mind, he was the type of guy to sleep with the maid of honour on your wedding night. Slow and deep and heavy and panting and then parting to finish with you. Or perhaps he was never a cold shoulder and he'd always had open arms, and I was too scorned by Madison, how he'd dropped me, to forgive him. I seemed to have forgiven him when I went to get my bag. I loved him then. I loved him when he didn't sleep with me, when he friend-zoned me, when I was his screensaver. And now he appeared out of the darkness, crashing carelessly into my life with compliments and embraces and craving a closeness, a fondness, a need to invite himself into my bed, I ran cold. I had spent nearly two years loving him each day that the sun rose, and in two years I had no pictures with the mysterious man with a rotten mind and a dangerous drive. I only harboured the pain of passing time. I'm sorry that I loved you, and I'm sorry that I was blind, and never has there ever been someone as miserably sorry that you were never meant to be mine. A Ghost in The Wind, a title from the very beginning before I got lost in time, a title that never made sense until the end—a title or a shrine?

Perhaps the biggest grief was that the empty hole that America once had sewn shut was unravelling. Everything was bleak, the whole world passed in one blank, beige, broken streak as I looked out the window, face pressed against the glass. Maryland, Delaware, New Jersey, Pennsylvania. Harriet Tubman's freedom run, I was leaving slave country and heading for the North. What misery this country was founded on.

God was nowhere to be seen, and I thought it my fault for always returning to America in the cold, in the winter, in the season of the wrung-out hearts and exhaustion. The traffic into New York was slow, red lights reflected off the backed-up traffic from Jersey City, crawling past the Statue of Liberty. Rain ran in red and blue, dizzy droplets down the panes, and panes they were, a pained picture, a plague, an opening to a sad void on a sad night. It took me seven hours at the back of the bus, bleary-eyed and quiet, sitting with nothing to do, no thoughts to mull over, and no view of the sullen American sky, to acknowledge the horror of the lost magic of this brazen land. My awe of Americana, the novelty wearing off. I thought perhaps it was better on a pedestal, from far away, from England, this country that I longed my whole life to be a part of, seemed increasingly plain.

I dared to admit that it had been Cody who had made it special. I had built that allusion, to the country boy, the fisherman, the adventurer, the friend, the warm hand holder, the heat in the cold, the truck and the country music, and the promise of something to believe in. He was now a shadow, a shady figure in the doorway, a stranger in the hallway, and who I knew faded away before my eyes, and they were too tired to cry. I missed the light. It was only when I crawled into bed and raised my palm to the nape of my neck and envisioned him there, that I noticed the necklace clasp, undone for weeks, had been screwed shut. Who would've thought I'd still be writing about him, shrouded in the New York night? All the times we shared running dry, dragged out with the low tide. Yet, he was the only one that had stuck around. Including me, inviting me, hugging me, touching me, moving within me. Yet when I returned from Virginia, I was left with the vague feeling of having simply seen someone I used to know.

***

After Virginia, I woke up to a whole world riddled with him. His aimless coming and goings had stripped New York of its enchantment. We were waltzing into a world of bad decisions, and I danced with the idea of flitting towards the very person I should've strayed from. My heart thudded as his crotch pulsed. And the desire was still there, enough to feel the punch, the authentic *thwack*, the startling slap of needing to write, daring to think, leaping into the night with spooling pools of crimson ink.

It didn't matter that I lived in America, nor did it matter that I worked for a boss who would give me her Amex card, or provide me with a designated desk in Soho House, for an American sleaze had reawakened me. It was far easier to hate him. I only felt alive when I was derived. I was the master juggler, and I wasn't worried. I had secured the job, I lived on the opposite side of the State, I had made friends, and I was on track. I could keep the flirtations under wraps. My mind spiralled though and I couldn't understand why I hated him so, for I hadn't last time. In his presence, I felt the absence of that friend.

His ache and my wrath and weakness and womanhood oozed from my chest with the hauntings of his Thanksgiving touch. Something within told me to be bolder, to be careless enough to let go and fall, and to see if he'd catch me, or if I'd crumple under the weight of a love gone wrong.

Seize youth before you get older, was the nagging voice on my shoulder. Though I doubted I was brave enough to face yet another great American heartbreak, another stifling summer, with hot air and sticky skin in the August heat, with a shivering coldness seeping and seeding and bleeding. Chilblains and chains and ice cream chimes of British summer time.

America was temporary and I had learned the taste wasn't worth the agony of soaring back across the sky. Hell, he had hurt me so bad that I had boomeranged across twelve countries in one year. And what a year 2023 had been. From Pisa and Florence and Rome, the coliseum and pizza to frozen lands of Iceland and bleak Berlin, grazing my hand across the ugly wall which had divided a city of Nazis and Jews and Germans and Europeans.

From the Burj Kalifa and the burning sun of Dubai to the month in the Philippines with Nanay and slums and barking dogs and tuk-tuks and private schooled doctors, to Malaysia in the tropical storms. From Portugal and petals and monasteries and yellow palaces and sheep's cheese. To Mexico and Mezcal, wonders of the world, cenotes and Mayan reserves, turquoise waters and mariachi, to Spain and the birthplace of my grandmother and her mother before her. From my cousin's flat in La Línea and my aunty's Paella in Gibraltar to seeing the Rock Hotel where my parents wed, to flying back to New York.

From graduating university and living with Meave, to meeting Tom and pubs and parks and beaches and havens and moving on. Nothing this year had struck me so hard, told me so vigorously to write, as three days in Virginia with Cody did.

The universe always knew when we had rekindled, for it reminded me with strange hums and low moans. The office and its music pulled me away from my work and up into the clouds of smoggy, sultry daytime slumber.

By the time I had fumbled for my vape deep sighed, filled up my water and done anything I could've done to rid him of my mind, I hid in the bathroom to draw in that long steady breath of nicotine. The Soho Works playlist refused my escape,

"Lying with you is like ecstasy."

But lying with him wasn't ecstasy, the aftertaste was. I had spent the whole day actively trying to shelf him, trying to escape into Tom, who only made me realise I was running towards the sweet boy, the kind boy, the ignorant boy, the boy with the small mind, and I bounced away from him. Ricocheting off the walls, debating and mulling and musing, considering whether I was too young to be so tired, too young to be so committed, too young to be high and mighty, proud and dedicated, loyal and loving. Perhaps womanhood was about lusting and lying and leaving? But that wasn't who I was. I wondered if Cody's mind too was racing or receding or retracing. If he knew how reckless he was?

I woke up the next morning, assuring myself the bus journey had simply worn me thin, and all the emotions I had felt the day before were just dust settling after a cataclysmic collision of a lost war. Though Cody or the universe or whoever my God was, wasn't finished with their reckoning.

"I miss you. How are you?"

Goddamnit.

If he wanted sentimentality, a love laced with nostalgia, a reassurance, then he should've picked yesterday. That was the problem. We were passing ships in the night, our emotions never aligning. My facade refused to crack and I decided not to speak to the man with the vulnerable heart, confused mind and beautiful burdens, but the Cody I had created. I was almost sorry that I had turned his identity into a character, for perhaps it stilted me from ever truly knowing him. I had likened myself to Miss Havisham, but now I was a cold and steely, unwavering Dr Frankenstein.

"Oh, am I living in your head rent-free?"

"Yes, Ma'am, and I wouldn't have it any other way."

"Hmm, doesn't that just make me your charity project?"

"No, Ma'am—you're my best investment."

He was funny. I'll give him that. Our replies back and forth were slow, either one not quite sure where to tread, or what to do with the cards in our hands. Toeing the line between the said and unsaid is forever a game. Cat and mouse.

"You could charm your way into anything with all those yes ma'ams and no ma'ams." I finally said.

"I never truly grasp how much peace you bring me until we're apart again."

I didn't want to be the little fish at the end of his hook. I'd much prefer to be the big pike, thrashing and wiggling and leaving him reeling.

"Why do you think that is?"

"I don't know. Care to enlighten me?"

"Maybe because you've been undervaluing me since the beginning of time."

Dicey move. Perhaps he wasn't playing and I was the queen of the game. The outward ice queen, the heartless, the walled-up woman. Inwardly, I was the damsel, the creator of my distress. We'd met each other in the dark, with the walls drawing in, with the hatch shut. Maybe we were simply confused, a moth to the light. He was my lamp and I was his, but our hearts hadn't caught up with our minds. The lamps had drawn cold, the bulb bust.

It dimmed sometime last year, somewhere in between Rochester and Cornwall. Somewhere thwarted. Perhaps it was better to lick our wounded wings on a cold bulb than to look up and see a sun shining, a sun beaming, a sun so hot we'd combust all together and return to that dark space. The cure was quality time and we'd never get that again. We hadn't had that since South Wedge. It felt now as though it never existed.

"I value you more than you know."

Fuck sake. Wrong move.

"Please don't be sad."

"I'm feeling down at the moment—probably just coming off the dopamine high from Thanksgiving."

"Thanks", I replied, disheartened that his pain was temporary and mine was harder to shift. The scorned lover, adamant in her refusal to be the side piece. Although I would have tentatively had him as mine.

"No, thank you."

Americans. Strangers to sarcasm. He told me he'd been looking at bus tickets to New York City, gushing about how cheap and easy it would be to hop on and to come see me. I felt a bubble of excitement and asked when he would, only he told me he didn't know—it would have to be spontaneous.

Of course. Madison. Too many saucepans on the pot.

Sizzle, sizzle, sulky sizzles.

I told him not to come.

Case closed. Conversation over. Triumph or tragedy? Traumatised kids trespassing the land of collateral damage, or two adults refusing to give up, to close the curtain, to let the flame die?

Wouldn't it be funny, simply hilarious if Cody was a projection of myself? If he was a simple man, and my complexities were so huge, a tsunami of years of unsureness that I had fashioned a complicated character, and blamed him for all my woes? That was a far easier denial than staring myself in the face, acknowledging that this book had been about me all along.

I wondered who hurt more, the one with the boyfriend who wasn't deserving of the lacerations his heart would have to suffer. Or the man, so lost, he saw it fit to chase a taken woman, a man with his own woman by his side, be-lining another?

I felt insufferably guilty, and unlike myself, unlike my morals to be committing treachery against love. Unable to be accountable for my actions, I blamed Owen. He was my first real-life love, after Leonardo DiCaprio, James Dean and Marlon Brando. He was my first real love, my first finance, and he taught me that love was nothing but fucking sorrow. Tom was a victim of everyone who had ever victimised me, and I wished he had never met me, for I wasn't the type of girl you should love so easily. Not now, not after Cody.

Tom should have loved me first, and I apologise to him, profusely, that he didn't pick Owen to the post. Tom should've loved me first, for I would never know the hard blow of a punch to the stomach, losing a fistful of hair for simply existing, or a forceful strike, and a back sliding down the wall, head fuzzy, knocked unconscious. Tom should've loved me first, for I would never know the torment, the torture of being held hostage in your own home, the viciousness of:

"Mongral"

"Rape"

"Fat"

"Disgusting"

"Ugly"

"Unwanted"

"Nothing."

"I'm sorry I resisted you", I replied after Cody's stretch of silence, *"I only resit you because I don't know how to navigate you."*

I should've loved Tom as I loved Cody, but I couldn't. Cody saved me, and Tom would always lose. Nice guys come last, that's the real tragedy. They come after the hurricane, to try and love a woman who's already been obliterated. No man, first, second, third, or even last, would ever match the love a daughter has for her Dad. And my Dad taught me that nice guys don't exist, and if they did, I wouldn't know how to treat one.

The oppressed becomes the oppressor. The hardest thing to accept was that if Tom hadn't been nice, if Tom hadn't allowed me to come to America, or to go to Virginia, or to travel, or to be myself, I would've been in England, tucked up in bed with him, thousands of miles away from any threats.

Although he slept under the English moon, unaware of my late-night stirring, breaking his trust broke any notion that I was good. I was worried that God knew what I had done. And if a love poet could cheat, then who couldn't?

I didn't think I would ever trust anyone again for as long as I didn't trust myself. I only wished he hadn't booked to come out, for I felt like I was a glue trap, and he was an unexpected mouse. It seemed so much worse that he was excited to see me. I should've broken it off in Mexico, but I was cowardly, just as I was cowardly to confess before he entered this forsaken land, and probably too cowardly to call it quits after he returned home. What's worse? For him to know before, or to know after?

My thoughts dwindled back to Owen, who I was glad to say had no reign over any corner of my heart. I could view our fucked up past with objective clarity. Although he adamantly denied it, I was completely certain he had cheated on me. I had the evidence. However, he had pecked out my eyes so ferociously that I couldn't see. He must've felt guilty, for he pressured me to have sex with other people, probably to cancel out his crime. But had he not, I would never have met Cody all those nights ago, on Main Street in Brockport.

Perhaps everyone was always cheating on each other. I hoped Tom would never find out, not for my selfish gain, but because he wouldn't deserve the pain. He deserved to be blissful and unaware and happy and to not have his heart tainted, not to stumble through relationships, unable to open up again.

"I don't know how to navigate you either."
"We should trade manuals."

***

The parts I didn't like about Cody were the parts I didn't like about myself. The floating about, the running towards something only to turn and flee the opposite direction, moving fast, moving slow, an inability to commit to anything but one's self.

You mustn't indulge in fruitless thoughts. For then how can you resist the temptation of the skewiff? It's tiring trying to avoid Groundhog Day when that's all the world ever knows. It's hard to let everything go. Impossible to slow when going fast is the only thing you've ever known. It's not easy to stop when you want to go.

It's desolate when everything you touch turns into a fever dream when life is a forever current, a rolling stream, and you watch the heads of those you love bob on by, eyes closed, trailing the current to another time.

How fast time goes. I missed Meave and Mexico, and it was unfathomable how that was simply two months ago. Sun-kissed and sizzled, cenotes and pools and lullabies of seas and skies, Cancun, the beauty was no surprise.

All I could ever see were figures walking away from me. Men with their backs turned, shoulders wide, arms by side.

I'd bolted up in the dead of night, and I was facing the mirror which as I'd slept had been behind me. I must've turned around in my sleep, for when I shuddered awake, sat up and startled, I thought I'd seen a ghost. I stared at it. Groggy and unsure and blinking, scared for a moment, heart beating. It was simply myself in the mirror, in the dark, confused and awry. I was released and collapsed back to sleep.

How uncomfortable. Always staring oneself down. Having foolish nightmares of your own reflection. At least I was young. I imagined it would be far worse to awake like that to a wrinkled face, sagging and old, and balding, eyes milky clouding blind.

I wished I had money, for when the States would inevitably kick me out again, I would've fucked off back to Asia. Anywhere but here, anywhere but there, a tale of tossing and turning and trying and crying and returning and revolving.

It was Meave's birthday. I looked at the ceiling fan, and I felt as though I was in a flat full of strangers. A flat which only knew my face and name. A land alone. Perhaps that's what homesickness felt like, a web of sadness, filtering around the room, ventilated by the fan, particles of poignancy, shifting through the air; invisible dust-laden orbs. Quiet.

I wondered how much would've been different, the clocks turning back, the hand spinning, whizzing, clicking, ticking. The shadowy man turned around.

Hi Dad.

I struggled to picture what it would've been like, if he had walked, or run— if he sprinted towards his children, swooping them up and holding them there, laughing rather than parting. The children with the ringlets and big brown eyes, the children deserving. But that was uncomfortable further still, and I made the shadowy man turn back around. I didn't want to see his face, for it was easier to slot another there.

I lay on my bed and played dead. I lay and thought of him every night, and wondered what it would've been like. So now, all I had was stories and a drawn-out life, where I was never home. I wrote a poem when I was 13, about a German boy, for first it was boys and then it was men that churned the words, sawing off my head and shoving it in a sack, flinging it up to the clouds, and never looking back.

She was a butterfly,
The more you tried to cage her,
The more she tried to fly.

And now I was always flying, a butterfly trapped between two sheets of glass, panicked and frantic, darting up and down, all around. I had to have nicotine before him and adventures after him. The only antidote was to be on the move forever, for if I stopped to look around, the violinist would've put down his bow and bowed.

DECEMBER 2023

We're all dying. It started the moment we were born, and that's why I always try to live carelessly, brashly, bravely, doing what I want when I want. It was ingrained in me that every day I woke up was a day less I had left. Live like your terminal, with the weight mortality in your heart, for, after all, you are.

That's why the job and the car, and the necessities and the niceties and the commute and the five days on the trot and two to recover and back again, forever and ever, for years and years is a sin. It's a deadly conception, and I will always cheat the corporate life, for I want no part in it.

I remember at school, my French teacher towered above me, thin and sombre and twisted and ugly, "Why didn't you do your homework?"

"I had better things to do."

And chaos ensued and I was kicked out of the class and bollocked in the corridor for everyone to hear. But, I couldn't have cared less, for it was true. I had better things to do. I will only ever do the things that serve me because damn your opinion, one day you'll be dead and I'll be dead too. How the hell will opinions matter then? Fear is the enemy, trust God.

Every time I returned to America I seemed to become vaguely religious. I think Americans need religion to live there, people always go looking for God but he doesn't show.

New York was melancholic and painful and sad. Strangers shouted and shoved and seethed, angry faces looking at me. New York belonged to the trash and rats and subways, with billowing smoke rising from grates. A sea of vermin, vicious and unwavering sent me caving inwardly.

I no longer liked the city of noise and smog, cars and creeps moving through the streets and the restlessness, the bustling, the bumping, the inability to walk ten feet. Every time I'd venture to Manhattan I'd retract back to Brooklyn again. New York stole my money and snatched my soul, and it took me six weeks to realise how unfair it was that companies could employ foreign staff and pay them nothing. How my boss always avoided handing over my stipend, $100 a week, she was begrudging and slow and moody, as if my work had no value and her pity had trailed off. Giving me a means to eat was merely a chore.

She'd given me a job offer one month in and I had accepted, but now I wasn't so sure. Her principles were twisted and like everyone I met, I was easily fooled. I was earning 40 cents an hour, in the most expensive city in the world, in 2023. The price to be in America. It was ironic because the happiest I had been this year was anywhere but America. It was Mexico, with Meave, lazing in a tropical daze.

I couldn't make up my mind as to whether I would ever come back to the land of the "free." Free labour. I probably would, once I got home and forgot about how empty, how hollow the world of New York truly is. I doubt anything good was ever written about New York by people who lived there, and if there was, they must've lived there long enough to forget anything about the outside world. The Empire State with the fallen city. New York, what a hoax. Home to the miserable. New York is the playground for the millionaires and the hell torn for the broke.

America was painting me bitter and dull. If I hadn't tricked myself with the terrible habit of finding anywhere and calling it home, I would've left America and told it to go fuck itself. I was so tempted to tell it anyway. I strode down the side walk in heavy stomps, *clomp clomp clomp.* My middle finger pointing to the ground.

The only saving grace was that I was back in Brooklyn, walking by brownstones and bins, run-down Dunkins and cracked-out groans. I'd choose Brooklyn over the cold empty skyscrapers of Manhattan, the steely blue, the tourist-laden, asshole cradle of the universe.

I was so unfathomably angry that once I returned home I'd have to find a new obsession, for I had been irreversibly stupid for ten years of my life, obsessing over the concrete cluttered, guttered, rotting jungle of human crap since I was a girl. If not America, then where? If not home, then where? I'd probably have to become a shaman and live in Nepal, eat rice and momos, deactivate all social media, become a Himalayan hobbit, living underground, for not even the sun could reverse my frown. What a distasteful thing this planet is. What a desolate world. What a waste, a garbage can overthrown. Curse you, New York. I'm glad you're going to be underwater at some point, hopefully soon. Even then people would hail it like they do Atlantis. That must've been a shit hole too.

I decided to officially fall out with New York.

So Hey, yeah you, America, *fuck you.*

Betty-Lou messaged me, detecting my strife from all those States away, she reassured me that I was part of her family. Oh how beautiful if that were true, and how somber that it wasn't. How sullen. How mistaken. How almost true. I was the Joker in Gotham City.

Cody messaged too. Growing tired of my ceaseless attempts at humour. Growing tired of feeling—me too.

He continued the conversation of the previous night:

"I'm exhausted."

"Get some rest, tired man. Dream something sweet."

"I didn't dream", he replied, *"That's the worst part of smoking— no dreams."*

"Come for a spontaneous weekend and smoke in the city of dreams." I had said this morning, as I felt New York changing and churning, preempting its vomit, its spray, it throwing me up.

"I would if I weren't drowning in work."

"That hurts", I sent, for he always knew how to reject me when everything else around me was rejecting me too.

"Do you want me to quit working and have nothing to spend on you, or work like crazy and have something to give?"

"Give your time to me", I typed adamantly. Americans and money, a concept that couldn't fuck me off more.

"Money makes time possible", he retorted, and I guess he wasn't wrong. Time is our currency.

"Guess I'm used to paying the price for missing you."

"Would you rather I waste my life at home, gaming my days away? You know how that story ends."

That's interesting, rolling Owen into this one, or perhaps he meant Tom, but if he did, he'd misjudged him. New York groaned some more and I was the rot in its gut. I felt myself vibrating against its sickly stomach lining.

"No, I'd rather have you exactly as you are", I typed, heading into Radio City, ignoring those around me, *"just do your humour research."*

Why is it he always misread me?

"There's nothing to laugh about."

Oh boy, and there it was, I was rising, rising, rising, rising with bile and slime and gone off hot dogs and smushed doughnuts by the wayside. New York was sick. New York was poison. New York had to get me out.

"I'm sorry I got it wrong. I don't know where I stand with you. I never know if you'll want to talk to me tomorrow or if you'll vanish.", I replied.

And New York gagged and I lurched.

"I've never been upset hearing from you—not once. I love talking to you."

I didn't reply to Cody for quite some time. I was on a Radio City tour with pretentious interns, dismissing conversation for I was too dejected to live in a falsehood of niceties.

"I just don't always know how to navigate you and my feelings are complicated because I always have you in my life temporarily and then we disappear again"

He took his time to reply, and I took my time to preempt mine.

"I don't know how to handle my feelings for you," he said and I was glad he was honest.

There were no trading manual jokes left, and New York ejected me, in a vile concoction of everybody it had ever swallowed, *"The human mind is interesting, how hard it can be to communicate with someone you feel you know so well."*

And I was splattered across the sidewalk, sprayed in sticky lumps. Left to be trodden on with disgust, scuffed and wiped away on the sole of a shoe until the sick hardened and turned to dust.

"I couldn't agree more."

"I'm sorry I'm complex to you, just as you're complex to me. Frustrating isn't it?" I replied once I was home, once safe, once recovered from my ejection.

And Tom messaged too. Everybody crawled out of the woodwork in my period of despondency. All I desired was a winter of hibernation, and yet, it seemed to be a winter of confusion and calamity.

"I love you so much. You're my beautiful angel and I really do miss you."

Oh how little I deserved that love, how much I craved to be left alone. Yet how much I needed everyone, and how little of myself I could give them.

***

I wondered what it was that I lacked. Which part of me wasn't enough, the sad part? The gloom which trailed after me in shadowy taunts? Or, the desolation, the vast expansiveness, the bareness, the blankness of knowing that fate is unchanging? To know I almost had it, but not enough?

I envisioned that to die would be to float away, to be high. To be cocooned in a cotton ball cloud, drifting off to classical music, strings and bows. I would meditate to practise dying and travel to practise living. What an art to live, what an art to die, what a colossal tragedy to love, and a comedy to be loveless.

The unhappiness was getting worse, the sorrow more paramount. It was because I was still. Stillness didn't serve me well. I was the most still I'd been all year. I was knotted up and sober, the most sober I'd been all year, and it was December. And I yearned to be high.

When Cody went distant I knew he was with Madison. I had no cause to be angry, for I had someone else too. I had no need to seethe, I simply sulked and hoped this longing would pass. New York was lonely. Loneliness too shall pass.

"Your writing is fucking magic", my sister had told me, after reading my angry excerpt about New York. Then suffering is magic. I knew the witchcraft of my dolour, my woe, all too well, for it was the only constant. If only the world knew my ache.

I wondered what it was like to win a victory, to conquer love, to be satisfied in a world of wanting. I needed to get my head back in the game. I needed to remember the shadow in the hallway, the stranger in the doorway. I needed to remember the Virginia struggle, the disappointment. I needed to remember he only compelled me from afar. But, that wasn't true.

I couldn't understand how he always chased me, in between spouts of nothingness. He'd water me and then a great drought. How when I saw him last year, I was single, we shared a bed for three long nights, and not once had he made an advance, a move. And in Virginia, he was all over me, I was riddled with him, with hands. He'd come into my room at night, and we'd sleep there together, and he'd hold my body, remove my clothes, and release fleshy, naked moans. We never kissed though. He requested that I marry him more times than any man ever had. More now, than even Owen. Yet, he was forever unobtainable.

"Marry me."

"You know I would."

"I'm still holding out for you."

I had spent the days in Virginia lonely in his company, rejecting his advances, balling my body and facing away. Now, from New York, my brush was waltzing, stroking his image across my canvas. It was better to have him there than nothing at all. I never did well with blank spaces. Travel was *my* escape, maybe somewhere, someplace, far away, in a hidden corner of the globe, I'd find him again. Women were *his* escape, maybe some woman, somewhere would be able to erase me, some kisses deep. Maybe Madison already had.

Perhaps it wasn't Cody I couldn't stomach, but knowing that if I allowed myself to feel, it would be to remain shattered in the knowledge that we had been doomed from that start. Perhaps we perfectly knew how to navigate each other, both daring not to. America had us on our knees.

Maybe it was the distance, the constant closing door which we didn't know how to steer around that fractured whatever there once was. Our love was always lost in translation, lost down a Brockport road. Lost in a breeze, in a *plop* of a lure and the *rustle* of the trees. Lost somewhere up in the sky. Lost in Letchworth, lost in Niagara Falls, in the roach motel, in Virginia. Lost in Madison, lost in Tom. Lost in Rochelle, lost in Owen. Lost even when we lay side by side. Perhaps had I been American there never would've been a book. I would've never had to write to keep him close. He would've always been there.

***

In four days I had slept a mere seven hours. I couldn't navigate the winds of change. I was slowly slipping away, losing my mind in the constant revolving door of careless time. America once eased my mind, but now it only reaffirmed my brokenness, and I couldn't prise myself from the floor. I lived in the dirt, looking up, ogling that American sky, watching that eagle soar towards the clouds. Three clouds: red, white and blue. The eagle straight on, its beak piercing through them one by one.

And they'd rip open, releasing shards of stars, which as they plummeted towards me, splintered and cracked, becoming ninja stars, slicing steel, severing my skin, turning that old good American soil, rich red.

I heard a great roar, an enormous engine. An Upstate truck? Firing onwards, steering through the night with loud laughs and quiet whispers and a thundering promise of a yellow-lined triumph…

Fuck.

I rolled my eyes up to the sky.

Who would've thought, this entire time, I'd been awaiting the kamikaze?

I closed my eyes and bid goodbye, and if I burned he was burning with me:

Cody DioGuardi.

***

I travelled to Toronto on a strange Sunday, the skies rolling grey. Spindly trees, bare and cold, shrouded in a December haze lining the highway. I left Rochester and had been crying into the window pane, watching miles of the yellow line roll on by, a ribbon racing the road.

It was Christmas Eve and I'd spent the morning at a diner with Cody, with pancakes and syrup and a lump in the throat. Four days in Rochester had raced on by as they always would. Each time I left, a piece of me remained behind. I wondered what was left of me now if anything at all.

It was a sombre Sunday, and at 3 pm the clouds came rolling in black. Headlights on the highway, dreary, foggy, dim-lit day. Afternoon disguised as evening, and forever the melancholy of leaving. We were miserable liars: I pretended not to care, whilst he pretended he'd always be there.

"Thank you for coming. I miss you every time we have to say goodbye."

"Our time together always feels so short, and the stretches apart feel endless."

"I know. But we always find our way back to each other."

***

I stood on the rooftop, having checked in, splitting the hostel payment between my credit card and debit card, having walked into the Christmas Eve dinner social, and having U-turned and walked away, down the street and into the only Kebab shop open on Christmas Eve night.

I stood on the rooftop and looked out at the misty skyscrapers, Toronto, buildings peeking above the clouds. I peered down at the street and up, at the charcoal oasis, and down to the street again. And for a long, curious moment felt the irresistible urge to up and throw myself off.

I wouldn't be seeing Cody again for months, and although only hours before, Rochester and The Sopranos, hiking and long night cuddles, lonely embraces in the arms of the only person who could fraud a feeling of love, seemed to have disappeared as suddenly as those days had begun. Cody was heading to Georgia in January. He'd spent four days convincing me to marry him.

In Rochester, I had believed him. He'd seemed so sure and so certain, so matter of fact that going to a registry office and filing for a visa seemed painstakingly obvious. And now, in Toronto, three hours away from Cody, his headlights blurring the night, the plan seemed further away than ever, and in four days Tom would be entering America. My life was a play and the curtain must've been hitched for it never seemed to fall.

I guessed Santa wasn't coming to the Hostel this year. And before I walked back inside, back to the cold, shoulders hunched, off to crawl into a bed in a room full of strangers, and not beside Cody's breaths and warmth flesh, another curious thing hit me. It almost winded me.

When I travelled with friends it was to roam the world with wide-eyed excitement, to exclaim and wonder and burn with the sensation of becoming alive. I knew I'd feel that again, with Meave, with Tom in New York City.

But I'd been travelling vastly on my own, walking the path by myself, forever trudging beside my grisly reflection. Travel was a crack of a whip, a punishment, an enslaved reminder that nothing is permanent. The days, the weeks, the months, the years. The job, the friends, the lovers, family. People aren't permanent. Everything can disappear. And the scariest thing of all is that if you travel as much as I have, it becomes quicksand, and the very thing that once freed you, drowns you until you're suffocating and anyone and everyone who could've pulled you out, disappeared home a long time ago.

***

I ate my pumpkin pie on Christmas Day in a bar in downtown Toronto, full and tired and weary.

***

I leant back and watched the sun roll up over the Canadian highway, pink mottling the stretch of blue. Dawn was here. I wondered how many other nomads were travelling onwards, one foot at a time, a bus and a plane, a thumbs-up hitchhike. How many big kids like me were roaming the world, having run away from home? How many other Mamas awoke each morning, thinking of their child, discovering something faintly important overseas? The world was big, and what I had seen was so small, so that must mean I'd have to explore forever.

I liked Canada, most probably because I liked America. And although I deeply loved Europe there was something about North America which dared me to stay.

I was on a fourteen-hour bus ride back to New York City. I'd been away for nine days. I was going back having shed the anxiety and heavy weight which had seemed to latch itself to me in the past few weeks. I could see why New York was full of crazies, there was something in the water there. I had been slowly losing myself to delusions and questions of reality. I was returning, refreshed. Ready to breathe life again. I was on my way to get Tom from JFK. Which meant one thing, I was halfway through my internship, and somewhere in Rochester, Cody was rolling up my green card, thrusting it up his nose, snorting lines. I had more travelling to do. I needed to test my hypothesis. To see if it was true— that I would love him on all corners of the Earth.

JANUARY 2024

I sobbed to Kings of Leon in a rickety single bed. In a hostel, in Chelsea. With my head to the ground floor window, strangers walking past, snow falling, feet cold. Homeless in New York City. Hardwood floors. The radiators clanging, neighbours banging, upstairs creaking, someone on the street shrieking.

Tom and Meave and Washington D.C and Times Square and a rooftop birthday and photos on Dumbo Street, all seemed to have flashed before my eyes and I wasn't sure if any of it had ever been real.

Cody had sent me 100 dollars for my twenty-third birthday, with a "Love you".

He had asked if I had missed him when Tom was here and I didn't give a straight answer. So, he gave me the silent treatment. Only to reveal,

"I've spent two years unsure I have feelings for you."

And I knew it to be true, and I had fallen asleep and woken crying. How little he had loved me all along, how grand I had imagined it to be. He was giving me money to get out of the hostel and to stay with him in Georgia, and I didn't even know why. What was the point, after everything?

***

"Hey", Cody announced into the room, as my cheek stuck to his stomach, my vape meeting his cigar, locking hands in smoky wisps above our heavy heads. I thought of palm trees, gold sand, and blue waves in the January sun. I wondered what it was that he thought about,

"Yeah?"

"You're beautiful."

"Thank you."

I sunk my head back down, hearing the page turn as he read his book, his hand massaging the knots from my back, the Rom-Com playing, the heat whirring, the motel creaking, the stars shining behind the clouds.

We'd come back from the bar where some countryman with a large moustache and a larger guitar, strumming Bruce Springsteen had called me a "Honky Tonk Woman". Cody demolished a plate of wings, his hands calloused raw. We watched the TV screens: Bills facing off against Kansas City in the New York snow, and I was glad I had run away, off into Georgia, off into another unknown. Cody was exhausted, working on the lighthouse for twelve hours a day, his eyes sunken, as I sat pretty, having done nothing but walk the stretch of blue. I'd spent the afternoon at the beach puzzling over how slave ships once rode the waves, but now they were a scenic escape.

I had walked with headphones, listening to Adele, young and wistful, stealing glances at the lighthouse, seeing figures hoisting buckets up and down and guessing which was Cody. I walked and thought, and I could hardly believe I was there. I could hardly believe we were still seeing each other at all. And I stayed on the beach, with those strings of thoughts, the sea birds, and the cargo ships rolling by. The waves lapped as I scanned the stretch of golden sand, the vast beach. The coveless beach. The cliffless beach. The American beach with surfers, fossil hunters and the grass growing from the dunes.

I sat on a swing seat, listened to sad songs, hit my vape and thought about so many things in such a peaceful current that I was glad I wasn't in New York. The sun dipped, and rain spotted the air. I watched the lens of the lighthouse flicker until the fog had fully submerged it, and it was time to walk home, against the waves, back to the lighthouse keeper. He picked me up at the gas station on the side of the road. He smiled, cracked a joke, turned the stereo up and drove us away, under a navy sky blackening from blue, under tall trees still green and a faint hopeful glow.

***

A woman needed her car jump started as we strolled out of the bar, bellies full, night becoming old.

"Hey, either of you got jump cables?"

"I'll be right over," Cody replied, and I marvelled at his ease to help, his willingness to assist a stranger after dawn to dusk labour, after buying my meal, after almost falling asleep at the bar. I also realised even if I had wanted to help, I would've had to dismiss the woman had I been alone, for I hadn't the faintest idea how to jump-start a car, and again I was impressed with his knowingness.

I told him he was kind and I hoped he knew I meant it.

And then he cleared his throat and I was back in the room with him, in the final bedtime stretch. I rolled off from his stomach, brushed my teeth and tied my hair. I was halfway through my stay in the Heartbreak Hotel in some distant coastal town of South Georgia. I was only halted in my sadness of saying goodbye in a few days for it meant Mama and Miami and margaritas.

I shuffled back into the room and lay on the bed, but I was too far for Cody who seemed to reach over in page-flicking intervals to rub my side or stroke my hair,

"Can you come back here please?", he finally asked, looking over, eyes wrinkled, face tired. I obliged and nestled back to my favourite resting place, and he ran his fingers through my curls, scrunching my hair and releasing them, palming circles on my scalp. He always said he liked my hair curly, I guess he did, for his hand nested in it, in rhythmic circles, until the lamp was shut off, and the lighthouse keeper turned off his lens.

Only, he slept and I didn't. I knew before I could blink I'd be an aeroplane ride away again, and his heavy sighs as he slept and warm sides would fade into memories, into words in a book. There was nothing I could do but lie there still, and wish it would never end. Staying awake meant feeling his kisses on my back each time he briefly stirred. Once or twice I'd roll over, open my eyes and see him lit up in the TV glow as it danced across his face. I wanted to reach out and hold him as easily as he did to me, but I never could, not even in Brockport, for I was never brave enough. Travelling the world on my own never once scared me; reaching out for the man I loved did. And so, I rolled away. I couldn't bear to look at him. He was the prettiest thing I'd ever seen.

***

"Don't forget your shell. I'll be sad if you forget that."

"I'm going to have a shell collection", I beamed.

"I'm going to get you one from every State I go to."

I sat in the Savannah airport, in my Rochester sweater, a six-hour stretch ahead of me before even boarding the plane, my Mum was already in the air and she'd be beating me to New York. I was glad to see my Mama, and empty to have left Cody, and one thing was clear, goodbyes never get easier.

"I love you." He had yelled out of the truck window.

"I love you," I yelled back.

And I raised my hands, cupped to a heart. And I faintly saw his, back at me, as he drove into the sky that had not yet turned yellow. Although goodbyes didn't get easier, the promise of returning always did. He hadn't given up on me yet.

FEBRUARY 2024

I had been bound by the shackles of Manhattan, and my heart twisted and torn with thorns that had bled over the streets of Brooklyn, it was February and I was older and worn and I was free.

I felt as though I should've come to New York City to fall in love and that it was a terrible pity that I hadn't found my maestro, my artist, my golden-fingered strummer. Though the true pity was, that I never did look, I never did seek him out, I just reopened old wounds with a familiar face, and the true pity behind it all was that I'd never find my maestro, for he was me, and I was too busy battling for air.

And if New York taught me one thing, the rising scraper in the pit of misery, is that if you define yourself as an artist, of any kind, then the only absolute must is freedom, to do what you want when you want to do it, the only exception being the obstacle of funds. But if you're brazen enough, that doesn't matter. Six months, unpaid, without an allowance, keeping afloat with a biweekly stipend of £200. Anything's possible if you're unhinged enough. The greatest balance of life is making sure you don't teeter too far, but if you do, perhaps you'll hardly notice.

I had gone from being wholeheartedly incapable of being on my own, but having trudged my bags through countries and States with the world on my shoulders, the heaviness of everything digging into me like an underseat bag slung over a shoulder, I couldn't imagine anything worse than being still with someone.

I liked to move on my own, the anonymity of it all. I liked to experience the world through my own eyes with my intellect, with my intuition, my fumbles and failures, and triumphs.

I enjoyed resting my sore feet at night, from having hit the concrete with my soles, one slab at a time for miles, musing. To stitch my wounds shut, to lick them, to let them bleed. I liked and enjoyed my stretch of solo travel, but there was only one person I'd ever stop running for, albeit if it was to run to him, into him, to grab his hand and get him to run alongside me, or behind me, so he could catch me. But the thing is, if he did, he'd be a person and we'd run until we'd be still. His allure was all wrapped up in what ifs and maybes and the magic of yearning, the tantalizing promise of something. And, I don't know much, but I like to think that's what nestled me into his special box too. We were too avoidant to be snared, both apprehensive to dare, needing not to spoil the lust which had rolled its way through two winters.

I looked forward to the day I would love someone else. To find the man with the balance I had always sought but always missed. To find the man who would adventure with me, not from me, the man who'd roam with me, not cage me. I wasn't in a rush to find him though, I first had to find myself, and that's not so simple when you're in the business of getting lost.

It's funny that sometimes when you speak to the universe, it talks back. After having written, "I was in the business of getting lost", I rolled over, hit my vape and sighed, ready to sleep again, to enter the night. I decided to open Facebook. Who doesn't reach for social media in the dark? A quote by Franz Kafka illuminated my screen,

"You are free, and that is why you are lost."

***

I had ended things with Tom. Not because I particularly wanted to, but because my conscience demanded it, so it was the season of Leonard Cohen again. He told me I had blindsided him and I had. I had just woken up and decided it was too much of a crime to continue to pretend, and hoped that letting him go would somehow absolve me of my sins. And so, I listened to *My Secret Life* and cried, and vowed I wouldn't get in another relationship again for quite some time. It was the hardest breakup, simply because he hadn't done anything wrong, and it wasn't right to keep him around, for he loved me so purely and I filtered that love into something dark, into a drug for my ego, a pitiful reassurance, a knowingness that I was valued. I was better than that betrayal and he was better off free, even if he didn't feel it.

I could never get used to breaking hearts, and I wished none of us had hearts, for it seemed careless for humans to have something so fragile beating beneath their chest or breast. I thought I'd feel a tremendous relief, but I only felt guilty and sad, and firm in the knowledge that I deserved the pangs of loneliness to follow.

I wondered if there'd come a day when Leonard Cohen couldn't fix my brokenness, and I'd have to flit to God. I was torn and twisted that Tom had waited for months for my return and that I had reassured him I only had seven weeks to go, the same day I told him it was over. And I thought of Owen, and how history repeats itself, and how Owen much more deserved the American breakup, and how Tom didn't.

I thought of Mum and Miami and showing her the Chelsea Hotel. I thought of how I wished everyone hadn't come to visit me, for I didn't deserve it. I thought of how I wished people didn't know I existed, didn't think of me, love me or look my way, how I shouldn't have come to America, and promised to return and leave someone hoping. The right thing never comes easy, and that's why millions of people wake up each morning comfortable with having chosen the wrong choice. Comfortable in their masked secrets, for being wrong and pretending it's right, will drive you mad one small drop at a time that you hardly notice at all. To be right when it feels wrong, will dowse you in some other emotion of an entirely different kind.

I knew the pain Tom was feeling, even if the only person to break up with me and break my heart, was the very man, who gave me the courage to end the relationships that weren't serving me. I thought perhaps my life was a punishment, perhaps life as a nomad, a rebel, a writer, a miserable woman who'd never settle down, would be a life of sacrifices and sorries and sad sounds.

My turbulent relationship with New York was rising and falling and I loved it as much as I hated it, and I was worried I'd return home empty and miss him. That the version of me here wasn't the version of me at home, and American me needed nothing, and English me needed everything. I was sure I had lost my mind, perhaps I was made up of multiple broken versions of myself and multiple survivor versions, the wounded child bobbing to the surface and disappearing again. Perhaps my mind was left in Bristol. Perhaps my mind was wrung out and left to dry on a clothing line, the bate on the hook at the end of the fishing line, perhaps it had oozed to nothingness when my Dad had left. Perhaps it was gone for good. Perhaps someone had flung it up to the moon and it rested there, perhaps nothing was real. New York and the taxis, and the streets and the bustle, and the emptiness and the loud and the quiet, the red and blue and the parked cars, NYPD sirens and Brooklyn brownstones would disappear and melt and wash away, down some plughole somewhere, and I'd be lying in Cornwall with a hole in my chest, having cut off everyone I'd left behind. But, I didn't want a place in anyone's heart, even if it meant being lonely, I couldn't bear it. I'd crave a spotlight and then convulse and contort in the warmth of the yellow hue and roll away, and catch a plane. I was far more comfortable in the clouds.

I was right, Leonard didn't suffice, and yet I called for God, and he wasn't there. I didn't deserve him either. God and happiness and Leonard had all escaped me.

I closed my eyes and I was back on the beach in Miami, pink and yellow streaking the sky, the ocean lapping blue. I was on the beach with my Mother. In New York, I had shouted at her at the NBA game and I didn't think I deserved her either. I didn't know what to do.

***

I was sinking. It was my mind. It was my sadness. I yearned to feel some sort of control in my spiral of doom. It was my need to be understood. It was the deep-seated desire to fuck off that seemed to have grown when I had left Owen, and only seemed to snowball since. It was that someone had to come to rescue me, for I seemed incapable of rescuing myself. I needed glue, a Band-Aid, a promise, a tangible wish. Perhaps I needed therapy.

I was glad I was in America. It may not have nursed me, but it breathed courage into me, bravery, it's where I wrote. I was a writer in America, I was brazen in America; I was independent in America. I had hope in America.

America. America. America. It was my toxic lover. I lived in America. I loved America. I needed America.

What America was, I was no longer sure. I had seven weeks to get a grip of myself, seven weeks to tape up any weakness, seven weeks to batten down the hatches and to buy shin pads and elbow pads and a hard hat helmet for my plummet through the sky before I crashed in a sad crumple into Heathrow arrivals.

I thought about being sick. Perhaps that would help. I thought about Tom. I was his sickness. I thought about Cody. He was mine. I thought about how I'd stopped going to the Intern excursions in December and it was February. How I was clumsy with time. How my Mother was here 2 days before, and now she was long gone, lost in the West Country somewhere on a farm or by the beach. How I broke Tom's heart. How I had pretended to be so many things for so many people, I'd lost sight of who the fuck I was. And how I didn't know where to find the answer to that. How I probably was going to watch Into the Wild the following day and eat candy, and cry.

***

"I loved you to the moon and back, but you're right, I didn't feel like your love stretched quite as far," Tom said.

And I thought it was beautiful and melancholic and poetic and true. And I cried. I balled and balled and balled, for he was right and there was nothing I could've done about it. Neither of us could change the amount of love we felt, and that's the thing, there's always someone who loves more and someone who can never quite love enough.

I wondered how much an Uber to the Brooklyn Bridge would cost, and if the price would matter if I hurled myself off. But my phone wasn't charged and neither were my headphones, and I'd probably just go and watch the stars, if there were any in this polluted land, and have a cigarette, and cry some more, and that was far easier from my bed. In the lonesome hours.

I forgot how the world stands still when you're going through a breakup. It always does. Steely stillness. A nothingness. A bottomless slowness. A teary-eyed silence. Deflated. All the air ever to have filled your lungs exhaled and released and broken. I understood I'd most likely be depressed everywhere I went. The next location would be far from winter in New York in the dark, it would be in the sun, with waves, where everything was bright and the light played tricks, where you almost mistook it for happiness. But even then, I'd panic and flutter and dive like a distressed bird into a window pane and knock myself right out cold, for the desperate fear of being trapped.

I walked through Prospect Park and Spring was bringing to shine through the trees, and I stopped to sit on park benches along the way, to smoke my stale cigarettes. Break up music blasting through my headphones which would routinely drop out and I'd look for them, pulling them out of leaves or from up under a bench, and I finally understood, this is what New York meant. And then I was walking again on concrete, sobbing as strangers passed me by, at least heartache proves you're alive.

***

I could hardly believe that it had only been a week and a half since I'd seen Cody. Since he'd given me a shell and kissed me. I felt as though I'd hardly seen him at all. This whole time. This whole stretch of America: Virginia, Rochester, Georgia. It was so hard to believe, I'd almost thought I'd made it up. I strained to remember him, when I last saw him a mere ten days before. It was hazy, almost black and white when I'd arrived and he'd picked me up from Savannah airport with a large grin, and beautiful eyes and carried my bags; when I said they were heavy, he said "Not really."

Oh how long ago it felt since he took me to Fort Pulaski, which I just had to google the name of, for I'd already forgotten it. Since he mucked around on my camera, I took snapshots of him with the cannon, with his sunglasses on and arms folded. I folded his clothes when he was at work and placed them on the bed since he ate my Skittles and I demanded he replace them. He gave me a great big "Mwah" of a kiss on my cheek each morning before work since he decided to come back to me after twelve-hour shifts and not his beach hut home. Since he took me fishing again, down a jetty with the sun burning hot, the yellow globe behind the clouds which were sinking toward the sea as dusk struggled to roll around. Since he drove me in his truck to the lighthouse and fought for permission to take me up. Since I climbed all those stairs, to reach the pink sunset at the top, only for the door to the deck to be jammed, and for him to hold my hand as I climbed towards the lens. Since he pinned me down with his strong arms and I wrestled playfully, since he kissed me for the first time since 2022, and came back to the motel black for all the grime of the arduous day had clung to his face.

Since I wrote him a letter with 26 reasons why I loved him on his 26th birthday. Since he brushed his teeth next to me and read in bed. How I tentatively rested my head on his stomach, and we fell asleep to Sex and the City or Creed or some action movie. I bought him surf boots for his birthday and watched as he tried on a wetsuit with the surf shop chick hitting on him. Since I zipped it up and unzipped it again. I watched him surfing the waves, with my camera, on the shore, sitting on his foreman's towel and talking to him about travel. Since we went to the Mexican restaurant, and the Wendy's, where he ashed in my fries. Where he'd strip off naked and talk to me, as if he wasn't naked at all, before he'd climb into the shower and throw on clothes and announce he was hungry, and we'd drive aimlessly as I turned snappy until he found someplace to go. Since he ordered pizza and ate it standing up, watching the television as I took off my shirt to eat mine because I couldn't spoil it with droppings off pizza toppings. Since I listened to music on the beach and chased the birds, and sat on a swing seat and listened to it creak and peer over my shoulder at the lighthouse and smile that he was on it, in it, on top of it. As he was me.

How he'd rubbed the small of my back at the bar, and told me he loved me. How I was beautiful. When he had asked me to cuddle him and I'd responded coyly, "Oh you want me to cuddle you?", and he retorted, "Oh yeah I forgot you were being mean." And how I hesitated and felt his arm against mine and how it'd always make my heartbeat. How I smiled and looked at him and said "Oh you like to be cuddled now?"

I flopped onto him, flinging my arms over his torso, and my leg over his legs and crushed him in comedic style, and how I caught a glimpse of his eyes lighting up with the smile he tried to hide, and then the page flick, and content hanging in the air. How he'd turned off a song on the radio in the truck after we'd been singing along because it'd reminded him of Madison. How I couldn't talk to him for the rest of the night after that, for I felt I'd never be good enough. How we'd lay side by side and then lay facing each other, how night after night we became closer, until one night, I was lying with my cheek pressed up to his chest, his head resting on my shoulder, and my arms around him and his around mine. I stroked his back shyly and he stroked mine hard, and how he kissed my neck and I felt like crying. How we started planting very small, very soft, almost not quite touching kisses on each other's lips, until we had to pull away and roll over and pretend that we didn't. Pretending we didn't feel the way we just felt. Pretending that the love was never there. For intimacy, for an embrace, the act of holding was something neither of us could endure. For in that moment, lying there skin to skin, holding each other as we felt the warm breath, was far too vulnerable for an affair.

And my brow furrowed as I wrote for I was completely and utterly perplexed how I could so simply forget. It felt now as if I hadn't seen him for years, as if I'd been without him the entire internship and I considered wholeheartedly the notion that I was eradicating him, compartmentalising him, shoving him in a box labelled, "does not exist". What a marvel, what a wonder, what an insane comprehension— the lengths of coping the brain turns to. How in a week and a half he'd texted me he missed me probably four times, but how I didn't believe he did. The next time I saw him, if I saw him at all, it would be to say goodbye as I waltzed off back to England.

How in a week and a half, I had seen my Mother and she'd already left. How in a space of ten days I had been in Georgia and New York and to Miami, walking the promenade in the heat with the crickets. To tacky gift stores and parasol lunches, to fairy lights wrapped around palm trees and swimming in a hot sea. With sharks. Lifeguards with a red flag and a purple flag and drinks by the hostel pool. Watching my Mum laze in an inflatable. And then to New York at a front-row NBA game, watching Saltburn with brie and bread and cider. Going to a comedy club and walking in the dark and the cold past the Chelsea Hotel. Showing her Dumbo and my office and Brooklyn, and the final bagel. How three days ago she was still here and now she was half the world away.

I hadn't straightened my hair since Cody had scrunched those curls. I didn't think I'd ever straighten it again.

***

I walked through Brooklyn on a sunny day, my coat too sticky hot, but I had tea in one hand and thought it too much of a fuss to carry the coat in the other. Winter seemed to have left us all at once. My boss had flown off to London without breathing a word to me and so I was left without any work and decided to walk two miles to Target. My days now as a Brooklyn bum were numbered. I left my headphones behind. I didn't want to drown out the noise. I craved to embody it. The wheels on the tarmac, the squeaks of the breaks of the yellow buses, the aeroplanes *soaring* overhead. The *clicks* of the cars locking and the birds in the bare trees *cooing*, the *toot toots* of impatient drivers and the far too often drawn out *honnnnnks*.

My tea turned cold in my hand. Microwaved tea often does. What a beautiful day, shadows casting the sun dazzled pavements. The sky is blue. It was as if a nutcracker had hit New York on the head, and Spring had come pouring out of the shell.

There was a makeshift book stool, somewhere between Nostrand and Atlantic Avenue, and I was compelled to stop and to look and to pick up and feel the books. To read the blurbs and to touch the spines. One or two I thought about buying.

I'd forgotten how much I enjoyed Brooklyn, and now I wasn't chained to Manhattan in cheap hostel rooms, I could finally breathe again. I could appreciate where I was. I was so busy walking and writing that I got lost, but the air felt fresh and I didn't care. The branches of the trees cast shadows over brownstones, over the arched windows and flat fronts. The sun bounced off the glass and I'd have to shield my eyes. I thought of the college girl who had longed to live here, and I'd pushed her aside. How easy it was to live in the middle of a dream, and to already be carving out the next.

***

The cider started tasting like I wished I had a cigarette, and then it was my last one, and then it started tasting like I'd be hungover. And like I was twenty-three, and like I only had six weeks left in the States, and like how leaving the States would hurt. It'd always hurt and I wished to figure out why. I had glass in my foot from where I'd accidentally smashed a vase in the night and didn't pick up all the pieces. I felt tired and everything mattered and nothing mattered at all.

I thought of Cody and Meave, and how they symbolised a bygone era. That I was in love with them both, for different reasons, and they were the two firmest friends I ever had. And that it felt like fate. How they were strings attached to Brockport. They were the sun, and I had felt their warmth, the first warmth for years. They had that golden glow, the heat that thawed the ice Owen had sewn. I only ever had room for them, and they'd grown, so, I meditated, and heavy heartedly wondered if one day they'd go.

***

I was heading to Boston. New York had eaten me alive, and I could no longer breathe. I had hidden in my room, slept with an

NYU student, and watched a Rangers game over a bowl of chilli with an Ice Hockey goalie in Long Island. I'd broken down to Cody and told him I was barely hanging on.

2:43 AM

Please come to Rochester. My apartment is waiting for you—it's yours. Just tell me you'll go.

2:51 AM

I can't stand to see you struggle. Go to my apartment, stay as long as you need.

3:38 AM

I'll send you money for whatever you need.

4:12 AM

I love you so much.

7:49 AM

I don't know what's ahead for us, but I know that I love you more than anything. I'd do anything for you, always.

4:03 PM

I want you here with me more than anything.

4:17 PM

We'll stay at the house, no hotels. You'll have the whole back porch, a big bed, and my desk if you need it. Whatever you want, I'll make it happen. Please, just come to me.

Who could've thought I'd be so tired?

I didn't know what I'd find in Boston or anywhere.

***

I met Cody for the last time, in South Carolina. I flew down, impatient to see him. I was always impatient, always wanting. It was his last day in Georgia and he was headed back to Rochester, to have a break before being sent to a different lighthouse, a different State.

The plane touched down in Myrtle Beach just before midnight. The air was thick with that Southern humidity, like walking into a wet wool blanket. I stood outside the terminal, chuffing my vape while awaiting a cab.

The motel I had booked was the type of place you'd find when you're not looking for comfort—just a bed and a door that barely locked. An abandoned vending machine whirred and the carpet stuck to my feet, cigarette burns in the sheets. I checked in, downed a Four Loko, and tried to sleep. But sleep wouldn't come, and every creak and shuffle outside the door made me weary. When Cody knocked sometime after 3 a.m., I nearly fell into him. His hoodie was soft, and he smelled like clean laundry and pine, a scent that felt out of place.

"Hey," he murmured, steadying me. His eyes flicked over my face, taking in the smudged eyeliner, and the way my hands trembled. "Rough night?"

I laughed bitterly. "Rough month."

He guided me inside, and I leaned into him, craving his warmth. We collapsed onto the bed and he turned on the TV. I drifted off to the sound of late-night commericals, his presence anchoring me in a way I didn't want to admit.

***

Sunlight pierced through the blinds like a blade, carving through my skull. My head throbbed, my mouth dry as sandpaper. Cody was already up, standing by the window, looking out at the world like it was a puzzle he couldn't quite solve.

"Surf's up," he announced, "You coming?"

I groaned, pulling the blanket over my head. "I'm dying."

He laughed, "Suit yourself. I'll be back soon."

And then he was gone before I could process that he had ever really been there, and I drifted in and out of sleep, waking only when he returned, dripping wet and grinning.

"Still dead?" he teased, tugging the blanket off me.

"Yes."

"Get dressed. I've got a surprise."

We ended up at the boardwalk, where he bought us tickets for the Ferris wheel. At the top, the world stretched out endlessly—blue sky meeting the ocean in a seamless horizon. Cody leaned back, watching me instead of the view.

"Better?" he asked, his voice soft.

I nodded, the tension in my chest loosening. For a moment, it was just us, suspended above the world.

***

"We should go," Cody said suddenly, as we walked back to the truck. "There's a spot in North Carolina. Great waves."

I didn't argue. He had that restless look again, the one that made it clear he wouldn't sit still for long. I glanced back over my shoulder, at the white sand, the beach I had so craved, but was too dejected to enjoy. Perhaps I was the only person ever to visit Myrtle Beach, without stepping a foot onto the beach itself.

He stopped at Taco Bell on the way out of town, promising it'd be quick. But minutes stretched into an hour, and when he finally returned, he was unbothered, sipping a soda like time meant nothing.

The drive north was long, the roads empty and endless. The sun hung low, casting a golden glow over the fields and trees. I watched the world blur past, the Deep South, the Bible Belt, the endless miles, the wee stops at the gas stations, the lack of conversation, the twitchiness, the numb bums, the road trip with oh so few words. Cody hummed along to the radio, tapping his fingers on the wheel. The air between us was low, not with tension, but something unspoken. I wanted to ask him what he felt, but the words wouldn't come.

As night fell, the road narrowed, flanked by trees that loomed like shadows, and all of a sudden the sky was slashed and torn, with streaks of red and radiating orange. The most magnificent sunset I had ever seen, and I viewed it only from the wing mirror, and my phone. And then, finally, we were in the Outer Banks, arriving at a beachside motel, the ocean a dark, and a gale roared, drowning out the waves beyond the dunes. Cody pulled me close in bed that night, his arm heavy around my waist. I felt his heartbeat against my back, steady and reassuring. Sometimes we didn't need words, I don't think we were ever very good at it, but back rubs, sighs, and sleepy cuddles sufficed.

***

Morning came with the sound of gulls and the smell of salt. Cody was up before me, eager to find a wetsuit. I tagged along, still groggy. It was too early for any store to be open, so we drove to a pier to kill time, but that was closed too, so it was McDonald's and dispense drinks, and tired eyes, and my rolling dreams. And then when the dreams rolled into 8 am, we washed up into a tiny surf shop.

The girl behind the counter lit up when she saw Cody. She was all long legs and sun-bleached hair, leaning in too close as she showed him the latest gear.

"You surf a lot?" she asked, twirling a lock of hair around her finger.

Cody shrugged, modestly. "Yeah, I guess."

I stood there, invisible. When he finally settled on a suit, I handed him a pair of surf boots. "Happy late birthday."

His eyes softened. "You didn't have to."

"I wanted to."

But, Cody decided the waves were, "Crappy", after plunging into the cold water, and rushing back out again. He didn't much want to be in North Carolina, and I didn't much have a say, so we packed up in the afternoon and headed for Virginia. I retracted further into myself when I realised he was hellbent on dropping me off in New York, wanting to rush back to Rochester, he seemed to be pushing us along. I was a truck buddy for the road, and I had hoped to be something else entirely. I had hoped for a holiday, for a Georgia reimagining, but that didn't seem to be on his agenda.

***

Virginia was quiet. Betty-Lou was at work, and the trees which had been bare over Thanksgiving had started blooming. I hoped one day I would have a big red-brick house in the countryside, with chickens and cats and all the lovely things Betty-Lou had. Cody slept through most of the visit, and seemed disinterested in me all together. I was unsure if he even wanted me there, I certainly didn't get invited to bed. I played cards with Memaw again,

"He's always been like this," she said, shuffling the deck. "Always looking for something."

I nodded and smiled, but I thought I might cry.

When I fell asleep, fully clothed, on top of the duvet, Cody underneath, I still didn't think that when I awoke, it would be to him shaking me awake, at the crack of dawn, as the house slept.

"Come on, the truck is packed. Let's go."

By the time we hit New Jersey, Cody was itching to move again. But I dragged him into the city, determined to make the most of it. Times Square was overwhelming—lights, noise, and people everywhere. We ended the night at a rooftop bar, overlooking the Empire State Building. The air was cool, and the city sparkled below us. A photographer offered to take our picture. We posed, arms around each other, the skyline behind us. When he asked if we wanted to buy it, we shook our heads.

Later, as we stumbled back to the subway, I felt a pang of regret. I realized I didn't have any photos of us. Nothing to prove we were here, that this had happened.

We planned to explore more the next day, but Cody was restless. By morning, he was ready to leave. At the New Jersey subway, we stood in silence. The air between us crackled with things unsaid, and then it all came out at once.

"You sure?" I asked.

He nodded. "Yeah. It's time."

I wanted to argue, to beg him to stay. But I knew it wouldn't matter.

He pulled me into a hug, his arms tight around me, and then the hug turned into a grip, and all of a sudden we were frozen in time, crying, gulping, deep breathing, red-eyed. Unable to move from that embrace, a reluctance to let go, and how I wished the last few days had been different. I wished he didn't always wait until we were parting to love me. How I needed him when he was with me, and how he didn't need me at all— until it was, "Goodbye."

Oh, how he always slipped through my fingers, how I never managed to claw back the Brockport time. I think he'd always been rushing away from me, and I'd always been rushing towards him, and that's why it never seemed to work.

"I never stopped loving you," I sobbed into his neck.

"I love you with all my heart."

APRIL 2024

MAY 2024

I got back with Tom, he was the only thing I had left.

JUNE 2024

If I could wake up and be anywhere, I'd be in America with the sun on my back. I'd have returned from a trip with Meave, with palm trees and sweat beads, with a passport stamp and a belly full, and money in my bank. I'd feel healthy and nimble and able. I'd feel free.

The sun was bending, echoing along the sides of the road, the hedges high. This is Cornwall, this is now, this is the walk, this is trying to flee. This is following the trail of Cody in my eye, following him in July yawns. And I had to keep walking, because if I walked it was not true. If I walked it would be a lie. The more I walked the less likely I was to die. The more I walked the more I would find him there. He'd be by the creek, skipping stones, and he'd turn around and embrace me, and I wouldn't have to set him on flames, and watch as he burnt and blew away.

I sat on a twisted trunk, from a fallen tree, and looked out upon the fields, feeling the droplets of the sky beginning to crack. Wearing my coat in the wettest summer of a hundred years. I hoped I had many more years of light, of sitting in a field in the evening before evening became night. The wind blew the far field white, long grass waltzing like waves. I wanted to share the field with someone, and maybe if he knew, he'd come. Only love would feel the weight of a gut punch.

And there he was, twitching his ears, a brown neck above the grass. A stag, looking back at me. And I trundled up through the field, wading waist-deep. Maybe if I got to him he'd stay with me. If he let me approach him, I'd let him fool me, for only fools are happy. And then I turned back, for the whimsical in the distance is just whimsy. Not even a touch is worth breaking that. And maybe if I sat with this rough bark against my pink skin for long enough, in a hundred years my wellies would still be placed, rubber in the rough.

AUGUST 2024

As I walked to the station in late August rain, I realised I missed New York. I didn't know if it was because the seasons had changed and I was back in the crisp of Fall, or if enough time had transpired for me to feel as if I was never there at all.

I'd move to Wiltshire, to commute to Bath. I had moved in with Tom briefly, better job opportunities, but the grass wasn't so green. Out of 180 applicants, I'd been successful and landed a 9-5 for a prestigious study abroad company. It was my job to look after a cohort of Americans, on their semesters abroad to Bath. Circular, I guess? Forever chasing that Brockport dream?

2017

I guess I didn't feel entirely kind and whole and open when it was a strange evening in the North of England when I envisioned the sky to be grey even though I couldn't see it. Perhaps it was that night, when the dusk had rolled in on the drive and all the buildings seemed blue, that I realised I didn't like goodbyes. Maybe it was the tinted windows which made the council flats seem bluer or my embarrassment at having been driven there. I'm not sure, but something tells me it was that night which kicked me in the stomach and cursed me to always fear goodbyes. It seemed to prove that nothing was permanent and everything was temporary, and you don't have time to catch your breath before a thunderous wave of life hits you square in the face, stinging your cheeks with salt and shock.

I thought that was my ultimate low, being sixteen years old in the North of England. I thought of the Angel of the North as I only grew sadder, and sadder still was that the girl in the car didn't know it wasn't the ultimate low, it was just a teaser for the life to follow. It was the first low of many, a glaringly obvious flashlight, a light so strong in such a thick blanket of darkness that it attracted moths to bounce around and ultimately die in its spotlight. Though the moths weren't moths at all, they were just other lows, waltzing about with itchy wings, and the light was my soul, and they all dropped dead in it.

"Is it up here?", Jane asked.

I didn't like her much and I didn't know why, perhaps because she was put together, and rich. I was taking her to somewhere crumbling, somewhere people like her turned her nose up at, or clicked their tongues out of pity. I should've liked her for she let me stay, and I was friends with her daughter Lola, and I thought Lola was a lot cooler than me, so that math would suggest her Mum was cool too. At least kind, for driving me there from their posh village, for "rescuing" me. Though I want it to be plain, terribly clear, irrefutably obvious, that I was spiteful for having been rescued, and it wasn't my idea at all. I have always been someone who likes to be in control of my whereabouts and happenings. If I had a therapist they'd probably tell me that's because I hadn't had much control in my life. I wonder how my imaginary therapist would justify the fact that for someone who likes to be in control, I always happen to find myself most definitely not in control, and most certainly enveloped in some sort of chaos. I probably wouldn't like their imaginary answer, and that's why I don't have one, as well as NHS waiting lists and not being able to afford privatised care. Then again, this is England, who can afford anything at all? Lola's Mum, that's who.

"Yeah", I replied, and my voice was quieter than I had expected, specks of rain ran down the windows, and I felt as small as one of those sulky drops. There was a click and then window wipers started and we turned a corner and the car started to slow and all I could hear above my heart thumping were the wipers swiping, slow and steady, rhythmic, heavy. That's exactly how I walked up to the door too, and into the lobby, and up the lift with my silent companions, my head hung in shame: slow and steady, rhythmic, heavy. My feet had dragged us to the welcome mat, and I could smell patchouli oil and misplaced guilt. I hesitated a moment and prayed to God he wasn't there. I prayed to God he was spending the night with his latest girlfriend. I prayed to God that He and he would both forgive me because I had spent much of my life sometimes not being able to tell the difference between the two. I prayed out of love and not out of fear, for if he were there the police would be called and then all would be lost. I didn't know how I'd be able to live with myself, and perhaps that's why the keys shook in my hands as I raised them to the lock.

***

We'd gotten the bus to the North, all the way from Cornwall—it was long and terrible— something like fourteen hours, and at sixteen that translates to a mini lifetime. My brother was fourteen and pressed his face to the window when we passed Bristol and took a picture of the Suspension Bridge. My sister was eighteen and we must've been in a thwarted sister phase for we didn't speak much, and my Mother spent the journey craving a fag, (it was before the days of Snuss and way before either of us quit fags).

At Leeds, the bus stopped for fuel and we ran out, lit up, and were shouted at by the conductor who had a Yorkshire accent which seemed to make the shouting that much more scary, so we ran back on and stayed sat and uncomfortable for the remainder of the journey. I had the grand idea to move to the furthest city in

England because I wanted to attend the best college for Film and TV production. At the time, it was the first grand idea of many grand ideas to come and possibly the worst one I had ever had. Then again, if I hadn't persuaded my Mum to allow me to move in with my Dad, or persuaded my Dad to accept me turning up out of the blue quite a few years overdue, nothing else in this story would've happened. And so that bus, crawling up the motorway, slow and steady, rhythmic heavy, was a catalyst of sorts. Maybe that's why it felt so terrible.

When we arrived, it was dark, and college kids were already drunk, in short skirts and sportswear, in caps, and fake tan, shouting and sprawling about. I felt grown up to know I lived here now. After devouring a cigarette or two, I tried to walk more grown up, past the gaggles of drunks, thinking to myself that in two years I'd be allowed to swig a bottle of Echoe Falls in public and squeal loudly too. We lugged several laundry bags, plastic and heavy, fraying white and red. My Dad met us with a smile, and I can't remember the course of our conversations, only he noted I was smoking now, so I offered him a rollie, and we climbed onto a bus, and ended up inside his council flat. We were all pretty hacked off and tired, and he showed us the new mahogany furniture he'd purchased when a factory down in Cornwall gave him £100,000 for doing his back in. My sister and I shared a room and argued about snoring. My brother wet his bed that night, and my Mum cleaned it up so Dad would wake none the wiser in the morning. It was paramount that he didn't know. Which is funny, because my brother is a Royal Marine now, the opposite of a bed-wetting boy. And, I'm manic depressive now which is far from the girl with stars in her eyes, so I guess we're both reformed.

My family only stayed for a couple of days. We got the whole Dad-special tour of the city and got scammed by a psychic reader in a gypsy wagon. Another one of my grand ideas. Seemingly, everyone goes along with these ideas, though they usually result in a loss of money and an unhappy ending. We'd also ventured to a tacky seaside town and ate fish and chips on the beach. There's a photograph of my brother and Father with their fish and my brother's hair is blowing and they both look pained. I'm not sure if they'd look happier or more pained if they knew that was the last time they'd see each other for almost ten years, and probably ever. The dread started kicking in when it was time for them to go and for me to stay. Dad and I dropped them off at the airport, and we waved them goodbye before completing the journey back to the flat in a peculiarly loud silence. Perhaps he wasn't a fan of goodbyes either. A lot rests on goodbyes, a lot more than people realise.

2019-2022

I hate goodbyes. Perhaps that's why I stayed. There seemed to have been a hundred reasons to stay, all of which evaded me now. The days in the dark, the days in bed, I guess they were good excuses to stay in my head, to disappear into my mind. I had stayed in that space for so long that even though years had elapsed, a new dawn dragging with every tide, a new wish upon each full moon, a new stone to weigh down an old pocket, I was still there, in the mirror, in the insults, in the bed. I had stayed in that space for so long, that I was sure that's where part of me would always belong. I guess you can't just escape a betrayal. It's not the type of thing you can avoid, a slap of the knees and a "Right, I'm off now", and a swift opening and closing of a door won't quite cut it. It's not that simple, at first you *run*, you run for your fucking life.

You run as though if you stopped running, you'd be hauled into the tower of London and racked, fucked, and poked before they shove your head through a loop, kick the stool and lick their lips as they watch you hang. But, running never works, and you willingly run back. Everyone asks you why, and you blame it on love. And then, the next time you escape, you're too wounded to run so you jog. A steady pace, a thorn in your side, blisters on the soles of your feet. Naturally, the finish line seems too far off, and it's easier to quit. So, you double back. The third time the taste of freedom comes calling, one of your legs is already broken, and so you limp, you limp and limp and limp, feeling deserving of the pain shooting through that fucked up leg with every step you take. But, you're slow. You're clumsy, and this time he comes for you, he does not wait. He fetches you, snatches you, a fist in your hair, yanks you on home, and snaps your good leg clean off.

In the morning, the rain falls in soft splatters. Drizzle. You watch it through the window, for you're not allowed outside. The doors are bolted, and the neighbours have turned their backs. Months go by like that, slow and steady, rhythmic, heavy. You forget why you ever tried to leave because he nurses you, he kisses you, he grinds above you, sliding in and out of you, he owns you as you fade away. You used to stare at the engagement ring, but now you stare off into the void, into the nothingness, it's safe there, you can't feel his breath there. You can't see anything, except the hazy face of someone else, as blood fills under his fingernails. He examines you closely, but you aren't even there. It's funny how months turn to years, and your eyes become dull. Even when you smile, they blink lifelessly, gazing upon a vast blanket of black. He smothers the hope from you as he chokes you. Your pink skin is white where his fingers dig. Then one morning, he forgets to lock the door and you're crawling. Carpet fibres and friction burn, and you drag your broken body onto the street, where the air is warm. There's soft music in the breeze and you realise not all is coated in dust, and an aeroplane leaves a white streak through the blue way above.

You can hardly feel the frog in your throat of a scratchy goodbye, you can only feel the gravel as it shaves your elbows and scrapes your knees. And then a shadow looms above and the last thing you think about is you as a kid. You don't feel the tear as it rolls from your sunken eye, but you feel the shame in your stomach for you didn't protect them and you don't know why. And then you're back again, he might as well have nailed you to the bed. At least he gives you a choice between a fist and a knife and you cry, and you can't feel pain anymore, and you choose the fist and he goes to work between your legs, and you don't know how you ended up like this. You can't tell the difference between hot flesh and the cold of death, and you overdose, and you pray it's over, only it's not. They save you, and you curse them and you're doomed to the pit of hell, living the same day over and over again. But then again, time keeps moving, it keeps ebbing and flowing, and you're shrinking and you're growing. You close your eyes, receiving the spit and wrath and hate, only to open them and those long dreary years have passed, and you've not spoken to him for two winters. You're crying on your bed, hunched up, face wet, your pillow between your gritting teeth, stuffing your mouth shut, as you fucking wail because you never forget.

You can't hold down a job, or a relationship, and friendships waltz on a revolving door, and you gain weight and you lose weight, you gain yourself and you lose yourself, and men are ugly and sex is scary, and no one knows who you truly are, except the prick who bent you and broke you and twisted you into an entirely new shape. You resent being a woman, for you resent being prey. You despise your body, for you feel the greedy eyes and the sweaty palms and you feel the hulking gaze of every man, and you smell the way he wants to bend you and contort you, and drill holes in your shoulders, so he can thrust you about on the end of a string. Any raspy breath sends you spiralling, and you lie there still, with a boyfriend you've had for quite some time, one whose kind, and you hate him. You hate him as he moves above you, and your eyes roll back and you're someplace else. You only trust that women are safe, and yet they make you sad because all you see is oppression and sexism and violence and thousands of years of rape and battery every time you look at them, and the world is empty, the world is cold, and all is lost. That's what they take from you, the good out of everything. The relatability is gone, the normalcy squashed, and who you were before any of it ever started is someone you call to, but someone you'll never see again, for they are dead than you that exist now. They take your soul and leave a shell.

The worst thing about leaving and staying gone is that the longer between now and then, the clearer you see. You realise that not only did they break you down to the bare bones of who you are, you're rebuilt. You're rebuilt meaner and uglier, angrier and entitled, spoilt and seething and unforgiving. You're rebuilt into a more broken version of them. Their brokenness is loud and yours is quiet. Their hatred is projected outwardly whilst yours shreds inwardly.

It takes a lot of love to hate so hard. Their DNA has become yours and you hate those who attach themselves to you, you look down on them for not being able to see the evil that festers in your heart and plagues your soul and soils your veins and rots your mind, and yet you desperately need them, and in moments of clarity you wonder if you've become the abuser, you see what they saw and you feel what they felt, only you don't act on it, you just brood and bury and burn. Your reflection changed somewhere along the way and you don't know how to let go, for you've been robbed, beaten and left for dead. You just want someone to understand you, to know you, to have been through what you've been through, but who has? Who'd have the stomach to know? Who could you even tell, and if you did find someone, would they look on with judgement and scorn? Would those who love you collapse under the weight of sorrow if they were to cut you open and hold your heart which beats with broken epiphanies?

But, you weren't always like this. You used to be young, and brave. You used to be kind and whole and open, excited and naive and beautiful and glowing. You were somebody entirely whole before they decided to snuff you out.

I hate goodbyes. Perhaps that's why I stayed. There seemed to have been a hundred reasons to stay, all of which evaded me now.

SEPTEMBER 2024

Everything seemed to be a blur, and that's just the way things had always been. One big blur, like a tornado, or dusty specs: in fact, prolonged and consistent enough to be dusty specs—a tornado is too bold, too striking, life isn't as such.

I was reading The Bell Jar under a dusky lamp in my boss' spare room. I was homeless. And I realised reading wouldn't cut it, I was back on the writing wagon—

I digress.

My dusty specs. You see, sometimes I take them off and clean them on some cheap fast fashion jumper sleeve, and pop them back on to see trees and seas, to see colours and plasmas and glaring adventures. Sometimes, the dusting off isn't so kind.

I was raped. I then hopped on a train to Bath and bounded into the office late, with a smile and niceties, and then was hauled off to Oxford for a residential, and caught a train right back to Bath to catch a flight to Copenhagen. Whilst my chest ached and my heart lurched.

Being raped isn't great, obviously—neither is being strangled. Try it homeless. Only a week earlier I had fled Tom because he'd been making weird contorted AI porn of my friends for two years, and I discovered a trove of photos whilst ordering a kebab on his phone.

So, that already was pretty shit, those specs were already suitably dusted. I was homeless in a different city, working remotely, and decided on a girl's night to shake my woes. The next thing I knew, I woke up in a hospital and the police seized my clothes. I didn't even have time to realise how fucked that all was until they were swabbing my vagina and body-mapping my injuries, and then it was only 48 hours until I was back in the office with coffee and students and bookings and pleasantries. But, he was in prison and they were preparing a trial. And, I was sleeping in a very nice, middle-class bedroom in a house big enough to have its own driveway, with baked apples for dessert. If that doesn't prove that life lacks a whole lot of seriousness, then I don't know what does.

I told Cody and at first, he was hellbent on killing the guy with his bare hands, and then he was hellbent on buying me a pink gun, and when that didn't cut it, he was hellbent on marrying me.

"Do you need me to come? Drop the charges, and I'll come over and handle him myself."

But, I think he'd always been hellbent on the latter:

"I love you more than words can say. Come to me, marry me. I'll buy your ticket right now. I can't stand the thought of you feeling unsafe ever again."

He continued like that all night, and into the next day:

"I miss you. I'm so sorry for what you've been through—you're incredible, and it breaks my heart to know someone hurt you like that. I'm so grateful you're safe. Come to America and marry me. I love you more than anything."

***

I was on my period and my stomach hurt, and I had taken up vaping again because fags are hard to pop out for when you're staying with the deputy dean. I'd switched out vaping for cigarettes three months prior, because I went on a health kick, as ironic as that seems.

I was five weeks into my new swanky graduate job, designing, organising and hosting the social and cultural program for Americans enrolled in a prestigious study abroad company. And here I was, bleeding in a very nice bedroom, at 10.44 pm with Oxford for a week stretching out in front of me. And then Copenhagen after that, and then a series of court dates and blurry-eyedness. I was surprised I hadn't had a complete breakdown — unless I was in the midst of one already. Perhaps a breakdown doesn't look like it does in the movies, perhaps it's working 10 days in a row with detectives and officers and rape specialists and sexual health practitioners calling me, and local news channels flashing images of my rape scene cordoned off, without me even remembering where it had happened. Perhaps it's listening to Joan Armatrading and eating baked apples out in the sticks, and writing about rape so colloquially.

***

I was on a bus to Oxford, with rain specs spritzing the front window. There was a dull ache in my stomach, and I was listening to Noah Kahan, and I couldn't believe that when I saw him live in London with Meave, that was the last time I'd feel any sense of normalcy, and seeing your favourite American folk singer with your favourite person, pissed on a £40 bottle of Chardonnay in London is anything but normal. She was in Boston, watching a Red Sox game. I longed for her. I longed for my American boy, and I thought of all the buses I had ever taken, and all the bags he had helped me carry on board, or put below. He was with me now, his Marlboro bag travelling in the under-bus storage as we cruised along rough British roads.

I couldn't feel anything except a meek despondency, a week ago I was waking up to a day that would come to choke me in the night. I had texted Meave in the club,

"I have just bought 15 tequilas to try and feel something but I feel nothing."

If I felt anything at all, I probably wouldn't be on a bus to Oxford.

***

15 hours later and I was still on shift. Amid an Oxford welcome disco, where they were blaring Murder on the Dance Floor. I thought of Saltburn, and I thought of my week, and I thought that one week ago today I hadn't even been raped and beaten and I was surprised at how I did it. Cody messaged me and asked how I was doing. I told him I was sad. He asked why. I never wanted to tell anyone I was sad again.

Meave was somewhere deep in America, and I wished I was deep somewhere else. My headphone wire was temperamental and I was back in the Oxford faculty suite, in bed, with a wire which kept pausing my music, and I wondered what the fuck was the point?

Cody had posted a photo of him leaving the island, he'd been in Michigan, slaving away since July, and it was September. I ogled at him, and the more I looked at his basketball hat grin, a flurry of waves behind him, his arms around two men I didn't know, the further away he seemed to disappear, until he was a spec in my mind, a spec on the phone, and a spec in the world, a tiny dot in the too vast of a planet, hurling backwards. *Hurling. Hurling. Hurling.*

I was going to go to the Bodleian Library, to a Kafka exhibition over the coming days. How I hurt like Kafka, how I bled like a poet, how clumsy my words. I read The Bell Jar on the bus to Oxford in the rain, not even Sylvia knew my pain. I wondered if everyone knew I was sad or if I masked it well, and the smoke alarm in the Oxford room blinked, and I exhaled a watermelon puff, and I didn't know how I ever preferred vapes over fags.

I signed off on a tenancy, £850 a month for a room in a house share, more than half my paycheck. I was sick and hungry, and tired, exhausted and contorted. I wish I had a bath, I'd drown myself, but all I could do was look at that blinking light instead.

I hoped Cody would save me before it was too late, but my childhood affinity with Romeo and Juliet warned otherwise. The prospect of love was a strange one. I was no longer sure if love had brought us this far, or if it was the continual fear of being alone. He wanted to get married, and flooded my phone with an array of compliments and adorations, gushing over babies and pregnancy, matrimony and 'Merica. We'd set a date for December and then he blew cold, pearly snowflakes cracking to ice blew bruised where he once stood, broken white butterflies with tears in their wings, they used to glide and now they faltered. Sombre snowflakes on a September day. Up in the dark, in the sky, on a plane to Copenhagen, I was tired, surprised by how the chill trailed after me.

He'd gone to Rochester, and Rochester meant Madison, and Madison meant sex and second choices and sentiments. Our paths were steering away from each other, mine headed towards heights and hopes and half aspirations. His towards some other destiny. I didn't feel as miffed as I had done before, I was anti-men and anti-Christ, and closed my eyes as my lids hung heavy, and dozed to a different, dreary dream.

OCTOBER 2024

I poured a glass of Merlot and laid back, the lamp off, the candles burning, the snug hue engulfing me on the bed with springs in my back. It was a good room, a big room in Bath. Posh, swanky Georgian-stone Bath. I was back again. I had the attic room with skylights, moss blotting the chimneys and a sun-stretched view. I had my toilet with a scuff on the mirror, and I'd already decorated it. Tom had his house for two years and had never decorated it.

I had virtually no money even though I worked all the time. I wasn't much better off than I was in New York. Oh skyscraper, cold-bitten, grey, vast New York. Magic on my tongue, or is it the Merlot?

My cheeks were damp and I realised I'd been crying. It was my first weekend in over a month in which nothing strange or twisted or dark had happened. I'd walked to Tesco for no good reason other than to buy milk for my coffee. Then again, I guess that is a good reason. I could've had my coffee black, but I wanted to get up and do something. I no longer knew what it was to be still. Mania had run away with me, anything to survive.

The BBC released an article stating we were the second most miserable country in the world, only beaten by Uzbekistan. I didn't much like the BBC since they'd blasted my rape scene on Spotlight News without my permission. Everyone who had tuned in knew I was raped behind some bins in front of a BetFred before I did. So, the BBC must equate the world simply to the Western world, because there is no way that the U.K. is more miserable than Lebanon, Palestine, Ukraine or the starving and dying populations in Africa. And, if we were, then that says all you need to know about Britain.

I was finally out of the office and my phone was silent, no ISVAs and police and court advisors. I texted both Tom and his Mum to return my car which was on his property and both had blocked me. Digitally raping my friends, violating me and being a dirty pervert didn't cut it. He had to steal my first car too. My five-year windswept road buddy who had ferried me to Owen's in our first stretch of dating, had moved me in and out of uni and had whizzed me around the winding country roads.

But, I was alive and breathing, breathing vapes because I guess when you're fucking slapped sideways by life, quitting vapes for three months no longer holds up and you're back to that poisonous *inhale* and *exhale*. But, I bought 50-factor sun cream alongside my milk. So, hopefully, that'll counteract the wrinkles. Then again, if I wrinkle that'll keep men away from me.

Cody had been messaging me a lot over my fucked up month, mostly to let me know he was serious about marrying me:

"I'm serious about marrying you. Get over here and start having my kids."

"Once we're married, you're going to be attached to me in ways you can't even imagine—like an invisible cord between us."

"I'm going to make you a mother."

"Come to America so I can give you kisses."

"I was planning to have you pregnant and settled by February."

"Marry me… right now… signed, sealed—you're mine. I mean it, so if you're ready, let's make it official."

So we started the process, and yet I still didn't truly believe him. I don't think I'd ever truly believe any man again. But, I thought that the worst thing that could happen is that it didn't happen. And it hadn't happened a few times before. So, I said I would marry him (for the hundredth time) because I couldn't truly apprehend what it would be like not to love him, and we agreed we'd do it in March, *"What makes you so certain now when you weren't before?"*

"It's the way our relationship has developed, the deeper talks we've had about what really matters. And honestly, there's no one else like you."

"I'm in for March, but it has to be in Vegas, all tacky and over the top. That's my only condition."

But I sure as shit wasn't going to be tied to anyone by an invisible chord. Not even an American cowboy. Women are tied to sugar and spice and all things nice. Our strength is our invisible chord. Maybe no one had ever told him that.

***

I wanted to run but I was wearing long black boots which were torn from the soles. I wanted to run but I didn't have the energy to run. I was too thick, too slow, too beat down, too pummelled into the pavement to pick up the pace, to sprint, to race. I thought of my Dad in London before I was born, punching out every wing mirror on the side of the road, and I thought I would too if my knuckles weren't so soft, if I weren't so tender. If my closed fist didn't reek of femininity. Being female was too furious— to punch was too futile. It wouldn't cause any weight, only a splintered rage, and blood would run thick and they'd herald me a hysteric.

I wanted to scream at men but they'd never care to listen, their black eyes would never blink, only glisten. My nerves were shot, my wrath neigh. All I could do to rectify any small part of myself was to get home as quickly as I could, drown myself in Merlot and write with fast, fucked off fingers as quickly as I could. A merciless attempt to self-exorcise, to yank the black from my soul and to knot it around manhood's neck, throttling the violence from their throats, bursting their Adam's apples, as if that were the only antidote.

Cody appeared to send me photos of strung-up pigs and fleshy meat. He was in Costa Rica, his second trip there in a couple of months, to surf. England hadn't seen him, neither had I.

"That's dysentery materialised", I typed.

I warned him to be cautious, knowing how easily things could go wrong. In the Philippines, I'd eaten some bad meat, and it ended up killing off all the good bacteria in my stomach. I reminded him of all the tests I had done: Celiac, Bowel Cancer, Diabetes, Chrones— and how they hadn't found the answer.

"What about sexiness, do they test for that?"

"No."

I was the stung-up pig with my fleshy meat, and fat-fingered men would caress my snout and fuck my mouth. Women are the meat and men prowl the market streets.

Not even the men you marry know the weight you carry, and the rain came hammering down. Down, down, hard and heavy on the skylights, and I shoved them shut. I lit my candles, pulled up the duvet and choked into a dead sleep, only reassured that no man was there, in the yellow hue of my bedroom, no man would hear me breathe, or hear me weep, or watch me sleep, defecating my pink, perfect, sheet.

***

Despair is a blackboard, life is the chalk, and it scratches in skeletal shivers, it drags in a deadbeat stretch. Frustration scratches along in chipped-off pallid quakes, and above the man shakes as he scribbles in faith.

Fiction splinters and fact falls in ash. The eye bags are embedded, and the days are pathetic, and what was known is poetic, and what's to come is hypothetic. The chalk is heavy, and your life is a lie. The winter sun has hung and the tears dry, and if you blink, none spill. You always feel full but the seams are yet to burst, and the picture you have drawn is a thorn. The petals are the chalky crumbles.

You want to climb high so you can weep and merge and absorb the view. You want to float in cold Cornish waters, ebbing grey, the waters which wade in and drag out against stormy rocks and charcoal blues. Your Grandpa is dead, he has been for quite some time. You lost him when you were drowning in the depths of disease, riddled with a man who wouldn't let you be.

Now the man you love doesn't love himself, and will never see you as sentient and savvy and small, and he comes from grills and autumn leaves, and redwood trees. He comes from smoke and you choke, and the days are long and the nights are short in your Dickensian fantasy. Nothing is real, everything is real, and there is something in your eye, something heavy in your mind.

Blindness rolls blurry. I stayed because I thought Tom was kind.

He never apologised. He left me in a cold sweat. He never apologised, and my writing hands turned old and gnarly, and I could see the liver spots emerging, and the age growing. I thought he was kind. I thought Owen was kind and Cody, and perhaps Cody wasn't kind, he wasn't mine, he was married when we met, and he never apologised. And I wrote Owen a love letter long ago, and I said sorry. What is to be sorry, to be sorrowful, to be woeful, to be wrong? I am sorry, for I was wrong. I was wrong about them, all of them. I was wrong about myself and the world, the world spun wrong, spun and spawned and scorned and sworn.

And the tears retracted—up the cheeks, in shame and salt. Grit was in your eye, the grit of loneliness and sunken people, shadow figures with sullen, sunken homesick scowls. Silky soldiers retreating into milky pools, for the eyes are strong and to feel was too strong for the weak. Stronger still was the urge to resist such a flow, for if it flowed freely and ferociously the tears would never stop flowing, until you were completely hell bound and drowned. I was turned away. To face the weight of the world would be to break, but I craved to break, I urged to break, I needed to break to be repaired, and because I was not broke, all I could do was choke. I choked because I thought he was kind.

If it were Owen I would've crawled back, because to crawl back is to omit the pain. Forgiveness is easier than hatred, and I couldn't hate, but how I wish I could. Tom, I thought you were kind. I thought you were kind, damn you for not being kind. You knew you'd never see me again, and you couldn't even pretend you were kind.

Heavy lies, empty goodbyes. I missed the freedom of expression, of countries, spices, elephants in the road, string lights, greasy burgers in sodden wrappers, secrets in dim lights. I missed feeling something other than flesh and bones. I missed what it's like to breathe, to breathe after a long cold, a breath in and a breath out. I missed Frat parties in the snow and mulled wine, and tentacles on a plate in Spain. I miss the dust in the sky, the heat. England is grey, and it always rains. Everyone's operating in pain. No one understands except for Mum, and one day she'll be gone. The thoughts are gone, and the well wishes are gone, and the stars are gone, and the day has come, and the day has gone, and the night appeared and disappeared, and no one cares, except for Mum.

Autumn leaves and zapped dreams, and sticky sap running from the tree, even nature bleeds.

"Are you spiritually aligned?", I asked him.

"No, are you?"

"No, I've been writing for three years and I was closer before I even started."

"What does that mean?"

It means I'll break alone, whilst waiting for an apology which will never come. I am exhausted by strength and anger, and I will sit and wait for an apology which will never come.

***

NOVEMBER 2024

The aurora borealis stretched pink across my skylights, purple brimming behind the clouds, on a random Thursday evening in mid-October, late. It was impossible to feel glum in a candle-lit attic room with ribbons of colour obstructed by stars and clouds. I slept with my blinds rolled up. I slept knowing the tides were turning, and that life was burning.

I wanted to cut loose. I wanted to fly free, over mountains, over the moon.

I wanted to dance. I wanted to dance loudly, and bravely, and brashly. I wanted to shake it off with a big grin, a cheesy grin that stretches and envelopes. I wanted to spin and jive and sway and play. I wanted to catch a plane somewhere far away and feel the warm sand on the soles of my feet. I wanted to stretch under the hot sun and run.

I hoped Cody would hurry up and marry me. I didn't have room for anybody else, but he was always running to everybody other than me. Perhaps that's why I was born to be a love poet, born to bleed. I tried to sleep, to cool the rushing thoughts, but a line from The Banshees of Insherin rattled in my head, and it wouldn't stop rattling, "Well, there goes that dream."

***

News broke the next morning that Trump had won the 2024 election, beating Kamala Harris. Had Harris won, the world would have welcomed the first female president of the United States, a woman of colour pathing a new dawn, a new era. But America had chosen the weight of history over the courage to begin anew. Donald Trump: 47th president of the United States.

DECEMBER 2024

The sky was orange, the waves a steely blue, lapping, drawing away with the flames and stretching back in again. Shadows stretched across the sand from dusky figures, hands in pockets, lonesome, wandering. I closed my eyes and I could see him there. I held onto his hand and told him I hated that I had to wait so long to see him again. It escaped my notice that my cheeks were wet, and if I hadn't looked to him I would never have looked to God. It seemed so unfair that I'd always have to wait so long. How raw the melancholy, how real the ache, how bruised I felt each time I opened my eyes to find myself awake. If this was love, then I was learning that to love is insufferable pain.

I wished he had loved me enough to stay, but he'd retracted so long ago, to a cold scape. He rose up like Ozymandius, tearing beyond the collapsing clouds and soft sounds. There goes my freedom break.

JANUARY 2025

It's hard to close a story when you don't know where to end when there have been so many endings and beginnings. My life had been a ritual of flirting between the two—ripping things open and stuffing them shut again. Cody had gone quiet and when he resurfaced, I knew what was on his tongue before he did, *"I love you more than anything, you have my whole heart. I'd marry you for a green card, but I'm just not ready to settle down yet. I want you to be able to live here, but I can't give you more than that."*

I'd come back from celebrating my twenty-fourth birthday in the Sahara Desert. Vast oranges and yellows, blue skies and dusky dunes. Camels and Berbers, tagines and tanlines had disappeared as though they had never existed at all. It was bleak and I was in Bath. The weather was turning and winter was growing. I had two wrinkles that hadn't been there before. How awful, I couldn't stop growing old. How I wish society hadn't told me I had an expiry date. How, untrue.

"It's fine, I guess I always knew it would end up this way. I could never marry you for a green card, I wanted to marry you for love."

I envisioned him getting into a car, seatbelt fastened, pressing his face up to the window, drawing hearts in the fog of his breath, and then driving away, on a journey of never returning.

"I'm with someone else."

He sent me a photo of his ex-wife. I was the same age he was when I met him, and he still hadn't quit her, after all.

"True love never dies."

The sarcasm was lost in translation.

"You've got that right."

How little he loved me after all. How humiliated I felt to have written this book. How small and sad I was in such a large and frightening world. How even Marie had trailed off.

I could already see him driving away, a faint shape in the distance, towards her and then onto someone else, dust flying behind the tyres. Crow lines, laughter. I guess that's where the story ends, in January, the day after my birthday, with a crushing blow.

I thought of the last time I saw him in New Jersey, bundling each other in a breaking hug, gripping each other by the subway barriers. Crying into each other's necks, a heavy, heaving sobbing. And now, I felt a deep sickness rise. All roads lead back to Rochelle. After all this time.

I had spent three years as a rebound, alone on the roadside.

Don't go falling in love with me now.

How I should've listened.

How I'm glad I didn't.

Sam Barber: Thought of You

in the wind highligh
ury while navigating

THE A

novelist, firm in the

an change the world.

xperiments with lyri

Printed by Libri Plureos GmbH in Hamburg, Germany